Reflections on the Marxist theory of history

Manchester University Press

Reflections on the Marxist theory of history

Paul Blackledge

Manchester University Press
Manchester and New York
distributed exclusively in the USA by Palgrave

Published by Manchester University Press
Oxford Road, Manchester M13 9NR, UK
and Room 400, 175 Fifth Avenue, New York, NY 10010, USA
www.manchesteruniversitypress.co.uk

Distributed exclusively in the USA by
Palgrave, 175 Fifth Avenue, New York,
NY 10010, USA

Distributed exclusively in Canada by
UBC Press, University of British Columbia, 2029 West Mall,
Vancouver, BC, Canada V6T 1Z2

British Library Cataloguing-in-Publication Data
A catalogue record for this book is available from the British Library

Library of Congress Cataloging-in-Publication Data applied for

ISBN 0 7190 6956 4 *hardback*
EAN 978 0 7190 6956 7

ISBN 0 7190 6957 2 *paperback*
EAN 978 0 7190 6957 4

First published 2006

15 14 13 12 11 10 09 08 07 06 10 9 8 7 6 5 4 3 2 1

Typeset in Sabon 10/12 pt
by Servis Filmsetting Ltd, Manchester
Printed in Great Britain
by CPI, Bath

To the memory of Brian Manning (1927–2004),
and for John and Matthew Marsden.

Contents

Preface and acknowledgements

The recent emergence of global anti-capitalist and anti-war movements has created a space within which Marxism can flourish as it has not been able to for a generation. Nevertheless, while, the anti-capitalist movement emerged in part as a protest against grotesque increases in global inequality that would have been readily recognisable to Marx, it did so in the wake of the break up of the Eastern bloc and the subsequent collapse of the Soviet Union which informed the belief, widespread among activists, that Marx's theory of revolution has little, if any, relevance to the modern world. More specifically, the collapse of Stalinism has been read by many historians as the concrete negation of the Marxist political project, such that, while many would accept that insights may be taken from the work of Marxist historians, the suggestion that there now exists a distinctive and defensible 'Marxist history' is widely regarded as anachronistic. Moreover, whereas Marx articulated a sophisticated epistemology, the Stalinist tendency to reduce Marxism to a crude form of positivism meant that the resulting bastardised form of historical materialism became highly susceptible to criticisms from theorists and historians associated with what has become known as the 'linguistic turn' in historiography. An aim of this book is to show that by disassociating Marxism from the legacy of Stalinism Marxist historiography need not retreat before these criticisms; and that, once rid of this incubus, Marx's theory of history can be shown to be sophisticated, powerful and vibrant.

In chapter 1 I argue that Marxism offers a unique, and scientific, basis from which to carry out historical research, and one that differentiates it from the twin failures of the traditional empiricist and the post-modernist approaches to historiography. As distinct from the former, Marxism offers a defensible basis for the selection of evidence, while it posits both a model of language and a method of research which, unlike the latter, are adequate to the task of conceptualising the socio-historical totality.

In chapter 2 I outline Marx and Engels' theory of history, and some of their attempts to actualise that approach in their historical studies. I argue that Marx and Engels offered neither a mechanically deterministic nor a voluntaristic approach to the study of history, but suggested rather a powerful method for grasping both the material parameters within which agents act and the historical nature of human agency itself.

I discuss the development of their approach within the Marxist movement in the half century or so after the deaths of Marx and Engels in chapter 3. Against much received wisdom on the subject, I argue that Marxists in both the Second and the Third Internationals produced powerful interpretations and applications of Marx's method, which culminated, on the one hand, in the publication of Trotsky's *History of the Russian Revolution* and Lukács's *History and Class Consciousness* and, on the other, in the emergence of the tradition of 'people's history', realised most famously in the work of the great historians who emerged from the Communist Party of Great Britain Historians' Group in the 1950s.

Chapter 4 offers a critical survey of debates on the application of Marx's concepts of 'mode of production' and 'relations of production' to the attempt to *periodise* history. Beginning with an analysis of V. Gordon Childe's discussion of pre-history, I move to outline debates on the slave, feudal and Asiatic modes of production, before examining contested conceptualisations of the transition from feudalism to capitalism generally and bourgeois revolution specifically.

Marxist debates on the perennial issue of structure and agency are considered in chapter 5. Beginning with a comment on Marx's classic solution to this debate as articulated in 'The Eighteenth Brumaire', I move on to survey the contributions of Sartre and Althusser, and the debates between Perry Anderson and Edward Thompson, before concluding with an overview of the contributions of Alasdair MacIntyre, in his early Marxist period, Alex Callinicos and the school of critical realism. I conclude that Marxists have made a series of powerful contributions to this question, which, at their best, successfully navigate between the twin errors of reductionism and voluntarism.

Finally, in chapter 6 I discuss competing Marxist attempts to periodise the contemporary – post-modern – conjuncture, paying attention to the suggestion that the post-modern world is one characterised by the defeat of the socialist alternative to capitalism. I argue that the notion of 'defeat' is itself somewhat slippery, as it is employed in the post-modern models of a series of *contingent* defeats for the labour movement and a *systemic* defeat of socialism as embodied in the collapse of the Soviet Union and its satellite states. Against those who claim that the demise of the Soviet Union marks the death of Marxism, I argue that the thesis that the Soviet regime and its sister states were 'socialist' is an inversion of Marx's understanding of socialism and that their collapse has little relevance to the fortunes of Marxism.

I conclude that Marxism remains as valid today as it has ever been, and that Marxist historiography offers a powerful tool for historical research that acts, first, as a potent critique of those who would attempt to naturalise capitalist rationality and, second, as a source both of inspiration for contemporary activists and, of political lessons from which radicals would do well to learn. The world may have moved on from 1871 in Paris, 1917 in Russia, 1956 in Hungary, 1968 in France, 1981 in Poland, etc., but capitalist social relations still prevail, and lessons can be learned by contemporary anti-capitalists from these and many other social movements.

Research for this book grew out of work I did for *Perry Anderson, Marxism and the New Left* (Merlin, 2004) and my essays in two collections I co-edited: *Historical Materialism and Social Evolution* (Basingstoke, UK, 2002), and *Alasdair MacIntyre's Marxist Writings* (Leiden, NL, 2006); it is informed also by essays I have had accepted for publication in the journals *Contemporary Politics*, *Historical Materialism*, *History of Political Thought*, *Studies in Marxism*, *Studies in East European Thought* and *Science and Society*. Writing this book was possible only because Kristyn Gorton endured my bizarre work patterns and read every word of the manuscript several painful times; my hat goes off to her. My understanding of the Marxist theory of history has been greatly improved by advice from and discussions with numerous people over the years. The list of those to whom I am thus indebted includes, but is by no means limited to, Alex Callinicos, Neil Davidson, Joe Hartney, Paul McGarr, Giuseppe Tassone and my comrades on the editorial board of *Historical Materialism*. Thanks also to Jonathan Bevan and Alison Welsby at Manchester University Press, and to Dave Packer, Ron Price, Roger Richardson and Ben Watson for their help with the manuscript of this book. Finally, I benefited greatly from my friendship with Brian Manning in the decade or so before his untimely death in 2004. Brian was a historian of the first rank; he was also a socialist activist, and from his early membership of the Labour Party, through his activity in CND and the New Left to his later membership of the Socialist Workers' Party, he successfully married political activity with a deployment of his command of the history of the English revolution to inspire as well as inform younger activists. It is to Brian's memory that this book is therefore dedicated.[1] I dedicate it also to my sons, John and Matthew, in the hope that they might, one day, be inspired by the kind of history that Brian, and those like him, wrote and continue to write.

Note

1 For my thoughts on Brian's contribution to the historiography of the English Revolution see my introduction to a review essay which he submitted to *Historical Materialism* shortly before his death: P. Blackledge 'Brian Manning: The People and the English Revolution' *Historical Materialism* 13:3, 2005.

1

Marxism and history

How are we to understand the nature of historical knowledge? The way that historians traditionally have answered this question has come under sustained attack since the 1980s in the wake of what has become known as the 'cultural' or 'linguistic turn'. This shift in perspective can be understood as a reaction to two developments. Negatively, as Bonnell and Hunt have argued, the old positivistic assumption about the nature of history – that it consisted in the accumulation of facts collected by diligent historians – came increasingly to be called into question as large research projects generated conflictual rather than cumulative results. More positively, the publication in 1973 of both Hayden White's *Metahistory: The Historical Imagination in Nineteenth-Century Europe* and Clifford Geertz's *The Interpretation of Cultures*, alongside the publication in the 1960s and 1970s of the work of 'Roland Barthes, Pierre Bourdieu, Jacques Derrida, Marshall Sahlins, Raymond Williams, and especially Michel Foucault', as Bonnell and Hunt maintain, 'changed the intellectual landscape'. Moreover, this new intellectual context challenged both the certainties of political history and the assumptions that underpinned the much more radical methods of social history, and partly as a response to this intellectual challenge there occurred a shift from *social* to *cultural* history. This shift marked much more than a change in methodological emphasis, for where social historians had attempted to explain historical processes by reference to underlying social structures, cultural historians inverted this relationship so that social categories are understood to be constructed not prior to but rather through language. Indeed, while many cultural historians could trace their research agenda back to an early interest in Marxism, the implications of the cultural turn seemed to be as damning of historical materialism as they were of traditional empiricist (positivist) history: Bonnell and Hunt argued that 'in the face of these intellectual trends and the collapse of communist systems in Eastern Europe and the former Soviet Union, Marxism as an interpretive and political paradigm has suffered a serious decline'.[1]

While Bonnell and Hunt are undoubtedly right to suggest that Marxism as a political and intellectual movement has suffered a number of setbacks over the period since the 1970s, it would be a mistake to equate Marxism with the Soviet system. As I have elsewhere criticised the theoretical weaknesses of the elision involved in the move from a critique of Stalinism to a rejection of Marx's political project,[2] and as I return to this criticism in the conclusion to this volume, at this stage of my argument I merely note that throughout the twentieth century there have emerged a number of vibrant anti-Stalinist interpretations of Marxism which did not mourn, but in fact rejoiced at, the collapse of the Soviet State in 1991.[3] Furthermore, few if any Marxists outside the direct influence of the Kremlin understood historical materialism as a form of positivism; and it was in fact from within Marxist anti-Stalinist milieux that the most exciting twentieth-century developments in historical materialism occurred. To ask what Marxism might add to the study of history, I therefore look beyond the Stalinist caricature of historical materialism to the powerful methods of anti-Stalinist Marxism.

Some contemporary debates

A student new to the discipline of history might be forgiven for feeling a little bewildered by the contradictory answers offered in introductory texts to the simple question of what Marxism might offer the historian. Arthur Marwick,[4] for instance, asserts that it would be wrong to consider Marx a proper historian because he attempted to squeeze the evidence he unearthed into 'an *a priori* conception of history'.[5] Marxism, for Marwick at least, would seem to have little to offer to the student of history. By contrast, John Arnold argues that 'practically all historians writing today are marxists (with a small m)'.[6] Perhaps, on Arnold's account, Marwick is one of the few remaining non-marxist historians. Unfortunately, Marwick certainly would not accept this characterisation of his colleagues, for he believes that even Marxist historians are not really Marxists in so far as they write good history: he asserts that it is the journalism of the acclaimed Marxist historian Eric Hobsbawm that owes most to his Marxism, while his historical studies escape from the constraints of Marx's theory of history.[7]

What are students to make of this disagreement? A decade ago Tony Judt, writing at Fukuyama's 'End of History', prefigured Arnold's comment when he wrote that 'the central tenets of Marxism . . . are so much a part of modern historical writing that it is hard to say what is and what is not "Marxist"'.[8] In apparent confirmation of this thesis, Ian Kershaw has recently suggested that 'Marx was right to argue that 'Men make their own history, but they do not make it as they please; they do not make it under self-selected circumstances, but under circumstances existing already, given and transmitted from the past.'[9]

While Kershaw might agree with Marx's formal solution to the structure–agency problem, he certainly is not a Marxist historian, excellent historian though he undoubtedly is. Indeed, once we look closely at contemporary history, the idea that almost every historian is in some sense a marxist (if only with a small m) seems implausible. For, on the one hand, as I have noted above, the last two or three decades have, through the medium of the linguistic turn, seen the rise of post-modernism in history, which grew, in part at least, out of a rejection of Marxist materialism; while on the other hand, the continuing dominance of naïve empiricism within mainstream historiography is reinforced by the current D.Phil culture, which, as Christopher Hill has argued, while teaching essential skills to prospective historians comes at the expense of generating a 'tunnel vision' by creating conditions where researchers learn 'more and more about less and less'.[10] Interestingly, in their struggle for the soul of history, both post-modernists and traditionalists are wont to attack Marxism as representative of the opposition. Patrick Joyce, for instance, argues that 'the ghost of Marx . . . unites the extremes of right and left in the most intemperate denunciations of the postmodernist scourge'; while Marwick writes that many Marxists have followed the lead of the post-modernists to make a metaphysical 'attack' on 'professional history'.[11] These polemical rejections of Marxism suggest that even if Judt and Arnold may have a point when they suggest that some of Marx's ideas have been sedimented into a common historiographic culture, it is far from being the case that all contemporary historians are marxists, let alone Marxists.

What then is Marxist history and what distinguishes it from other types of historical enquiry? I argue that Marx and, later, Marxists offer three key contributions to historiography through which we might develop a sophisticated answer to the historical relativism associated with post-modernism, without collapsing into the naïve empiricism of traditional history. First, Marxists have elaborated an anthropology and a corresponding theory of language through which we might grasp, contra the post-modernists, the nature of the real world. Second, Marxists have developed a scientific method through which we might enquire into the nature of the world beyond language. Third, Marxists have developed a series of concepts through which this scientific enquiry could adequately be realised.

Customarily, historians have claimed, when called on to justify their profession, that they seek human self-awareness. Many historians have accordingly understood their goal as adding to our knowledge of ourselves through a careful examination of the evidence of what our ancestors did. Furthermore, from the time of the great nineteenth-century German historian Leopold Von Ranke onwards, they have attempted to realise this project through a systematic study of primary and secondary sources, with a view to producing knowledge of what actually happened. It is in this sense that Marwick locates history as 'a cumulative and cooperative activity', and characterises himself, not as this or that kind of historian, but as a historian, pure and simple.[12]

Marwick does not, though, address adequately the claim that different historians, while remaining true to Rankean principles, can produce very different interpretations of the past. In fact, it is a sign of the weakness of his case that he does not attempt to provide a systematic critique of post-modern relativism, but simply accepts its logic when he asserts: 'I have no chance of convincing anyone who is already a confirmed postmodernist. Our basic assumptions are different.'[13] While a statement such as this certainly would not convince a post-modernist of the error of her ways, it might convince an empiricist that the post-modernists had been right all along: our conclusions, apparently, are embedded in the assumptions from which we begin our enquiries.

This sense of hopelessness in Marwick's position is reinforced when we read that this supposed representative of the broad profession of historians believes that neither Marxists nor feminists can be trusted with history because they are 'so determined to read off predetermined lessons . . . that they scarcely get round to analysing the evidence'. Nevertheless, while Marwick is keen to berate Marxists for their supposed attachment to dogma, his real venom is reserved for the feminists, whose 'propaganda' he contrasts with his own 'reasoned conclusions'.[14] This absurd argument serves merely to further reinforce the belief that, if this is its best defence of objectivity, then history must be a field of incommensurable interpretations.

For those who wish to defend a more sophisticated version of the claim that history can reach objectively verifiable conclusions, Richard Evans[15] provides a much more cogent case than that which is to be found in Marwick's book. Where Marwick defends a similar version of epistemological empiricism to that outlined in Geoffrey Elton's *The Practice of History* (1967),[16] Evans shows, in his postscript to the second edition of Elton's book, that even when this book was first published, its thesis that history concerned itself with the search for absolute truths through an engagement with empirical sources was 'not really representative' of history as it was then practised, and is certainly unrepresentative of more contemporary history.[17] In contrast to the crude claims made by Elton and Marwick, Evans argues that 'to search for a truly "scientific" history is to pursue a mirage'.[18] By this Evans means that the desire to let the facts 'speak for themselves' through the neutral historian is impossible, as most facts can be deployed as evidence for competing interpretations of particular events: 'Elton is completely wrong in his view that there is only one legitimate way to read a given document.'[19] Despite this claim, Evans shuns post-modern relativism when he argues that 'surely the past does impose its reality through the sources in a basic way. At the most elemental level, one cannot simply read into documents words that are not there.'[20]

Evans gives two examples of recent controversies within history to support this claim: the first is an example of sloppy scholarship; the second, a wilful misinterpretation of documents. Evans's first case concerns the Marxist historian David Abraham. In the early 1980s it was discovered that Abraham, in *The Collapse of the Weimer Republic* (1981), had made numerous errors in his deployment of sources. Evans believes that the reason for these errors was Abraham's weak research skills, rather than a systematic attempt to falsify the documents: many, if not most, of the errors involved Abraham's incorrectly reading evidence that might have supported his thesis as actually contradicting it. Irrespective of Abraham's motives, his case allowed historians to show that by documenting his errors the scope for valid interpretation of evidence was narrow.[21]

While the case of Abraham created little consternation outside of the academy, the political implications of Evans's second example of the power of traditional historiography to confront myth was of qualitatively greater significance: revisionist historians were seeking to provide a pseudo-academic defence of Holocaust denial. Beyond noting the embarrassment of post-modernists when confronted with their inability to even conceive of an adequate riposte to these revisionists, Evans made relatively little of this debate in his *In Defence of History*.[22] However, in 2000 he acted for the defence in a libel trial brought by David Irving against Deborah Lipstadt and Penguin Books. The case rested on the charge, made by Lipstadt, that Irving had systematically misinterpreted documents in his 1977 book *Hitler's War*, within which he claimed that 'far from ordering it himself, Hitler had not known about the extermination of the Jews until late in 1943, and both before and after that had done his best to mitigate the worst excesses of his subordinates'.[23] Evans showed that Irving's book was unreliable, as it included 'massive falsification of evidence', through his moulding of 'the "facts" so that they appeared to support his opinions even when in reality they did not'.[24]

Evans suggested that Irving's case was different from Abraham's, for Abraham accepted that he had erred, and his errors, while generally tending to give credence to his thesis, did not systematically support it. Irving's 'errors', by contrast, were systematically and universally designed to substantiate his defence of Hitler's role in the Holocaust: his motives were less ambiguous than were Abraham's – he sought to misrepresent the documents as part of a project to rehabilitate Hitler's reputation.

The strength of Evans's case against Irving was built on a painstaking search through the sources used by the latter, which showed that Irving had systematically distorted the meaning of documents. Unfortunately, while Evans is right to reject Judt's claim that Irving's method paralleled that of other historians, in that he merely selected evidence to support his case, he did not outline an alternative, *scientific*, method of selection.[25] In fact, despite his critique of post-modern theory,[26] in *In Defence of History* he praised 'the best postmodernist history' – among which he counted Simon Schama's *Citizens: A Chronicle of the French Revolution* and Orlando Figes's *A People's Tragedy: The Russian Revolution 1891–1921* – for reinstating 'good writing as legitimate practice'.[27]

Unfortunately, while these books could not be faulted for systematically *moulding* facts, they did *select* facts to substantiate particular political, indeed counter-revolutionary, arguments. Now, in as much as Evans legitimises this practice, its consequences are much more problematical for the concept of historical truth than can be gauged from his comment that 'neither pretends to be definitive'.[28] For the arbitrary selection of evidence suggests that the narratives so produced have no more explanatory power than does a well researched historical novel.

For instance, if the French revolution is read as a drama involving a relatively small number of key actors, then its place within the broader movement of history is obscured. This is precisely the function of Schama's study, which Eric Hobsbawm described as the latest version of a pornography of Terror that stretched back to Dicken's *A Tale of Two Cities* and Baroness Orczy's *The Scarlet Pimpernel*. Hobsbawm perceptively argued that Schama's 'choice of narrative focused on particular people and incidents, neatly sidesteps the problems of perspective and generalisation'.[29] In effect Schama's method leaves the revolution meaningless except as a rather compelling (and bloody) soap-opera. A number of Marxist reviewers of Evans's book made the similar criticism that his refusal to engage in a debate over the nature of the selection of evidence left his criticisms of post-modernism fundamentally flawed. Unfortunately, while Evans noted these criticisms in the second edition of his book, he did not engage with them.[30]

Marxism against post-modernism

According to post-modernists such as Keith Jenkins the gap between history, understood as our discursive re-creation of the past, and the past itself, as the infinite number of events and processes that have happened before now, is insurmountable: 'The past and history float free of each other.'[31] Similarly, Patrick Joyce has argued that 'the major advance of "postmodernism" . . . [is] that events, structures and processes of the past are indistinguishable from the forms of documentary representation, the conceptual and political appropriations, and the historical discourses that construct them'. According to Joyce, because post-modernists recognise 'the irreducibly discursive character of the social' they are also aware that 'there is no overarching coherence evident in either the polity, the economy or the social system'.[32] So, for the post-modernists, there is no single *story* (or grand narrative) to tell of the past, only a series of *stories* about it. Further, the myriad stories about the past suggest that there is no single truth to tell either. Jenkins actually relishes this conclusion: 'it is really brilliant news that historians can never get things right'.[33]

The idea that the social world is irredeemably discursive such that there can be no privileged vantage point from which we might grasp 'real' underlying relations was forcefully argued in Britain by Gareth Stedman Jones in *Languages of Class* (1983). Stedman Jones suggested that historical enquiry should begin from a realisation that language is not to be understood simply as 'referring' back to some 'primal anterior reality'. Following the logic of this suggestion, he argued, in opposition to Marxism, that rather than attempt to look through language to underlying real interests, historians must 'study the production of interest, identification, grievance and aspiration within political language themselves'.[34]

The Marxist historian Neville Kirk responded to this challenge to historical materialism by pointing out that Stedman Jones's method was 'idealistic' because it 'effectively dissolves reality back into language'.[35] That may be so, but if Stedman Jones is right about the nature of language, then it would be fruitless to maintain the belief that a materialist alternative to their approach is viable. Fortunately, Marxists have developed an alternative materialist theory of language that offers the possibility of overcoming the dualism between empiricism and post-modernism.

Stedman Jones argued that

> language disrupts any simple notion of the determination of consciousness by social being because it is itself part of social being. We cannot therefore decode political language to reach a primal and material expression of interest since it is the discursive structure of political language which conceives and defines interest in the first place.[36]

In a later essay he argued that what historians had found significant in the revolution in linguistics inaugurated by Saussure was not the claim that they should take language seriously, but that from within the new perspective language was understood to be 'a self-contained system of signs the meaning of which were determined by their relationship with each other rather than to some primordial or transcendental extra-linguistic terrain'.[37]

Where it had been traditionally argued that words, specifically, and language, more generally, were a relatively transparent set of references to distinct things in the real world, Saussure, in his *Course in General Linguistics* (1915), argued that words (signs) gained their meaning not through their positive reference to real things in the world but through their structured relationship within language to other signs. To substantiate this claim he divided language between a relatively static *langue* and a more dynamic *parole*. He defined langue, as Callinicos argues, as 'the whole set of linguistic habits which allow an individual to be understood', whereas parole was the actual historical use of language in speech. Saussure argued that a science of language was possible only if the study of langue was prioritised over the study of parole. This argument marked an undoubted advance on previous approaches to the study of language. Nevertheless, while Saussure believed that language thus understood could illuminate extra-linguistic practices, his conception of words (signs) as constructed through a combination of a concept – the signified – and a sound image – the signifier – suggested that there was no way through which one could perceive an unmediated reality behind language. This was the point made by the post-structuralists in the

1960s. They argued that the concept, or the signified, was just as much a part of language as was the signifier, and, in Jacques Derrida's famous phrase, they concluded that 'there is nothing outside the text'.[38] Post-structuralism therefore emerged out of the radicalisation of structuralism.

In 1983 Perry Anderson argued that post-structuralism could be understood through its embrace of four movements. First, there was the 'exorbitation of language': where Saussure had stressed that his model was of strictly limited reference to the analysis of language, structuralism had generalised it and argued that it had a universal validity. Second, and as a direct consequence of this, there was an 'attenuation of truth': by contrast with Saussure, who had understood language to be constituted through a series of signs, each of which is, in turn, made up of a signifier and a signified, post-structuralism 'repressed the referential' element of the sign. Third, this led to the 'randomisation of history': once language was understood to be the general paradigm of society, then the concept of causation was lost. Finally, there is the 'capsizal of structures': as the linguistic paradigm consists of a series of signifiers, unconnected to the 'real' world, then the real world cannot operate to limit the structure.[39] The outcome of this fourfold movement was a theory that tended, as with Stedman Jones, to invert the traditional Marxist conceptualisation of the priority of social being over social consciousness: 'The deconstructive turn', Raphael Samuel argued, 'treats material practices as effects rather than causes, ideas as constitutive rather than reflective'.[40]

In its most extreme form the Derridean influence on historiography has informed the trajectory of postcolonial theorists such as Gayatri Spivak. In an influential essay, 'Can the Subaltern Speak?', Spivak redefined the concept of subaltern, which had been introduced by Gramsci as a means of bypassing his fascist censors by writing about the working class in suitably Aesopian language, to mean those working-class and peasant women whose voices were excluded from the archive. Thus defined, Spivak famously argued that the subaltern could not in fact speak, and that those historians who claimed to write the kind of history from below which aimed to give voice to these groups actually imposed their own rationality on the silent object of their analyses.[41]

Aijaz Ahmed has argued, however, that this thesis involves a tautologous conceptualisation of subaltern as those who leave no direct trace on the archive while, conversely, defining elites as those that do leave archival imprints. He claims, further, that Spivak elides over the way in which historians, in the wake of Edward Thompson's path breaking study of the English working class, have 'prised open' archives that were created by dominant groups to 'assemble' genuine histories from below.[42] Indeed, in contrast to the work of historians like E. P. Thompson, Spivak's argument negates Gramsci's suggestion that 'every trace of independent initiative on the part of subaltern groups should therefore be of incalculable value for the integral historian'.[43] More generally, while historians influenced by the linguistic turn have undoubtedly produced interesting studies of the past, the results of their studies are limited: as Samuel insisted, 'the historical record cannot be read only as a system of signs', for historians must look beyond language if they are to measure 'words against deeds'.[44]

If historians are to realise this goal then they must give evidence that they possess an alternative model of language to that propounded by the post-structuralists. More specifically, if Marxists are to defend an alternative model of social causation then they are beholden to offer a more powerful model of the relationship between language and the real world.

As I discuss at greater length in the next chapter, in *The German Ideology* Marx suggested an alternative theory of language, one built on his conception of human nature. Men and women, he and Engels argued, 'begin to distinguish themselves from animals as soon as they begin to *produce* their means of subsistence'.[45] Where previous thinkers had tended to distinguish humanity from animals by our ability to reason, Marx and Engels looked instead to the point in history at which humans distinguished themselves from animals, suggesting that this occurred at the moment when we began to act productively on the world so as to consciously transform it to meet our needs. They suggested that this process was a form of social practice which demanded some form of language to enable it. Generally, they made the materialist point that 'the production of ideas, of conceptions, of consciousness, is at first directly interwoven with the material activity and the material intercourse of men, the language of real life . . . Consciousness can never be anything else than conscious existence.' Further, they argued that language, as the concrete form taken by consciousness, 'is as old as consciousness, language is practical consciousness that exists also for other men, and for that reason alone it really exists for me personally as well; language, like consciousness, only arises from the need, the necessity, of intercourse with other men'.[46]

This argument was developed by the Russian linguist – and victim of Stalin – V. N. Volosinov, who argued that Saussure's prioritisation of langue over parole effectively rids language of its human content. Alternatively, language, according to Volosinov in *Marxism and the Philosophy of Language* (1929), is best understood as the practical activity of people speaking to each other.[47] He argued:

> Every sign . . . is a construct between socially organised persons in the process of their interaction. Therefore, the forms of signs are conditioned above all by the social organisation of the participants involved and also by the immediate conditions of their interaction. When these forms change, so does sign. And it should be one of the tasks of the study of ideologies to trace this social life of the verbal sign. Only so approached can the problem of the relationship between sign and existence find its concrete expression; only then will the process of the causal shaping of the sign by existence stand out as a process of genuine existence-to-sign transit, of genuine refraction of existence in the sign.[48]

So, against Saussure's prioritisation of langue in his study of language, Volosinov prioritises speech because, as he argued, 'words are always filled with content and meaning drawn from behaviour or ideology'; or, more simply, 'the utterance is a social phenomenon'.[49] Whereas Saussure's approach lent itself to abstract formalism because it divorced the study of language from its concrete expression in dialogue, Volosinov's focus on speech as a concrete activity allowed him to conceptualise language in all its richness, precisely because it is conceived as a part of social being.

In fact Marxists share with Stedman Jones and others influenced by the linguistic turn an awareness that language is a central part of social being, but differ from them in their interpretation of how best this relationship is conceptualised. No Marxist historian of any stature believes that language is an unproblematically transparent medium through which we can view an underlying reality. Yet, Marxists do believe that we can cognise reality, at least approximately, through language and other media. Moreover, Marxists argue that if underlying forces are downplayed by historians in their research, then the fruits of their enquiries will be severely undermined.

Neal Wood makes this point in his critique of the 'idealism' of the Cambridge School of the history of ideas. What has been described as the 'manifesto' of this school was penned by Quentin Skinner in 1969 – 'Meaning and Understanding in the History of Ideas' – in which its author challenged what he believed were two misconceived approaches to the study of intellectual history. The first of these methods was 'dictated by the claim that the text itself should form the self-sufficient object of inquiry and understanding'.[50] According to Skinner, partisans of this model, who read classic texts as timeless artefacts whose wisdom shone down the ages, were wont to miss that which is unique and interesting about a text, being forced into a procrustean bed constructed from later concerns. By contrast, Skinner stressed the central importance to the historian of recognising the intentions of classical authors, which could be understood only within their historical context.[51] To an extent, Skinner's method would appear to cohere with a sophisticated interpretation of historical materialism. Nevertheless, in contrast to Marx's method, Skinner insisted that the context within which agents acted should be understood not as an anterior material context, but primarily as being 'essentially linguistic'.[52] Skinner therefore differentiated his approach from both the ahistorical method traditionally associated with the history of ideas and the perceived reductionism of Marxism.[53] Similarly, John Pocock, Skinner's colleague at Cambridge, has argued, in Saussurian language, that 'the performance of a text is its performance as *parole* in the context of *langue*'.[54] Whatever the undoubted power of the history written from within this perspective, because of the limited nature of language thus conceived, the method associated with the Cambridge school is weakened in that, as Wood argues, it 'seldom examines in detail and depth the precise nature of the interrelationships of the political ideas with the realities of human activity'. Wood recommends as an antidote to the limitations of this school's 'philosophical idealism . . . an increased recognition of the material world of society and politics and a greater acknowledgement that life is much more than language, and that politics, historical and contemporary, involves much more than verbal signs'.[55]

More substantively, Christopher Hill challenged Pocock's argument that 'men cannot do what they have no means of saying they have done'. Hill argued that 'things precede words . . . new words were needed because new things happened'.[56] This claim relates to Hill's discussion of the use of the word 'revolution' in seventeenth-century England. According to Raymond Williams, the word first entered the English language in the fourteenth century to denote the technical process of *revolving*, and, while it has since maintained this earlier meaning, 'revolution' in the sense of social and political transformation evolved in a complex process from the fifteenth century onwards.[57] Of particular importance to this process was the way in which political upheavals were understood to create a 'world turned upside down' – the link here between the technical and the socio-political denotation of 'revolution' is readily apparent. Hill pointed out that a turning of the world upside down was only half a revolution – for the wheel to come full circle would mean a restoration of the old order.[58] Nevertheless, he argued that despite the ambiguity attached to it, the notion of revolution did begin to take on its current denotation in the mid-seventeenth century, as actors involved in making a revolution were compelled to develop their language in order that they might make sense of these novel events: 'men groped for new words to describe what they were experiencing'.[59]

According to Hill, to adequately understand seventeenth-century politics the historian must analyse language and changing social practice in their dynamic relationship; for to analyse only one side of this process would be to commit the sin of reductionism. While I have suggested that Volosinov points to a way out of this reductionist trap, it is also the case that Volosinov's arguments imply a methodological starting point from which historians can justify their approach to the selection of evidence. For in developing Marx's argument that language is practical consciousness, Volosinov points back to Marx's productivist anthropology as a basis from which evidence can be justifiably selected.[60]

If we agree with Marx that humans re-create themselves through their socially organised engagement in the process of producing to meet their needs, and if we also agree with him (see chapter 2 of this book) that in producing to meet those needs humans develop new needs and capacities, then we are drawn to accept his conclusion that the production and reproduction of human life lies at the centre of the historical process.[61]

This suggestion leaves unresolved the problem of how to use language and other media to illuminate the underlying historical processes. Marx's answer to this problem is unique in the social sciences, because he insisted that his method was not neutral but could be realised only from the point of view of the working class.[62]

The most sophisticated articulation of this argument was made by Lukács in *History and Class Consciousness* (1923). He suggested that even those intellectuals who in all honesty aimed to tell the truth as they saw it from their own perspective in effect naturalised that which is historical: their own individual frame of reference. In viewing society from the false concrete of the individual, they remained trapped in a bourgeois perspective unable to comprehend capitalism either as a totality or as a historical mode of production: 'the individual can never be the measure of all things. For when the individual confronts objective reality he is faced by a complex of ready-made and unalterable objects which allow him only the subjective responses of recognition or rejection.'[63] While Lukács insisted that the most important form of this failure was the inability of bourgeois economists to adequately conceptualise economic crises, he also argued that it was manifest in the empiricism of bourgeois historiography.[64] Specifically, he maintained that 'one of the most terrible memories of every sober observer' has been 'the total inability of every bourgeois thinker and historian to see the world-historical events of the present [1914–23] as universal history'. More generally, he claimed that 'we see the unhistorical and antihistorical character of bourgeois thought most strikingly when we consider *the problem of the present as a historical problem*'. So, Lukács argued, it was the individual frame of reference of traditional intellectuals which, in tending to naturalise capitalist social relations, entailed that they were incapable of seeing 'the present as history'.[65] Conversely, because the proletariat is actually at the centre of the constant reproduction of bourgeois society it is able to conceive of both the creation and the transcendence of that mode of production. Therefore,

> historical materialism is the theory of the proletarian revolution. It is so because its essence is an intellectual synthesis of the social existence which produces and fundamentally determines the proletariat; and because the proletariat struggling for liberation finds its clear self-consciousness in it.[66]

Given that the majority of proletarians are not consciously revolutionary most of the time, Lukács argued that the standpoint of the proletariat must necessarily be 'imputed' to the working class. This imputation was possible from a Marxist point of view, as Marx understood the proletariat to have an 'essence' out of which its empirical reality emerged but to which it could not be reduced.

> When socialist writers ascribe this world-historic role to the proletariat, it is not at all, as Critical Criticism pretends to believe, because they regard the proletarians as *gods*. Rather the contrary. Since in the fully-formed proletariat the abstraction of all humanity, even of the *semblance* of humanity, is practically complete; since the conditions of life of the proletariat sum up all the condi-

> tions of life of society today in their most inhuman form; since man has lost himself in the proletariat, yet at the same time has not only gained theoretical consciousness of that loss, but through urgent, no longer removable, no longer disguisable, absolutely imperative *need* – the practical expression of *necessity* – is driven directly to revolt against this inhumanity, it follows that the proletariat can and must emancipate itself. But it cannot emancipate itself without abolishing the conditions of its own life. It cannot abolish the conditions of its own life without abolishing all the inhuman conditions of life of society today which are summed up in its own situation. Not in vain does it go through the stern but steeling school of *labour*. It is not a question of what this or that proletarian, or even the whole proletariat, at the moment *regards* as its aim. It is a question of *what the proletariat is*, and what, in accordance with this *being*, it will historically be compelled to do. Its aim and historical action is visibly and irrevocably foreshadowed in its own life situation as well as in the whole organization of bourgeois society today. There is no need to explain here that a large part of the English and French proletariat is already *conscious* of its historic task and is constantly working to develop that consciousness into complete clarity.[67]

While the negative power of Lukács's critique of the false objectivity of bourgeois thought is readily apparent,[68] it is less obvious how the notion of 'the standpoint of the proletariat' is not itself just another individual perspective masquerading as the total viewpoint of the working class.[69] Certainly, Marx himself argued that with the movement from the formal to the real subsumption of labour to capital, the working class became fragmented and workers themselves tended to become dehumanised by the technical division of labour, such that, typically, they accept their own exploitation and oppression. Nevertheless, Marx also recognised that, despite their fragmented situation, workers regularly engaged in collective rebellions against their condition.[70] It is this constant process of struggle at higher and lower levels which is the basis for the Marxist perspective on society. The 'standpoint of the proletariat' is best understood as signifying a point of view generalised from the high points of a century-and-a-half of such struggles.[71] This notion is different from, and more powerful than, the idea of class interests, contra Peter Burke's suggestion,[72] because the generalised lessons from past struggles embodied in the concept of the standpoint of the proletariat signify a democratic relationship to the practice of the working class which is missing from the cruder conception of class interest. The reason for this is that the concept of interest is itself contested. As Stephen Perkins has pointed out, from an individual perspective workers act 'rationally' when they conceive their interests in opposition to other workers', yet collective struggles reflect an alternative rationality which emerges spontaneously, much to the chagrin of rational-choice theorists, throughout history.[73] Despite the many criticisms made of Lukács's early work that suggest the contrary, because the notion of the standpoint of the proletariat is grounded in the history of the labour movement it would be a mistake to conceive of it as an intellectual imposition on workers. As Lukács himself argued, 'in no sense is it the party's role to impose any kind of abstract, cleverly devised tactics upon the masses. On the contrary, it must continuously learn from their struggle and their conduct of it.'[74] The standpoint of the proletariat is therefore a perspective generalised from the history of working-class struggles against capitalism; struggles which have taught Marxists that the priorities of capitalism can be challenged, and that there is an alternative to the status quo. Beyond the political lessons that can be drawn from them, these struggles suggest a prior social structure which Marxists have sought to understand so as to overcome.

With regard to the method by which Marx attempted this analysis, he wrote that the 'only way in which thought' might 'appropriate' the 'concrete in the mind' was through a process of 'rising from the abstract to the concrete'.[75] By this process Marx did not mean to eliminate the need for empirical research; quite the opposite. He argued that the social scientist must start with the totality as it appears – he gives the example of a population of a given society – and then by slow process break down the totality into the many constituent parts that determine its nature. Only then could the social scientist reconstruct the original totality from its many determinations. At the start and end of this method there would exist a population, but where at the beginning of the process this was a 'chaotic' concept, once it was thus analysed it could be reconstructed as a 'rich totality of many determinations and relations'.[76] The power of this method lies in its ability to inform the replacement of bad, unanalytical, concepts, such as that of an undifferentiated population, with analytically powerful concepts such as social class. The difference between these two types of concept is fundamental to Marxism, for where a richly determined concept could be used to explain social dynamics, a chaotic concept could not. Marx therefore differentiated between his real, or concrete, abstractions and the false, or abstract, abstractions deployed by other theorists.

Marx's careful deployment of concepts does not, contra his empiricist critics, imply the his approach eschews empirical description while embracing one form or another of reductionism. In fact, as I argue in the next chapter, in his historical studies Marx reduces neither human agency nor non-economic structures to underlying economic processes. Furthermore, as Geoffrey de Ste. Croix has powerfully argued, and as many Marxist historians have demonstrated in practice, there is no necessary contradiction between Marx's conception of social structure and the demand that historians attempt to richly describe historical processes.[77]

In its most sophisticated presentation, the Marxist conception of underlying structures is not in the least reductive. The philosopher of science Roy Bhaskar has argued, in terms compatible with Marxism, that explanatory structures operate as 'causal powers' beneath our empirical observations of the world. A causal power is a mechanism immanent to something through which it may or may not bring about change in the world.[78] A man carrying a gun in a crowded street, for instance, has the capacity to kill, but may choose not to realise this potential. The power to do something does not therefore entail that it will be done. Similarly, while the shared experience of exploitation might tend to provoke workers to see themselves as a distinct social class, countless of other forces will mediate against this eventuality. As Bhaskar argues, in complex systems underlying powers can act only as tendencies because they exist in 'open systems', within which many different powers interact with each other in a complex and dynamic manner.[79] The unifying experience of class oppression and exploitation, for instance, is typically countered by other tendencies, including the equally economic, but fragmenting, experience of competition for jobs. These underlying powers obviously will be experienced through their interaction with myriad other tendential powers, such that there would be no sense in reducing history to the operation of just one of those underlying powers. Nevertheless, that class struggles occur demands explanation, and Bhaskar argues that science is interested in inferring those explanatory powers that must be present in the real world if such empirical results are to be explained.[80] This process of inference is not equivalent to the reduction of empirical events to underlying causes, but rather suggests a research agenda: if social class, for instance, can be inferred from the existence of class struggles in the real world, then it is incumbent on historians to ask questions of the class structure of a society when examining it. More generally, if Marx was right to define humans as social producers, then the power of his insight is to be realised through historical research which sets out from the concept of the mode of production.

Andrew Collier has incorporated this approach into his discussion of Marx's theory of history. He argues that as historical materialism posits the existence within society of a series of underlying relations, each with its own causal powers, history is best understood as an open system within which those powers may or may not be actualised by real actors. Accordingly, in so far as Marx makes seemingly inevitablist statements, these are best understood as referring to 'open-ended inevitability'. Collier describes this form of inevitability as being more akin to predictions of the sort involved in the claim 'On the basis of the geography, drainage system and climate of an area that sooner or later it will be subject to serious flooding', in opposition to the closed system claim 'Water kept at standard pressure will boil if sufficiently heated'. He concludes that historical materialism 'is not a theory of inevitable stages through which history must pass'.[81]

Marxist historiography aims to provide a framework through which past processes can be understood and to inform analyses of those causal powers in the present system whose operation tends to foster or to impede the struggle for human liberation. Marxist studies of the past relate to contemporary struggles, therefore, both by locating them within the broad parabola of human history and by discerning relevant lessons from which the contemporary movement might learn. This is neither a reductive nor an empiricist project. Rather it is a theoretically and politically informed research agenda, which demands a clear understanding of the past to help inform contemporary socialist practice.

Conclusion

Marx liked to repeat the Lancashire phrase 'The proof of the pudding is in the eating', perhaps because it was somewhat pithier than his own similar second thesis on Feuerbach:

> The question whether objective truth can be attributed to human thinking is not a question of theory but is a *practical question*. Man must prove the truth, *i.e.*, the reality and power, the this-sidedness of his thinking, in practice. The dispute over the reality or non-reality of thinking which is isolated from practice is a purely scholastic question.[82]

The point of this thesis was to defend revolutionary practice against scholastic contemplation, but it can be equally generalised to justify the power of historical materialism through its practical application in the work of a series of powerful historical studies, from Marx's *Eighteenth Brumaire*, through Trotsky's *History of the Russian Revolution* and James's *The Black Jacobins* to the work of the British Marxist historians[83] and, more recently, the history produced by Perry Anderson, Guy Bois, Robin Blackburn, Bob Brenner, Neil Davidson, John Haldon, Jim Holstun, Neville Kirk, Brian Kelly, Peter Kriedte, Peter Linebaugh, Tim Mason, Marcus Rediker, Benno Teshke, Chris Wickham, Howard Zinn and many others. In this book I argue that Marx, alongside the socialist activists, historians, philosophers, political scientists and social theorists who have been influenced by his ideas, have made fundamentally important contributions to our understanding of the past, and to the nature of ongoing social processes. To that end I aim to outline Marx's contribution to the theory of history, and the contributions and debates that have been made by those who have built on his insights. My work therefore operates, in the first instance, as a practical refutation of the suggestion that historical materialism is a form of either economic reductionism or naïve positivism that died with the Soviet Union in 1991, and, second, as a contribution to the debate within Marxism as to the most powerful of the competing interpretations of historical materialism.

Notes

1 V. E. Bonnell and L. Hunt 'Introduction' to V. E. Bonnell and L. Hunt eds *Beyond the Cultural Turn* (Berkeley, CA, 1999). The discussion above is based on this essay; the quoted matter is taken from pp. 3–4.

2 P. Blackledge 'Realism and Renewals' *Contemporary Politics* 7:4, 2001; P. Blackledge *Perry Anderson, Marxism and the New Left* (London, 2004); see also M. Perry *Marxism and History* (London, 2002), pp. 22–7.

3 A. Callinicos *The Revenge of History* (Cambridge, 1991).
4 Arthur Marwick is professor of history at the Open University.
5 A. Marwick *The New Nature of History* (London, 2001), p. 9.
6 J. Arnold *History: A Very Short Introduction* (Oxford, 2000), p. 85. For a number of similarly appreciative comments on the influence of Marxism on contemporary history see the various interviews collected in M. L. G. Pallares-Burke *The New History: Confessions and Conversations* (Cambridge, 2002).
7 Marwick *New Nature of History*, p. 7.
8 T. Judt 'Chronicles of a Death Foretold' in A. Ryan ed. *After the End of History* (London, 1992), pp. 115–16.
9 I. Kershaw 'Facts Don't Reflect Myths of Power' *Times Higher Education Supplement*, 16 January 2004, p. 23.
10 C. Hill 'History and the Present' in C. Hill *A Nation of Change and Novelty* (London, 1990), p. 246.
11 P. Joyce 'The End of Social History?' in K. Jenkins ed. *The Postmodern History Reader* (London, 1997), p. 346; Marwick *New Nature of History*, p. 5.
12 Marwick *New Nature of History*, pp. 8, 3.
13 Ibid., p. 2.
14 Ibid., pp. 7–8.
15 Richard Evans is professor of modern history at Cambridge University
16 Marwick *New Nature of History*, p. 17; G. R. Elton *The Practice of History* (London, 2002 [1967]), pp. 52–60.
17 Elton *Practice of History*, p. 49; R. Evans 'Afterword' in Elton *Practice of History*, p. 202.
18 R. Evans *In Defence of History* (London, 2000 [1997]), p. 73.
19 Ibid., p. 84.
20 Ibid., p. 115.
21 Ibid., pp. 116–23; David Abraham *The Collapse of the Weimer Republic: Political Economy and Crisis* (Princeton, NJ, 1981).
22 Ibid., p. 124.
23 R. Evans *Telling Lies About Hitler* (London, 2002), p. 11.
24 Ibid., pp. 246–7.
25 Ibid., p. 247.
26 Evans *In Defence of History*, p. 112.
27 Ibid., p. 244.
28 Ibid., p. 245.
29 E. Hobsbawm *Echoes of the Marseillaise* (London, 1990), pp. 5, 97.
30 Evans *In Defence of History*, pp. 265–6.
31 K. Jenkins *Re-Thinking History* (London, 2003 [1991]), p. 7.
32 Joyce 'The End of Social History?', p. 247.
33 K. Jenkins *Refiguring History* (London, 2003), p. 5.
34 G. Stedman Jones *Languages of Class* (Cambridge, 1983), pp. 20, 22.
35 N. Kirk 'History, Language, Ideas and Postmodernism: A Materialist View' in Jenkins ed. *The Postmodern History Reader*, p. 333. For Marxist criticisms of Stedman Jones see N. Kirk 'Class and the "Linguistic Turn" in Chartist and Post-Chartist Historiography' in N. Kirk ed. *Social Class and Marxism* (Aldershot, 1996); J. Foster 'The Declassing of Language' *New Left Review* no. 150 March–April 1985; J. Saville *1848: The British State and the Chartist Movement*

(Cambridge, 1987), pp. 217ff.; D. Thompson *Outsiders* (London, 1993), pp. 35ff.; A. Callinicos *Making History* (Leiden, 2004), pp. 143ff.
36 Stedman Jones *Languages of Class*, pp. 21–2.
37 G. Stedman Jones 'The Determinist Fix: Some Obstacles to the Further Development of the Linguistic Approach to History in the 1990s' *History Workshop Journal* 42, Autumn 1996, p. 20.
38 A. Callinicos *Is There a Future for Marxism?* (London, 1982), pp. 25–52.
39 P. Anderson *In the Tracks of Historical Materialism* (London, 1983), pp. 40–51.
40 R. Samuel 'Reading the Signs' *History Workshop Journal* 32, autumn 1991, pp. 104, 106.
41 G. Spivak 'Can the Subaltern Speak?' in C. Nelson and Grossberg eds *Marxism and the Interpretation of Culture* (Urbana, IL, 1988); G. Spivak 'Subaltern Studies: Deconstructing Historiography' in D. Landry and G. MacLean eds *The Spivak Reader* (London, 1996). On the journal *Subaltern Studies* see P. Jani 'Mapping Subaltern Studies and the Postcolonial' *Historical Materialism* 11:3, 2003, pp. 271–88; V. Kaiwar 'Towards Orientalism and Nativism: The Impasse of Subaltern Studies' *Historical Materialism* 12:2, 2004, pp. 189–247.
42 A. Ahmed 'Postcolonial Theory and the "Post-" Condition' in L. Panitch ed. *The Socialist Register* 1997, p. 378. Cf. M. Bunzl *Real History* (London, 1997), pp. 77–83; B. Palmer *Descent into Discourse* (Philadelphia, 1990), pp. 26–37; W. Thompson *Postmodernism and History* (London, 2004), pp. 102–5; A. Callinicos 'Marxism and the Crisis of Social History' in J. Rees ed. *Essays on Historical Materialism* (London, 1998).
43 A. Gramsci *Selections from the Prison Notebooks* (London, 1971), p. 55.
44 R. Samuel 'Reading the Signs: II. Fact-Grubbers and Mind-Readers' *History Workshop Journal* 33, spring 1992, pp. 245–6.
45 K. Marx and F. Engels *The German Ideology* (London, 1970 [1845]), p. 62.
46 Ibid., pp. 47, 51. In chapter 2 I show that Engels developed this argument in his 1874 essay 'The Part Played by Labour in the Transition from Ape to Man'.
47 D. McNally *Bodies of Meaning* (New York, 2001), p. 111.
48 V. N. Volosinov *Marxism and the Philosophy of Language* (Harvard, 1986 [1929]), p. 21.
49 Ibid., pp. 70, 82.
50 Q. Skinner 'Meaning and Understanding in the History of Ideas' *History and Theory* 8, 1969, p. 4.
51 Ibid., p. 37; cf. Q. Skinner *Foundations of Modern Political Thought* (Cambridge, 1978), p. xi.
52 Skinner 'Meaning', p. 49.
53 Ibid., p. 42. For more on Skinner's relationship to Marxism see the interview with him republished in Pallares-Burke *The New History*, pp. 218–21.
54 J. G. A. Pocock *Virtue, Commerce and History* (Cambridge, 1985), p. 14.
55 N. Wood *Reflections on Political Theory* (London, 2002), pp. 103, 109.
56 C. Hill 'The Word "Revolution"' in C. Hill *A Nation of Change and Novelty* (London, 1990), pp. 97–8; see also E. P. Thompson *Customs in Common* (London, 1991), pp. 274–5.
57 R. Williams *Keywords* (London, 1976), p. 226.
58 C. Hill 'The Word "Revolution"', p. 88.
59 Ibid., p. 100.

60 This anthropology is discussed in chapter 2.
61 See K. Marx *Capital* Vol. I (London, 1976 [1867]), pp. 175–6.
62 Marx *Poverty of Philosophy*, p. 120.
63 G. Lukács *History and Class Consciousness* (London, 1971), pp. 69, 50, 63, 193.
64 Ibid., pp. 54, 48.
65 Ibid., pp. 157–8.
66 G. Lukács *Lenin* (London, 1970 [1924]), p. 9.
67 K. Marx and F. Engels 'The Holy Family' in K. Marx and F. Engels *Collected Works*, Vol. 4 (London, 1975 [1845]), p. 36.
68 For Marx's biting critique of the academic frame of mind see his 'Notes on Adolph Wagner' in *Karl Marx: Texts on Method* ed. T. Carver (Oxford, 1975 [1879–80]).
69 See I. Mészáros *Beyond Capital* (London, 1995), p. 322.
70 On the division of labour and working class struggle see P. Blackledge 'Marx and Intellectuals' in D. Bates and P. Reynolds eds *Marxism and Intellectuals* (London, 2006).
71 J. Rees *The Algebra of Revolution* (London, 1998), p. 236; S. Perkins *Marxism and the Proletariat* (London, 1993), pp. 15–45.
72 P. Burke *History and Social Theory* (Cambridge, 1992), p. 60.
73 Perkins, *Marxism and the Proletariat*, p. 52.
74 Lukács *Lenin*, p. 36 quoted in Rees *The Algebra of Revolution*, p. 228.
75 K. Marx *Grundrisse* (London, 1973 [1857]), p. 101.
76 Ibid., p. 100.
77 G. de Ste. Croix *The Class Struggle in the Ancient Greek World* (London, 1983), p. 90.
78 A. Collier *Critical Realism* (London, 1994), pp. 20–7.
79 Collier *Critical Realism*, pp. 61–8.
80 R. Bhaskar *Plato etc.* (London, 1994), pp. 23, 30. A. Sayer *Method in Social Science: A Realist Approach* (London, 1992), p. 107.
81 A. Collier *Marx* (Oxford, 2004), pp. 144, 36.
82 K. Marx 'Theses on Feuerbach' in *The German Ideology*, p. 121.
83 Cf. H. Kaye *The British Marxist Historians* (London, 1995) which contains essays on Maurice Dobb, Rodney Hilton, Christopher Hill, Eric Hobsbawm, and Edward Thompson, and H. Kaye *The Education of Desire: Marxists and the Writing of History* (London, 1992) which contains essays on George Rudé, Victor Kiernan, Edward Thompson, Leslie Morton, John Berger and the American Leo Huberman. There is a stimulating essay on Geoffrey de Ste. Croix in P. Anderson *A Zone of Engagement* (London, 1992). On Thompson see P. Anderson *Arguments within English Marxism* (London, 1980), and two books by Bryan Palmer: *The Making of E. P. Thompson* (Toronto, 1981) and *E. P. Thompson: Objections and Oppositions* (London, 1994). I have discussed Anderson's historiography in *Perry Anderson, Marxism and the New Left* (London, 2004). Additionally Jim Holstun provides a stimulating overview of Brian Manning's contribution to Marxist historiography in *International Socialism* 2:103, 2004, while I have offered a more modest overview of John Saville's work in *International Socialism* 2: 105, 2004. See also V. Kiernan 'Problems of Marxist History' *New Left Review* no. 161, January–February 1987.

2

Marx, Engels and historical materialism

Introduction

In this chapter I outline Marx and Engels's theory of history and its relationship to their revolutionary political practice. Many commentators would cite two reasons for dismissing such a project: first, Marx and Engels were not a unity, their ideas and arguments diverging markedly; and, second, neither Marx nor Engels individually produced a coherent and singular *oeuvre*. While there is obviously some truth in these claims, I have reservations about both of them. As to the suggestion that Marx's and Engels's interpretations of historical materialism diverged sharply, I follow Draper and Hobsbawm in recognising differences in stress between these two collaborators, while finding it somewhat implausible that two men of such obvious intellectual capacities could work so closely together for four decades without noticing that they were not in close agreement.[1] However, it is the view that there are a plurality of Marxes (or, less frequently, Engelses) from which we might cherry pick to construct the Marxism of our choice that I am most concerned to reject. Something of the weakness with this approach is evident in two recent studies of historical materialism: Steve Rigby's *Marxism and History* and Gerry Cohen's *Karl Marx's Theory of History*.[2] Rigby claimed that the discovery of a series of 'internally coherent but mutually contradictory Marxes . . . is the inevitable result of a variety of readers making sense of Marx's extensive works'; and, given the multiplicity of Marxes thus conceived, Rigby pointed out that his aim was not to outline what Marx actually said but to reconstruct what is most useful from Marx's 'ambiguous legacy'. Similarly, Cohen made clear that his aim was to 'reconstruct' from Marx's messy legacy 'a less untidy version' of historical materialism.[3] Nevertheless, despite these shared aims, Cohen and Rigby reconstruct two diametrically opposed Marxisms from Marx's legacy. Whereas Cohen defends a strong version of productive-force determinism, Rigby dismisses the relevance of that interpretation of Marxism and defends the power of Marx's critique of economic reductionism.[4] The methods of Cohen and Rigby would appear to imply that we can reconstruct the Marx(ism) of our choice from the writings of Marx (and Engels).

I am not convinced of the validity of this claim; for while it is obviously the case that Marx, like any other great thinker, can be quoted against himself; it is less obvious, in the absence of a careful contextualisation of each statement, that such a method can achieve much more than the trivialisation of the subject. For instance, Rigby quotes Marx's comment, from the Preface to volume 1 of *Capital* (1867), that within the book he treats individuals only as 'personifications of economic categories' as evidence of the worst form of economic determinism from which he seeks to liberate the best of Marx's historiography, without commenting on either the theoretical or the historical context within which this statement was made. By contrast with his dismissal of this seemingly reductionist formulation of Marx's method, Rigby approvingly quotes Marx and Engels's anti-reductionist argument articulated in *The Holy Family* (1845): 'History does nothing, it possesses *no* immense wealth, it wages no battles. It is man, real living man who does all that, who possesses and fights, "history" is not, as it were, a person apart, using man as a means to achieve *its own* aims; history is nothing but the activity of man pursuing his aims.'[5] Despite the superficial plausibility of this contrast, we can be certain that Marx had not rejected his earlier methodology when he wrote *Capital.* As the first volume *Capital* was in press, Marx was presented with a copy of *The Holy Family* by his friend Kugelmann, and on reading this long-lost work he reported in a letter to Engels – 24 April 1867 – that he was 'pleasantly surprised to find that we have no need to feel ashamed of the piece'.[6] Such a response to his reading of his earlier arguments demands some explanation: either Marx had misunderstood the gap between his contemporary structuralism and his earlier humanism or the relationship between the two articulations of his understanding of history is more complex than Rigby suggests. A more sympathetic reading of the gap between these two statements would begin by noting the different levels of abstraction at which they were written.[7] As Marx argued that the 'only way in which thought' might 'appropriate' the 'concrete in the mind' was through a process of 'rising from the abstract to the concrete', then it is plain that his writings will include a series of abstract postulates, which, if taken out of the context of the totality of *oeuvre*, will lend themselves to ahistorical parody.[8] This, unfortunately, despite its great power, is the trap into which Cohen's book falls: for he defends an interpretation of historical materialism according to which revolutionary transitions from one mode of production to another occur with a functional necessity.[9] Cohen locates Marx's 1859 Preface to the *Contribution to the Critique of Political Economy* at the centre of this reconstruction of Marxism. Unfortunately, while this is a fundamentally important text, it was written with an eye to the censor and correspondingly tends to downplay the active side of Marx's thought.[10] While this would be unproblematical if the Preface were read in the context of Marx's revolutionary practice, Cohen fails to do this and defends, as I argue in chapter 5, an interpretation of historical materialism which is systematically fatalistic in a way that is quite alien to Marx. In opposition to both Cohen and Rigby, I follow Draper in arguing that if Marx's revolutionary method is judged as a totality, rather than by decontextualised statements, then a much more powerful interpretation of historical materialism is possible.[11] I also agree with Hobsbawm, Hill and Mészáros that Marx's theory of history 'had already found its mature formulation in the mid 1840s, and remained substantially unchanged in later years'.[12]

Production and history

Marx's theory of history is so often derided as an, indeed the, archetypical form of economic reductionism that it seems almost churlish to point out that the very core of his project involved a rejection of the reification of the concepts of the economic, the political and the sociological, etc., as distinct levels in society. As Lucio Colletti argued, 'never in Marx do we find economic categories that are purely economic categories. All his concepts, on the contrary, are both economic and sociological.'[13] Throughout his life Marx insisted that it was *production*, understood as a social, political and historical process, that was at the centre of the social totality. He repeatedly distinguished his theory of history from all others by placing the production process, not 'the economy', at its centre.

Perhaps the classic statement of this approach is to be found in *The German Ideology*, in which Marx and Engels wrote that men and women – that is real, concrete, historical men and women rather than the abstractions beloved of social Darwinists – 'begin to distinguish themselves from animals as soon as they begin to *produce* their means of subsistence'. They insisted that in producing socially, these 'definite individuals . . . enter into definite social and political relations', the concrete form of which can not be deduced *a priori* but must be ascertained through 'empirical observation'.[14] So, from the very beginning, Marx and Engels counterposed their *materialist* interpretation of history to idealistic models, generally, and more specifically to what they perceived to be the idealism of the Young Hegelian circle out of which their ideas evolved. Marx and Engels therefore contrasted their theory of history, within which language and ideas grow out of the production process, to the Hegelian idealistic view according to which history is the teleological story of world spirit (God) realising itself: 'in contrast to German philosophy which descends from heaven to earth, here we ascend from earth to heaven'.[15]

One key consequence of their demand that historical generalisations be empirically grounded was that they rejected both religious interpretations of history and also crudely materialistic approaches. So, in contrast to Feuerbach's[16] crude materialism – according to which history is the story of man's encounter with nature – Marx and Engels argued that it was only through history that men and women create themselves as social beings. If the first action of history is that which aims at satisfying some basic needs –

to eat, drink, maintain warmth, etc. – then in satisfying those needs real historical men and women, as opposed to humans understood as a transhistorical category, would create new needs.[17] By historicising human needs in this way, Marx historicises the concept of human nature itself: for if it is our nature to aim at satisfying our needs, and if our needs capacities' change through history, then so too does our nature itself change. This suggestion does not lead Marx to reject the concept of human nature *tout court*, but rather he seeks to attain a more powerful analysis of it than that implied by those whose methodological starting point is the individual. Accordingly, he differentiates between a fairly basic and transhistorical 'human nature', or 'species being', and a more malleable 'nature of humanity', or 'social being'.[18] Marx expressed this view most systematically in *Capital* through a critique of Bentham's utilitarianism in which he argued that both the historical and transhistorical components of human nature must be uncovered:

> To know what is useful for a dog, one must study dog-nature. This nature itself is not to be deduced from the principle of utility. Applying this to man, he that would criticise all human acts, movements, relations, etc., by the principle of utility, must first deal with human nature in general, and then with human nature as modified in each historical epoch. Bentham makes short work of it. With the driest naiveté he takes the modern shopkeeper, especially the English shopkeeper, as the normal man.[19]

To understand history, Marx insisted, we must learn to view it as a process of change and continuity: certain transhistorical features of humanity are realised throughout history in specific determinate conditions. Any historian who downplays either the common or the specific features of any epoch would necessarily produce an inadequate history of the period. However, of these two failings it was the latter which was by far the more significant; for the failure to adequately periodise the past would have the effect of dehistoricising history. This, in effect, is the Marxist critique of the dominant strand of historiography from antiquity to the present day. Thus, political history – that which the nineteenth-century English social historian J. R. Green dismissed as 'drum and trumpet' history, and which Marx and Engels scathingly criticised as 'the high-sounding dramas of princes and states' – had the effect of not only writing out of the historical record the vast bulk of humanity , but of obscuring the historical specificity of each period under investigation.[20]

It was the 'absurd' ahistorical consequences of this 'conception of history' which informed Marx's critique of the crass empiricism of the Rankean kind. While Marx criticised both Hegel's idealism and Ranke's empiricism, he did not judge their failings to be equally severe. Indeed, despite his criticisms of Hegel, he distanced himself from those who regarded this idealist philosopher as a 'dead dog' by openly avowing himself a 'pupil of that mighty thinker'. Conversely, he was much more dismissive of Ranke's empiricism; and, in a letter to Engels – 7 September 1864 – he described the father of modern historiography as a 'weed' and a 'capering little troll'. More substantively he argued that Ranke's 'mere root-grubbing' history had as a necessary consequence the attribution of 'great events to "mean and petty causes"'.[21]

Marx's criticism of Ranke gets to the heart of a fundamental problem of historiography: on what basis should facts be gathered and assessed? Marx was scathing in his criticisms of the Young Hegelians for ignoring the facts of history, but if anything his criticism of the empiricists was even more severe, because, while they collected facts diligently, they could not justify their choice of which facts to collect. By contrast, Marx's general answer to the problem of the historical method lay in his anthropology: if men and women distinguished themselves from nature through social production, then the fundamental questions to ask of any historical period would include those regarding the nature of production within that period. Marx was to reiterate this point endlessly throughout his life. In *Capital* (1867) he noted that 'writers of history have so far paid very little attention to the development of material production, which is the basis of all social life, and therefore of all real history'.[22] Similarly, in his *Notes on Adolph Wagner* (1879) he criticised Wagner's supposition that people begin by 'standing in that theoretical relation to the thing of the external world'. On the contrary, Marx insisted, 'they begin, like every animal, by eating, drinking etc., hence . . . by relating themselves actively, taking hold of certain things in the external world through action, and thus satisfying their need[s]'.[23]

Marx provided his most complete outline of this argument in the *Grundrisse* (1857). In this manuscript he suggested that because the production process changed over time, despite the fact that 'all epochs of production have certain common traits', there did exist specific qualities whose 'elements . . . are not general and common [but] must be separated out from the determinations valid for production as such, so that . . . their essential difference is not forgotten'.[24] Against the suggestion that it is consumption which determines the nature of production, Marx argued that while the desire to satisfy human needs within nature is the starting point of history, because consumption could not occur without their first being some form of production and because the act of production creates new needs both within the production process and for the producer, 'production and consumption are . . . moments of one process, in which production is the real point of departure and hence also the predominant moment'.[25] More generally, he insisted that production, distribution, exchange and consumption all form part of a 'totality' within which 'production predominates'.[26] So, according to Marx, each social structure is best understood as a whole within which production is of fundamental importance. While this model does not deny the historical significance of political and ideological moments within the totality, it refuses to reify politics and ideology, etc., as distinct and separate levels. So, while Marx was keen to stress that 'the concrete is concrete because it is the concentration of many determinations, hence unity of the diverse',[27] his model, as Hobsbawm has pointed out, is much more than a pluralistic account of the reciprocal interaction of factors within history.[28] Marx attempted to create a methodological space between reductionism and pluralism: for, where reductionism negated the study of history, pluralism tended to descend into simple empiricist descriptions of events that have little analytical value.[29]

The importance of this methodological innovation should not be underestimated, because it suggests a solution to the post-modernist challenge to contemporary history. For where contemporary empiricist historiography cannot justify its claim to aim at, in Ranke's words, telling history as 'it really was' in the face of the post-modernist argument that all descriptions are necessarily partial and biased, Marx implies that by rooting historical enquiries within the process of production the choice of the historiographical starting point can be anthropologically justified: he offers a guide by which historians might navigate the treacherous path between what Pierre Vilar labelled the equally treacherous 'abyss of empiricism' and that 'abyss of idealism'.[30] However, to start a historical analysis with an investigation of the production process obviously does not guarantee the power of the history thus produced. It was to guard against the error of reducing history to production that Marx insisted that the study of concrete moments in history demanded an analysis of the 'concentration of many determinations' in those periods. More specifically, he and Engels insisted that when

> viewed apart from real history, these abstractions have in themselves no value whatsoever. They can only serve to facilitate the arrangement of historical material and to indicate the sequence of its separate strata. But they by no means afford a recipe, or schema, as does philosophy, for neatly trimming the epochs of history.[31]

Similarly, in the context of the rising socialist movement in Germany in the years after Marx's death, Engels felt compelled to distance his and Marx's arguments from those of their epigones. In a letter to Joseph Bloch – 21 September 1890 – Engels argued:

> According to the materialist conception of history, the *ultimately* determining element in history is the production and reproduction of real life. Other than this neither Marx nor I have ever asserted. Hence if somebody twists this into saying that the economic element is the *only* determining one, he transforms that proposition into a meaningless, abstract, senseless phrase. The economic situation is the basis, but the various elements of the superstructure – political forms of the class struggle and its results, to wit: constitutions established by the victorious class after a successful battle, etc., juridical forms, and even the reflexes of all these actual struggles in the brains of the participants, political, juristic, philosophical theories, religious views and their further development into systems of dogmas – also exercise their influence upon the course of the historical struggles and in many cases preponderate in determining their *form*. There is an interaction of all these elements in which, amid all the endless host

> of accidents (that is, of things and events whose inner interconnection is so remote or so impossible of proof that we can regard it as non-existent, as negligible), the economic movement finally asserts itself as necessary. Otherwise the application of the theory to any period of history would be easier than the solution of a simple equation of the first degree.

More specifically, Engels, in a letter to Conrad Schmidt – 27 October 1890 – argued that the state, in contrast to economic reductionist readings of historical materialism, would enjoy a degree of 'relative independence' of the economic base, such that 'political power can wreak havoc with economic development'. Engels stressed the importance of political, ideological and other 'factors' to the explanation of the historical process. However, rather than outline a detailed map of his and Marx's method, he suggested that if Bloch wanted to understand historical materialism he should read Marx's 'Eighteenth Brumaire' (1852) and *Capital*, and his own *Anti-Dühring* (1877), and *Ludwig Feuerbach and the End of Classical German Philosophy* (1886). Engels commented in that letter to Bloch:

> Marx and I are ourselves partly to blame for the fact that the younger people sometimes lay more stress on the economic side than is due to it. We had to emphasise the main principle *vis-à-vis* our adversaries, who denied it, and we had not always the time, the place or the opportunity to give their due to the other elements involved in the interaction. But when it came to presenting a section of history, that is, to making a practical application, it was a different matter and there no error was permissible.

Ignoring Engels's suggestion, most commentators on Marx have chosen not to delve too deeply into their historiography, but to analyse Marx's famous 1859 Preface to his *Contribution to the Critique of Political Economy* as a surrogate for his entire oeuvre. Unfortunately, if taken out of its context, this essay can suggest a particularly reductionist model of history. According to the Preface;

> In the social production of their existence, men inevitably enter into definite relations, which are independent of their will, namely relations of production appropriate to a given stage in the development of their material forces of production. The totality of these relations of production constitutes the economic structure of society, the real foundations on which arises a legal and political superstructure and to which correspond definite forms of social consciousness . . . At a certain stage of development, the material productive forces of society come into conflict with the existing relations of production . . . From forms of development of the productive forces these relations turn into their fetters. Then begins an era of social revolution. The changes in the economic foundation lead sooner or later to the transformation of the whole immense superstructure. In studying such transformations it is always necessary to distinguish between the material transformation of the economic conditions of production, which can be determined with the precision of natural science, and the legal, political, religious, artistic or philosophic – in short, ideological forms in which

> men become conscious of this conflict and fight it out. Just as one does not judge an individual by what he thinks about himself, so one cannot judge such a period of transformation by its consciousness, but, on the contrary, this consciousness must be explained from the contradictions of material life, from the conflict existing between the social forces of production and the relations of production. No social order is ever destroyed before all the productive forces for which it is sufficient have been developed, and new superior relations of production never replace older ones before the material conditions for their existence have matured within the framework of the old society. Mankind thus inevitably sets itself only such tasks as it is able to solve, since closer examination will always show that the problem itself arises only when the material conditions for its solution are already present or at least in the course of formation. In broad outline, the Asiatic, ancient, feudal and modern bourgeois modes of production may be designated as epochs marking progress in the economic development of society. The bourgeois mode of production is the last antagonistic form of the social process of production – antagonistic not in the sense of individual antagonism but of an antagonism that emanates from the individuals' social conditions of existence – but the productive forces developing within bourgeois society create also the material conditions for a solution of this antagonism. The prehistory of human society accordingly closes with this social formation.[32]

As Prinz argues, Marx was keen in this essay to stress the scientific objectivity of his enterprise, and to play down his practical revolutionary intentions so that he could bypass the Prussian censor and therefore speak to socialist activists in Germany. So, rather ironically, practical revolutionary reasons explain the dry anti-humanist prose of this passage. Nevertheless, once we take this context into account we can learn much from this passage, for in it Marx articulates his understanding of the process of production as it had been deepened in the years after 1845. In *The German Ideology*, in addition to rooting ideas and politics, etc., within the production process, he had divided production itself into two separate analytical spheres: the forces of production – the means of production and the labour power required to utilise those instruments and raw materials[33] – and forms of intercourse – an early articulation of his concept of relations of production. While the concept of forms of intercourse betrayed a certain level of technological determinism in Marx's early thought, with his articulation of the concept of relations of production in *The Poverty of Philosophy* (1847) his mature theory of history is for the first time elaborated in full.[34] The concept of relations of production was central to this project because through it, as Therborn has argued, Marx realised his aim of periodising history.[35] Accordingly, if humans were defined as socially producing animals, then distinct productive epochs could be differentiated by the relations of production that dominated within each. Hence Marx periodised history into a series of modes of production, each of which he understood as a distinct articulation of forces and relations of production.

According to Marx, relations of production were economic relations of effective control; that is essentially exploitative relations between classes.[36] Marx argued that class grew out of the division of labour. In hunter–gatherer societies a rough division of labour existed between the sexes: women, because of the demands of pregnancy and child-rearing, predominantly gathered, while men hunted. However, the development of the productive forces tended to generate an increasingly complex division of labour. At first this division merely reflected natural 'predisposition', but as it expanded so it took the form of a division between mental and manual labour. Henceforth, a certain group of individuals coalesced out of the division of labour as a new class which slowly took control of the production process. Moreover, the division between mental and material labour helped generate a scorn for manual labour on the part of mental labourers, and a corresponding and one-sided anti-intellectualism on the part of manual labourers. This division informed the self-consciousness of intellectuals, who could flatter themselves that consciousness 'is something other than consciousness of existing practice': the disdain shown among many modern historians for Marxism's stress on the importance of production to the understanding of social practice is but one example of this self-deceit.[37] As I point out below, Engels fleshed out this schematic account of the consequences of the division of labour in *The Origin of the Family, Private Property and the State* (1884). For the moment, it is enough to say that Marx explained class as a historical phenomenon through his analysis of the division of labour.

Class, for Marx, can be reduced neither to status nor to consciousness; it is rather, in Geoffrey de Ste. Croix's words, an objective 'expression of the fact of exploitation', and a class is a 'group of persons in a community identified by their position in the whole system of social production, defined above all according to their relationship (primarily in terms of degree of control) to the conditions of production . . . and to other classes'. As Ste. Croix points out, class conflict 'is essentially the fundamental relationship between classes involving exploitation and resistance to it, but not necessarily either class consciousness or collective activity in common'.[38] According to Ste. Croix, the appeal of the Marxist conception of class lies in its analytical power: Marx's model explains class conflict in a much deeper sense than, for instance, Weber's conception of status, which, because it is a static concept, 'hardly helps us to understand or to explain anything except in the most trite and innocuous way'.[39]

As a mode of production is a distinct articulation of forces and relations of production, to define the mode dominant within any society is to provide the framework from within which the class struggle, politics, ideology, etc., of that social formation can be explained. However, to define the dominant mode of production within a specific social formation is only the first step along the process to articulating the many determinations of a specific concrete process, and lest Marx is interpreted as suggesting more than this, then

Engels's admonitions to Bloch, quoted above, should be bourne in mind. Indeed, even in an abstract formulation of the relationship between society's productive base and its political and ideological superstructure, in volume 3 of *Capital*, Marx is keen to stress that the exact structure of any given social formation can be discovered only through careful empirical analysis.

> The specific economic form, in which unpaid surplus-labour is pumped out of direct producers, determines the relationship of rulers and ruled, as it grows directly out of production itself and, in turn, reacts upon it as a determining element. Upon this, however, is founded the entire formation of the economic community which grows up out of the production relations themselves, thereby simultaneously its specific political form. It is always the direct relationship of the owners of the conditions of production to the direct producers – a relation always naturally corresponding to a definite stage in the development of the methods of labour and thereby its social productivity – which reveals the innermost secret, the hidden basis of the entire social structure and with it the political form of the relation of sovereignty and dependence, in short, the corresponding specific form of the state. This does not prevent the same economic basis – the same from the standpoint of its main conditions – due to innumerable different empirical circumstances, natural environment, racial relations, external historical influences, etc., from showing infinite variations and gradations in appearance, which can be ascertained only by analysis of the empirically given conditions.[40]

So, in his theory of history, Marx posited a method of historical analysis – to start from the mode of production – but not *a priori* answers to this analysis. While the deterministic language of the 1859 Preface might appear otherwise, it need not be read so; and if the context discussed by Prinz is taken into account it should not be.[41] For instance, against a unilinear reading of Marx's comment that history has moved through 'the Asiatic, ancient, feudal and modern bourgeois modes of production', Eric Hobsbawm has suggested that those stages be understood as a logical, not a historical, progression. In the *Grundrisse*, which was written around eighteen months before the Preface to the *Contribution to the Critique of Political Economy*, Marx had deepened his analysis of pre-capitalist economic formations so that the number of such modes had expanded since he had written *The German Ideology*, while he reiterated his belief that these various modes offered alternative paths through history. So, whereas the list of pre-capitalist modes of production was not intended to represent a unilinear path through history, it was meant to convey the idea of a logical progression towards the growing 'individualisation of man'.[42]

If the culmination of this process was to be the victory of the socialist struggles of the proletariat – 'we call communism the real movement which abolishes the present state of things'[43] – Marx's embrace of a multilinear theory of history meant that he was prepared to contend that, in certain circumstances, there could be a movement from lower to higher forms of communal ownership without an intervening capitalist stage. Because his research into the nature of pre-class societies had convinced him of their general vitality, Marx became convinced that, in favourable international conditions, it would be possible for some groups to leap across the logical stages of historical individualisation.[44]

Marx concretely developed this idea in his discussion of the Russian peasant commune. Responding to a letter from the Russian revolutionary Vera Zasulich – 16 February 1881 – asking his strategic advice regarding Russia's peasant communes, Marx spent weeks penning a series of draft responses before sending his considered reply. These comments were the considered fruits of a decade-long research programme into Russian history and politics. In fact, so serious was Marx's attempt to master the Russian situation that he taught himself Russian – according to his wife Jenny, 'as if it was a matter of life and death'.[45] The conclusion of this project was Marx's reply to Zasulich – 8 March 1881 – within which he argued that

> the analysis in *Capital* . . . provides no reasons for or against the Russian commune. But the special studies I have made of it, including a search for original source material, has convinced me that the commune is the fulcrum for social regeneration in Russia. But in order that it might function as such, the harmful influences assailing it on all sides must first be eliminated.

He argued that his suggestion, made in the Preface to the first volume of *Capital*, that English social development showed less developed countries 'the image of [their] own future'[46] referred to those West European countries in which capital accumulation had begun, not to states which had yet to start down that path.

Numerous commentators have argued that in making these claims Marx finally broke with the procrustean unilinear model that he had previously embraced.[47] Kingston-Mann argues, for instance, that until 1870 Marx was convinced that the bourgeoisie were a necessary agent of modernisation, but after that he came to accept a much more nuanced model of social evolution.[48] However, as Chattopadhyay has recently argued, that analysis misunderstands the level both of change and of continuity between Marx's mature framework. For, Marx did not hold to a unilinear model of history prior to 1870, and after 1870 he continued to believe that capital accumulation, on a world scale, remained a necessary precondition for socialism.[49] In the 1882 Preface to the Russian edition of the *Communist Manifesto*, for instance, Marx and Engels argued that 'if the Russian revolution becomes the signal for proletarian revolution in the West, so that the two complement each other, then Russia's peasant communal land-ownership may serve as the point of departure for a communist development'. Idiosyncratically, Wada dismisses the explicit linkage in this passage of the success of the Russian communes with the success of a West European revolution with the suggestion that Marx, in the wake of the death of his wife, was 'in low spirits' at the time, which explains why he allowed Engels to subvert his new multilinear model with vestiges of his older framework.[50] This claim is, to say the least, as Sayer and Corrigan pointed out, 'highly speculative'.[51] It is surely much more plausible to argue that in making these comments on the Russian commune, Marx was not rejecting his earlier materialism, but was deepening it by making it both more international[52] and more attuned to the vitality of pre-capitalist forms of communal production.

One of the central claims made in *The German Ideology*, which is a defining claim of Marxism, is that the

> development of productive forces (which itself implies the actual empirical existence of men in their world-historical, instead of local, being) is an absolutely necessary practical premise because without it want is merely made general, and with destitution the struggle for necessities and all the old filthy business would necessarily be reproduced.[53]

If Marx had rejected this argument, then he surely would no longer have been a Marxist in any meaningful sense. This is not so, suggests Rigby; or at least it need not be so, if we are to rescue something of value from historical materialism.

In so far as Rigby defends this argument, it rests on an elision: to accept 'productive force determinism', he claims, is by implication to accept that it is the productive forces rather than human actors that make history.[54] But this claim is true only if we accept a particularly mechanical model of determination. However, as Alasdair MacIntyre argued, Marx understood determination in a Hegelian sense, as denoting the process through which the economic base of a society provides 'a framework within which superstructures arise, a set off relations around which the human relations can entwine themselves, a kernel of human relationships from which all else grows'.[55] Given that the distinguishing characteristic of human production, according to Marx, was that it was a form of 'purposeful activity', it makes little sense to contrast productive-force determination with free action.[56] Rather, because we exercise free will within determinate material contexts, it is much better to follow Hegel in conceiving determination and freedom as two sides of the same coin: 'freedom is the appreciation of necessity', as Engels put it.[57]

At different moments in his younger days Marx argued that both 'labour' and 'freedom' were the 'the essence of man'.[58] These two conceptions should be understood to be complementary, and to flow from Marx's Hegelian inheritance. Marx insisted that freedom was a potential inherent in humanity that came to be realised through history; it was thus something that evolved over time through a process of collective struggles, and these struggles could best be understood against the background of the development of humanity's productive forces. Freedom should therefore not be reified as either one moment of this process or as an attribute of individuals against the social. Rather, the meaning of freedom evolves through history, as both the material parameters for its realisation expand and as groups form through struggle to fight for the realisation of those expanding demands.[59]

As to the first of these two preconditions for the realisation of expanded freedoms, Marx famously wrote in the third volume of *Capital* that 'the realm of freedom really begins only where labour determined by necessity and external expediency ends'. He insists that humanity must unceasingly struggle with nature to realise its needs because, first, there will always remain a 'realm of necessity' which demands labour if needs are to be met and, second, the expanded productive forces constructed to meet one set of needs will tend to generate new needs. So while Marx equates freedom with socialism, he does not allow us to forget that there will never be a free lunch – only meals that are more or less efficiently acquired: 'The reduction of the working day is the basic prerequisite' for the realisation of freedom.[60] So, contra Rigby, productive-force determination does not entail that productive forces, rather than human agents, make history.

Neither, despite Engels's remark at Marx's funeral that 'just as Darwin discovered the law of development or organic nature, so Marx discovered the law of development of human history', can Marx's evolutionary model of social development be reduced to a form of social Darwinism.

Marxism and evolutionism

In 1980 Margaret Fay finally put to rest the myth that Marx had sought to dedicate the first volume of *Capital* to Darwin.[61] However, that the myth had survived for the best part of a century, and continues on today despite its refutation, is evidence of its plausibility, based, as it was, on the admiration that both Marx and Engels undoubtedly shared for Darwin's 'epoch-making work'.[62] Marx argued in a letter to Engels that, despite Darwin's 'crude English style', his book 'contains the basis in natural history for our view'.[63] But if Darwinism did 'contain' historical materialism's 'basis in natural history', what was the actual relationship between the two theories?

The emergent relationship between cultural and biological evolution in Marxist theory was nowhere more eloquently expressed than in Engels's 'The Part Played by Labour in the Transition from Ape to Man' (1874). In this unfinished masterpiece Engels took issue with Darwin's interpretation of the evolution of modern humans. Darwin had argued that the decisive moment in the evolution of humans occurred with the development of large brains, after which, he assumed, the other human characteristics of upright gait, free hands and language evolved. In contrast to this hypothesis, Engels suggested that massive brain development followed on the evolution of an upright gait:

> Climbing assigns different functions to the hands and the feet, and when their mode of life involved locomotion on level ground, these apes gradually got out of the habit of using their hands [in walking] and adopted a more erect posture. This was the decisive step in the transition from ape to man.[64]

Once the hands of our ape ancestors became free then they could increasingly be used to fashion tools; and once the evolutionary advantage no longer lay with hands used for climbing, and instead moved to favour hands that could work tools, then it was only a matter of time before simian hands evolved into something resembling those of the modern humans. This fact is of great importance because it shows that 'the hand is not only the organ of labour, it is also the product of labour'.[65]

This evolutionary adaptation had profound cultural and biological consequences for the further evolution of humans. Engels notes that while social man must have evolved from a gregarious forebear, because 'labour necessarily helped to bring the members of society closer together . . . men . . . arrived at a point where they had something to say to each other'.[66] Labour therefore reinforced any tendencies towards the evolution of social behaviour, up to and including the adaptation of the larynx, facilitating the development of language. Finally, labour and language together became the two most important stimuli of rapid brain expansion.[67] Increased intelligence and technological know-how then led to the development of a more varied diet. The broadening of our ancestors' diet, in turn, underpinned further expansions of the brain, which then facilitated the conquest of fire and the domestication of livestock.[68] So, the basis for social evolution was the natural evolution of an upright gait in our simian ancestors. Social and natural evolutionary processes from then onwards reinforced each other in a positive feedback loop to propel forward the evolution of our ancestors towards our modern form. Engels argues that Darwin's inability to grasp this process was a consequence of the 'ideological influence' on his thought which tended to demean the importance of labour to social history more generally.[69]

Weikart argues that in 'The Part Played by Labour in the Transition from Ape to Man' Engels confused Darwinism and Lamarckianism.[70] In a sense this would be unsurprising, as Ernst Haeckel, Germany's foremost Darwinian at the time, accepted that acquired characteristics could be inherited. However, I do not think that Engels meant that culturally evolved characteristics could be inherited directly, and certainly his argument need not be interpreted in that way.[71] Rather, he posits a dialectical relationship between cultural and natural evolution, whereby an important part of the 'natural' environment, within which humans compete for survival, is culturally constructed, such that cultural structures will act as part of the context within which natural selection takes place.

Once humans had evolved to their modern form then natural evolution gave way to cultural evolution as the most dynamic force in human history. Engels analysed this phenomenon in *The Origin of the Family, Private Property and the State* (1884). He famously opened this popularisation and slight Marxist translation of Morgan's *Ancient Society* with the claim that through his anthropological studies, Morgan had

> discovered afresh . . . the materialistic conception of history . . . according to [which], the determining factor in history is, in the final instance, the production and reproduction of the immediate essentials of life. This, again, is of a twofold character. On the one side, the production of the means of existence, of articles of food and clothing, dwellings, and of the tools necessary for that production; on the other side, the production of human beings themselves, the propagation of the species. The social organization under which the people of a particular historical epoch and a particular country live is determined by both kinds of production: by the stage of development of labour on the one hand and of the family on the other.[72]

While Engels was attracted by Morgan's method, he reiterated his and Marx's belief that theory should be empirically grounded, and therefore attached a caveat to his argument: 'so long as no important additional material makes changes necessary, his classification will undoubtedly remain in force'.[73] For his part, Morgan had periodised human history into three main epochs – savagery, barbarism and civilisation – eras which modern scholars would label hunter–gatherer, agricultural and urban societies. Engels drew on this schema to argue that the classes, the state and women's oppression were not universal features of human history.

Specifically, Engels argued that it was only at the point in history when the productivity of labour exceeded that necessary for its own 'maintenance' that the exploitation of man by man, and the existence of social classes, became a possibility.[74] Developing the discussion of the division of labour as outlined in *The German Ideology*, he argued that the early egalitarian division of labour within the family between (male) hunters and (female) gatherers became transformed into a power relationship as the move to pastoralism dramatically increased the status of the man without changing the division of labour within the family: for as the woman's domestic position brought less and less wealth into the household relative to the man's new wealth in livestock, so too did the position of women deteriorate relative to the position of men.[75] Furthermore, with the increased productivity of labour and the existence of surplus product, warfare became endemic as people stole both livestock and other people to use as slaves. Wars over the control of social surplus in turn begat warriors; and a new division of labour between men developed atop that between men and women. This division had a twofold character: on the one hand men could now become the spoils of war, creating a new class of unfree labour; while a second division arose between more and less powerful men within the victorious groups. Engels argued that 'from the first great social division of labour arose the first great cleavage of society into two classes: masters and slaves, exploiters and exploited'.[76] It was at this point in history that the concept of private property emerged to delineate the control of particular individuals over parts of the social surplus. Once private property emerged, the problem of how to reproduce it over generations became a concrete issue. Where, previously, descent had been measured through the mother, now the needs of fathers to pass on their property to their children demanded that they have sole sexual access to specific women. In this context, the family developed not as a realm of domestic bliss 'which forms the ideal of the present day philistine', but as a property right bestowed on the man. Engels points out that the etymology of the word 'family' can be traced back to the Roman word *familia* which referred to 'the total number of slaves belonging to one man'.[77] So, in contrast to the reproductive structure of savage and barbarian groups, the emergence of civilisation marked 'the overthrow of mother right', which was itself 'the world historical defeat of the female sex'.[78] After a protracted process, the new inequalities and divisions were solidified, and with the birth of civilisation there emerged 'a class which no longer concerns itself with production'.[79] However, as class exploitation and sexual oppression emerged through history, then so did the struggles against them. In this context, the state grew as a structure that was needed to stabilise society – and to do so in the interests of the new ruling class.

> The state is . . . a product of society at a particular stage of development; it is the admission that this society has involved itself in insoluble self-contradiction and is cleft into irreconcilable antagonisms which it is powerless to exorcise. But in order that these antagonisms, classes with conflicting economic interests, shall not consume themselves and society in fruitless struggle, a power, apparently standing above society, has become necessary to moderate the conflict and keep it within the bounds of 'order' . . . [However], as the state . . . also arose in the thick of the fight between the classes, it is normally the state of the most powerful, economically ruling class, which by its means becomes also the politically ruling class, and so acquires new means of holding down and exploiting the oppressed class. The ancient state was, above all, the state of the slave-owners for holding down the slaves, just as the feudal state was the organ of the nobility for holding down the peasant serfs and bondsmen, and the modern representative state is the instrument for exploiting wage-labour by capital. Exceptional periods, however, occur when the warring classes are so nearly equal in forces that the state power, as apparent mediator, acquires for the moment a certain independence in relation to both. This applies to the absolute monarchy of the seventeenth and eighteenth centuries, which balances the nobility and the bourgeoisie against one another; and to the Bonapartism of the First and particularly of the Second French Empire.[80]

Hence Engels explained the rise of classes, the state and sexual oppression within the context of the change in the mode of production from hunter–gatherer societies through agricultural societies to the emergence of urban societies. Research has moved on since 1884, and many of Engels's arguments have been superseded – it had moved on by 1891 when Engels noted in the Preface to the fourth edition of the book that this research had 'disproved' some of Morgan's minor hypotheses. Nevertheless, as Eleanor Burke Leacock has claimed of Engels's book, 'despite its shortcomings, it is still a masterful and profound theoretical synthesis'.[81] Conversely, other commentators, while praising Engels's work, have rejected his main theoretical claim. Juliet Mitchell observed: 'it is, I think, ultimately, this search for historical origins that mars' Engels's thesis.[82] Similarly, Jules Townsend has suggested that the key weakness with Engels's thesis is that it cannot explain the 'universality' of 'patriarchy'.[83] However, Lise Vogel has said that Engels's methodological Preface is suggestive of a possible solution to this problem: whereas Engels claimed that, according to historical materialism, 'the determining factor in history is, in the final instance, the production and reproduction of the immediate essentials of life', this perspective opens up a fruitful line of research into the dialectical histories of class and sexual divisions which does not reduce the latter to the former. According to Vogel it has been an unfortunate characteristic of the post-Engelsian left that while they have embraced Engels's general history of sexual oppression, they have not taken seriously his deepening of historical materialism to include social reproduction in addition to social production.[84] By contrast, Lindsey German has claimed that feminists who read Engels as positing the existence of the two distinct modes of production and reproduction misrepresent his views, as he plainly goes on to suggest that 'as human beings developed production, so the family became relatively less important', to the point at which, in Engels's words, family structures become 'completely dominated by the system of property'.[85]

Whatever the relative merits of these arguments, it is surely misjudged to claim, as does Wally Seccombe, that 'anthropological research lends no support' either to Engels's historical account of the rise of patriarchy or to 'many radical feminist' alternatives. Seccombe supports this claim through the suggestion that because the 'anthological evidence on foraging people indicates a frequent (but by no means uniform) pattern of rough parity between the sexes', and also evidence in 'some pre-class societies [of] strong and persistent patterns of male dominance', then both feminist patriarchy theorists and Engels are equally wrong. But this is surely mistaken, for Engels's claims and those of patriarchy theorists are of a different order. Thus, while patriarchy theory is tied to a universal model of male dominance, Engels's key interest is in showing that the contemporary political and sexual 'facts' are themselves products of history. Therefore his general claims, in stark contrast to the claims of patriarchy theory, seem not to be refuted but rather to be deepened by the evidence deployed by Seccombe.[86]

More generally, Engels distinguished his evolutionary theory from contemporary attempts to reduce human behaviour to their transhistorical ape-nature. He dismissed the precursors of contemporary socio-biologists with the argument that 'even the mere contemplation of previous history as a series of class struggles suffices to make clear the utter shallowness of the conception of this history as a feeble variety of the "struggle for existence". I would therefore never do this favour to these false naturalists.'[87] But how does this difference affect the relationship between Marx's theory of cultural evolution and Darwin's theory of natural evolution?

In Darwin's model, evolutionary change in the natural world is the product of the combination of variation between individuals, heredity, selection and the struggle for existence.[88] Perry Anderson has criticised the application of Darwinism to social history, arguing that social structures do not exist which can reasonably be related to the selection process operating in the natural world: for whereas genes mutate randomly and have no relation to the forces that select them, in the social world 'innovation belongs to the same plane as selection . . . both . . . always involve the common material of conscious human agency'.[89] Thus, 'social [and natural] innovations . . . are utterly different in both the scale of the variation they represent and the speed of the changes they unleash'.[90] Similarly, Callinicos has argued that Marxism includes an evolutionary component that is closer to the developmental model of Lamarck than it is to Darwin's variational model.[91] Nevertheless, despite the incorporation of an evolutionary component within historical materialism, Marx did not embrace a unilinear model of historical progress.

Progress and tragedy

In *Orientalism*, Edward Said famously dismissed Marx's writings on India as an instance of a more general racist discourse within which 'orientals' were depersonalised as a step towards legitimising European colonialism. To substantiate this claim, Said quoted from Marx's newspaper article 'British Rule in India' – 10 June 1853 –in which Marx seems to excuse imperialism by the fact that through it England had acted as 'the unconscious tool of history'.[92] Accordingly, Said accuses Marx of ignoring the suffering of the Indians and of falling victim to the discourse of orientalism through the medium of his theory of social revolution.[93] The iron laws of progress, it appears, had blinded Marx to the real 'empirical' suffering of the Indians.

Unfortunately, this interpretation of Marx's analysis of Indian history involves Said in ignoring both the broader theoretical context of Marx's argument and the reception of his thesis in Indian anti-imperialist circles. To take the latter point first: as Aijaz Ahmad has pointed out, whatever the undoubted crudities of Marx's formulations in this essay, most Indian anti-imperialist writers have agreed that capitalism did play a partially progressive role in India.[94] Moreover, when Marx developed his analysis of the role of imperialism in the sub-continent he looked to the Indians both as victims of imperialism and as potential agents of their own emancipation. In 'The Future Results of the British Rule in India' – 22 July 1853 – he argued that the 'English bourgeoisie . . . will neither emancipate nor materially mend the social condition of the mass of the people'. He insisted that for the Indians to achieve emancipation one or other revolution was necessary: either a proletarian revolution in England or a national liberation movement of the

'Hindus . . . to throw off the English yoke altogether'.[95] Whatever might be said of this analysis, it most certainly is not a racist dismissal of the humanity of Indians. Quite the reverse: as Ahmad argues, Marx's discussion of capitalist development in India can best be understood within the context of his broader analysis of the transition from feudalism to capitalism: Marx conceived the likely prospects for India's peasantry as paralleling those experienced by the European peasantry a few centuries earlier. Accordingly, far from being an apologist for capitalist progress, Marx understood the immediate situation of the Indian peasantry to be 'tragic'.[96] He concluded 'The Future Results of British Rule in India' with the observation that the condition of the Indian peasantry paralleled that of all other exploited and oppressed classes through history, and that nineteenth-century apologists for capitalism acted to deliberately ignore the fact that 'human progress . . . would not drink the nectar but from the skulls of the slain'.[97]

The concept of tragedy, as Ahmad is well aware, does much more in Marx's oeuvre than inform his analysis of colonialism. In *The Poverty of Philosophy*, Marx wrote that 'the very moment civilization begins, production begins to be founded on the antagonism of orders, estates, classes, and finally on the antagonism of accumulated labour and actual labour. No antagonism, no progress.'[98] More concretely, Engels wrote in *The Peasant War In Germany* (1850), his history of the Anabaptist revolt of the early sixteenth century:

> The worst thing that can befall a leader of an extreme party is to be compelled to take over a government in an epoch when the movement is not yet ripe for the domination of the class which he represents and for the realisation of the measures which that domination would imply. What he *can* do depends not upon his will but upon the sharpness of the clash of interests between the various classes, and upon the degree of development of the material means of existence, the relations of production and means of communication upon which the clash of interests of the classes is based every time. What he *ought* to do, what his party demands of him, again depends not upon him, or upon the degree of development of the class struggle and its conditions. He is bound to his doctrines and the demands hitherto propounded which do not emanate from the interrelations of the social classes at a given moment, or from the more or less accidental level of relations of production and means of communication, but from his more or less penetrating insight into the general result of the social and political movement. Thus he necessarily finds himself in a dilemma. What he *can* do is in contrast to all his actions as hitherto practised, to all his principles and to the present interests of his party; what he *ought* to do cannot be achieved. In a word, he is compelled to represent not his party or his class, but the class for whom conditions are ripe for domination. In the interests of the movement itself, he is compelled to defend the interests of an alien class, and to feed his own class with phrases and promises, with the assertion that the interests of that alien class are their own interests. Whoever puts himself in this awkward position is irrevocably lost.[99]

It was from within this framework that Engels analysed the situation of 'the magnificent figure of Thomas Munzer'[100] – the leader of the sixteenth-century peasant movement – in terms drawn from *The German Ideology*, in which he and Marx had argued that 'the development of productive forces . . . is an absolutely necessary practical premise because without it want is merely made general, and with destitution the struggle for necessities and all the old filthy business would necessarily be reproduced'.[101] So while Engels traced Munzer's inspiring attempts to win freedom for the German peasants, he showed how it was Munzer's tragedy to find himself in a historically hopeless situation which guaranteed the ultimate defeat of his movement.

Returning to Rigby's claim that historians 'have been able to make little use of' Marx's 'productive force determinism',[102] Engels's application of this method in this essay implies that this is surely not true. Indeed, any reputable historian should attempt to contextualise the actions of the human agents they study, and part of that context would include the level of economic development within which they found themselves. For productive-force determinism does not, contra Rigby, imply that it is the productive forces that make history; rather, as Ball argues, the level of the development of the productive forces sets the parameters of the possible outcomes to an event: productive-force determinism is thus best understood as a form of 'political possibilism'.[103] And while the development of the productive forces implies that our abilities to realise various aims increases, it in no way entails that we will realise those potentials. More generally, without an understanding of the constraints set on human action by the level of development of the forces of production, as Engels argued in a letter to Lassalle of 18 May 1859 paralleling Marx's comments on Ranke, noted above, then historians risk reducing 'the tragic conflict to smaller dimensions'.

From Feudalism to capitalism

On comparing Marx's comments on the Russian peasant commune with his earlier discussion of colonialism in India one is immediately struck by a superficial contrast between his earlier vision of history as tragic necessity and his later embrace of historical multilinearity. On a similar note, Robert Brenner has argued that there is a break between the Marx of *The German Ideology*, *The Poverty of Philosophy* and *The Communist Manifesto* and the later Marx of the *Grundrisse* and *Capital*. Brenner suggests that the model of the transition offered in Marx's earlier writings parallels Adam Smith's approach, and like Smith, the young Marx does not in fact develop a theory of societal transformation, for he assumes that which he aims to explain: 'the bourgeoisie's rise to power is quasi-automatic'.[104] Specifically, the young Marx's unilinearity is inherited from Smith as a tacit acceptance of a trans-historical model of capitalist human nature fighting to break the fetters which feudalism had placed on capitalist development. By contrast, Brenner argues that the 'master principle' through which the later Marx develops a powerful theory of social transformation is 'the mode of production, conceived as a system of social-property relations'.[105]

Unfortunately, while Brenner is undoubtedly correct to stress the centrality of the related concepts of mode of production and relations of production to Marx's theory of history, his attempt to delineate between the theories of history expounded in *The Poverty of Philosophy* and *Capital* is unconvincing for a number of reasons. First, as I noted above, while Marx deployed the concept of forms of intercourse in *The German Ideology*, he had developed the concept of relations of production in *The Poverty of Philosophy*. Second, he reasserted his model of productive-force 'determinism' in the 1859 Preface – written eighteen months after the *Grundrisse*. Finally, as late as the 1882 Introduction to the *Communist Manifesto*, he and Engels continued to reaffirm the importance of the development of the productive forces in history. More generally, Marx's comments on Russia in the 1880s were premissed on his analysis of its unique position in the world – as yet untouched by capitalism and colonialism it was free to a degree unknown to those areas where capitalism was enforcing its terrible logic. Nevertheless, while it is implausible to contrast the young with the old Marx, as Brenner does, in *Capital* Marx undoubtedly deepened his analysis of the origins of capitalism.

The first volume of *Capital* famously closes with Marx's discussion of the 'primitive accumulation of capital'; that is, his discussion of the creation of the historical prerequisites for the emergence of capitalism. Up to this point, Marx had shown that capital accumulation is a circular process which seems to have no start point.[106] However, if Marx was to provide a historical analysis of capitalism, he needed to show how capital arose and what forces were tending towards its dissolution. On the later point, Marx's theory of value and his associated theory of the tendency of the rate of profit to fall were intended to show that capitalism generated the conditions for its *possible* overthrow.[107] Second, Marx explained the rise of capitalism as a function of the separation of human labour from the means of production – the primitive accumulation of capital; and his discussion of this process is among the most celebrated sections of *Capital*. Marx argued that capitalism arose when the peasantry was separated from the land and made into 'free' wage labourers, for it was only within a framework of free wage labour that capital could be freely accumulated. The 'classic form' taken by this process was in England, where the enclosure of the commons resulted in the destruction of the old peasant way of life, and thenceforth the ex-peasants were forced to sell their ability to work so that that they might earn the money needed to buy such commodities as were necessary for their continued existence.[108]

Through this historical analysis of the rise of capitalism, Marx debunks one of the key myths of bourgeois economics: that consumers and producers meet in the marketplace as free and equal agents. For Marx shows that the free market was created through the violent proletarianisation of the peasantry: 'capital comes dripping from head to toe, from every pore, with dirt and blood'.[109] According to Marx, a violent revolution in England's relations of production occurred between the fourteenth and sixteenth centuries which gave birth to capitalism.[110] Commenting on this argument, McNally points out that Marx exposed the 'great evasion at the heart' of any defence of the free market: that it is premissed on the violent expropriation of the common people.[111]

While Marx outlined a sophisticated history of the brutal creation of an English proletariat, he failed to produce a similarly powerful model of pre-capitalist modes of production which could explain why the English proletariat emerged when and where it did.[112] This is not to suggest that Marx had no such theory; he did. However, in his mature work he did little more than suggest that a prior development of the forces of production was a prerequisite for the proletarianisation of the peasantry. The closest Marx came to an explanation of those prerequisites is in the third volume of *Capital*, in which he wrote that a certain level of commercial capitalist development 'is itself a historical precondition for the development of the forces of production (1) as a precondition for the concentration of money wealth, and (2) because the capitalist mode of production presupposes production for trade'. So, in his mature work, as in *The German Ideology*, Marx continued to explain the general course of history as a consequence of the development of the forces of production, while resisting the temptation of embracing historical inevitibilism: he insisted that the development of commercial capital, 'taken by itself, is insufficient to explain the transition from one mode of production to another'.[113]

Marx argued that while trade and merchant capital always had a 'solvent effect on the pre-existing organisations of production', in and of itself merchant capital could not explain the transition from feudalism to capitalism: 'how far it leads to the dissolution of the old mode of production depends first and foremost on the solidity and inner articulation of this mode of production itself'.[114] While the 'revolutions' in trade of the sixteenth and seventeenth centuries 'were a major moment in promoting the transition from the feudal to the capitalist mode of production . . . the modern mode of production in its first period . . . developed only where the conditions for it had been created in the middle ages'.[115]

However, if Marx's dismissal of the revolutionary consequences of merchant capital seems unequivocal in this passage, later in the same chapter his argument is more ambiguous. Famously, he claimed that the 'transition from feudalism to capitalism takes place in two different ways'. The first, 'really revolutionary', way involves the producer becoming a merchant and a capitalist; whereas the second way involves the merchant taking 'direct control of production'. While this argument seems to imply that the merchant's capital could dissolve feudalism from within, Marx immediately takes back this suggestion and argues that merchant capital 'cannot bring about the overthrow of the old mode of production by itself, but rather preserves and retains it as its own precondition'.[116] Nevertheless, on the following page, Marx suggests that the transition can take not two but three forms, the two mentioned above and a third where 'the merchant becomes an industrialist directly'.[117] So while on the one hand Marx explicitly denies merchant capital a revolutionary role in the transition from feudalism to capitalism, on the other hand the implication of this comment appears to sustain a radically divergent interpretation of the relationship between merchant capital and the emergence of the capitalist mode of production. In fact, whereas the dismissal of the revolutionary role of merchant capital coheres with Brenner's approach, noted above, Marx's claim that merchants could directly foster the dissolution of feudalism by becoming industrialists themselves recalls his earlier argument, articulated in *The German Ideology*, that towns grew out of feudal production and subsequently developed an antagonistic relationship to feudalism, and that this conflict between town and country eventually gave rise to the bourgeois revolutions by which capitalism burst the fetters of feudal society.[118]

The space created by this ambiguity has generated a considerable literature in recent years. For whereas, on the one hand, commentators such as Comninel have argued that Marx's concept of a bourgeois revolution is best 'dropped' from the Marxist theory of history, more orthodox Marxists have insisted that in *Capital* Marx deepened, and certainly did not reject, the interpretation of historical materialism articulated in *The German Ideology*.[119] One problem affecting this debate is a tendency to reify Marx's discussion of bourgeois revolutions. Comninel argues that the 'definitive statement of the concept of bourgeois revolution comes in the *Communist Manifesto*'.[120] There Marx and Engels argued that

> each step in the development of the bourgeoisie was accompanied by a corresponding political advance in that class. An oppressed class under the sway of the feudal nobility . . . the bourgeoisie has at last, since the establishment of modern industry and of the world market, conquered for itself, in the modern representative state, exclusive political sway. The executive of the modern state is but a committee for managing the common affairs of the whole bourgeoisie.[121]

It is this schematic comment that has come under sustained attack over recent decades, for largely political reasons, from revisionist historians.[122] However, neither Marx nor Engels wrote any systematic treatment of the French revolution, and their comments on bourgeois revolutions are best understood through an examination of their actual historical studies of such movements.

With respect to Marx and Engels's analyses of the 'Great French Revolution', Michael Löwy has pointed out that their comments were not meant to be 'an exercise in academic historiography', but were rather aimed at highlighting the need for a 'new revolution'.[123] So, through a comparison of Marx's arguments of the pre-1848 period – within which the French bourgeoisie were represented in 'much less heroic' terms – with those of the period around 1848, Löwy argues that Marx and Engels 'only extolled the virtues of the revolutionary bourgeoisie of 1789 the more effectively to stigmatize the "misbegotten" German version of 1848'.[124]

More generally, Marx's most famous comment on the French revolution – made in what was perhaps his finest work of contemporary history, 'The Eighteenth Brumaire of Louis Bonaparte' – suggests, contra those who regard his analysis on 1789 as a simple model for the coming socialist revolution, a fundamental structural difference between bourgeois and socialist revolutions. Whereas 'The Eighteenth Brumaire' was a study of French politics from 1848 to 1851, Marx opened the essay with a claim regarding the nature of the revolution of 1789 (and the English revolution of 1649). He argued that 'unheroic though bourgeois society is, it nevertheless needed heroism, sacrifice, terror, civil war, and national wars to bring it into being'. He claimed that not just any form of heroism would suffice; 'the heroes as well as the parties and the masses of the old French Revolution, performed the task of their time – that of unchaining and establishing modern bourgeois society – in Roman costumes and with Roman phrases'. Not that the language of the revolutionaries need necessarily have been that of the Roman Republic. Commenting on the English revolution of 1649, he wrote: 'similarly, at another stage of development a century earlier, Cromwell and the English people had borrowed from the Old Testament the speech, emotions, and illusions for their bourgeois revolution'. The common characteristic of these bourgeois revolutionary movements were not their specific ideological garb. Rather, it was the fact that they needed such a mask to cover their true purpose. In fact, once the English bourgeoisie had won their revolution, 'Locke supplanted Habakkuk'. The problem for the bourgeoisie, Marx argued, is that while some such ideals of freedom and self-determination – whether borrowed from the Old Testament, the Roman Republic or wherever – were needed to mobilise the masses without whom bourgeois victory against the old order could not be realised, their true Lockean spirit could never act as this ideology. Specifically, because the bourgeoisie was but another minority class that would exploit the 'people' it claimed to represent, the popular mobilisations demanded by the classic bourgeois revolutions could not be realised if this antagonistic relationship was revealed. In order to win popular support for its revolution, representatives of the bourgeoisie were compelled to sell its revolution as the people's revolution. This is not to imply that Cromwell and Robespierre were dishonest; rather Marx suggests that bourgeois revolutions required such utopians if they were to succeed in mobilising the masses necessary to overthrow the old order; and once they had played their role such men could be discarded as the bourgeoisie got on with business.

Conversely, because the proletariat did not exploit any class below it, 'the social revolution of the nineteenth century cannot take its poetry from the past but only from the future':

> Bourgeois revolutions, like those of the eighteenth century, storm more swiftly from success to success . . . Proletarian revolutions, like those of the nineteenth century, constantly criticize themselves, constantly interrupt themselves in their own course, return to the apparently accomplished, in order to begin anew; they deride with cruel thoroughness the half-measures, weaknesses, and paltriness of their first attempts, seem to throw down their opponents only so the latter may draw new strength from the earth and rise before them again more gigantic than ever, recoil constantly from the indefinite colossalness of their own goals – until a situation is created which makes all turning back impossible.[125]

So, Marx argues, the form, if not the content, of the ideology of bourgeois revolutions could be explained by the gap between the interests of the bourgeoisie and the interests of the mass of the people below them. Commenting on Marx's comparison of bourgeois and proletarian revolutions, Callinicos argues that the self-consciousness required of the proletariat in its revolution demanded that Marxists, in contrast to bourgeois revolutionaries, approach the facts of their situation with the utmost honesty, and reject any unifying myths, in particular the myth of nationalism, as politically debilitating.[126] Because the socialist revolution could be realised only as the self-emancipation of the working class it demanded a degree of self-consciousness on the part of workers that was historically novel. Conversely, because the primary concern of the bourgeoisie was to create an environment conducive to capital accumulation, then so long as the state under which it operated removed any fetters to the accumulation process then the bourgeoisie would be largely content. So, whereas the socialist revolution necessarily involved a self-conscious movement of the masses, bourgeois revolutions, and bourgeois states, could take on a variety of distinct forms.

One 'bourgeois revolution' that Engels analysed in depth was the unification of Germany under Bismarck in the 1860s. Written over the winter of 1887–88, Engels's unfinished essay *The Role of Force in History* aimed to give concrete expression to the method outlined in his book *Anti-Dühring*. At the heart of the essay were three pertinent points. First, the German bourgeoisie had shown themselves to be too cowardly to realise the demands of their bourgeois revolution – to unify Germany's fragmented political structure within in a liberal constitution. Second, in the context of heightened global competition Bismarck had, using the methods of the Prussian *junkers*, unified Germany for the bourgeoisie. Finally, Bismarck had shown that while 'great men' could act in congruence with the 'objective needs' of history, he had also shown that he could frustrate these forces. At all these levels, Engels managed to locate Germany's political history within the context of the development of the forces of production without reducing the former to the latter.

To take these points in reverse order, Engels argued that Bismarck 'never exhibited even the ghost of an original political idea'. Nevertheless, 'this narrowness was his good fortune' for it meant that he took decisive action to realise the demand – made for their own reasons both by the Prussian junkers and the German bourgeoisie – to unify Germany.[127] However, once this historic demand was realised, Engels suggested that the negative consequences of Bismarck's junkerism came to the fore. With the defeat of the French in the Franco-Prussian war, Bismarck moved not to stabilise Europe, but to 'extort' reparations from the French. At this point 'Bismarck appears as the independent politician for the first time . . . And, as a result he committed his first colossal blunder.'[128] The blunder was not so much the demand that the French pay the Germans monetary compensation, though that was bad enough; rather it consisted in Bismarck's seizure of Alsace and Lorraine which had the effect of pushing France into the arms of Russia and ensuring that, at some point, Europe would once again be plunged into war – which for the Germans would be on two fronts.[129]

Regarding the class nature of Bismarck's rule, Engels was adamant that in unifying Germany Bismarck had realised the tasks which the German bourgeoisie were too cowardly to carry through: the bourgeois revolution had been carried behind the backs, so to speak, of the bourgeoisie: 'the worst excesses of *Kleinstaaterei* were finally eliminated: those which had been the main obstacles to capitalist development, on the one hand, and to Prussian ambition on the other'.[130] However, at his moment of glory, Bismarck was faced with a choice, either use his authority to establish fully the power of capital in Germany, use it to Prussify the rest of Germany or use it to maintain his own domination.[131] In the event, Engels argued, Bismarck chose the third option, to create a new Bonapartist regime, and while he satisfied the economic demands of the bourgeoisie, he continued to thwart bourgeois political aspirations.[132]

Interestingly, Engels had prefigured this argument in the 1874 Preface to *The Peasant War in Germany* (1850), his analysis of the German peasant uprisings of the sixteenth century. There he claimed that while the German bourgeoisie was a historically late arrival, growing in economic weight in a period when the proletariat had already started to bite at its heals, the cowardice of the German bourgeoisie in 1848 and 1870 could not be reduced to this material condition, for 'our big bourgeois of 1870 still act exactly as the middle burgers of 1525 acted'.[133] Bourgeois cowardice, at least in Germany, was to be understood as the norm; a far cry from the vision of the revolutionary bourgeoisie outlined in the *Communist Manifesto*.[134] Consequently, with no revolutionary bourgeoisie 'it has been the peculiar fate of Prussia to complete its bourgeois revolution . . . in the pleasant form of Bonapartism'.[135] In characterising bourgeois revolutions by their consequences rather than by the agency through which they are realised, Engels prefigured more recent discussions of the concept of bourgeois revolution that has been embraced by Callinicos, but mistakenly described as a late twentieth-century response to revisionism by Comninel.[136]

Conclusion

At its heart, historical materialism is a theory of historical change through the evolving contradictions between the forces and relations of production of various modes of production. In *Ludwig Feuerbach and the End of Classical German Philosophy*, Engels argued that human history is 'the uninterrupted process of becoming and passing away'. He suggested that Hegel's great contribution to Marx's materialism was to posit the world not 'as a complex of ready-made things, but as a complex of processes'. These processes do not exist in opposition to human agency, nor do they merely operate through passive human agents; but rather, as 'everything which sets men in motion must pass through their minds', then human agency is at the centre of the social totality.[137] Hence, Engels insisted, 'productive force determinism' and humanism should not be conceived of as two alternative approaches to the understanding of human history, but should instead be seen as mutually constructive: humans constantly make and remake themselves through history in a material context.[138] History is much more than the stories of kings and wars; it is the realm of human self-creation which constantly reminds us, contra Margaret Thatcher, that there is always an alternative. However, the parameters of realistic alternatives at any historical juncture depend, *ultimately*, on the productivity of labour at that moment. Nevertheless, there is a large gap between what is possible and what is realised, and that gap cannot be comprehended except through detailed empirical studies of the evidence, starting from the forces and relations of production but certainly not limited to them. Nonetheless, what can be achieved politically is also in part a reflection of what people believe it is possible to achieve. Marxist historiography therefore aims not only to understand the world, but to generate historical examples of other, better, ways of doing things. As Engels argued in his history of land-ownership in Germany, *The Mark* (1892): 'it is necessary to contrast the misery of agricultural labourers of the present time and the mortgage-servitude of the small peasants, with the old common property of all free men in what was then in truth their "fatherland", the free common possession of all by inheritance'.[139] Similarly, in *Capital* Marx aimed to show that while the division of labour had once required that workers become reduced to the level of machinery, with the industrial revolution 'the technical reason for the lifelong attachment of the worker to a partial function is swept away'.[140] The possibility for a better world grew within capitalism, but this was only a possibility; and despite some ambiguous formulations to the contrary, the general thrust of both Marx's and Engels's work was as a critique of political and historical fatalism. As Hobsbawm has argued Marxist historical analyses stemmed, always, from a 'commitment to politics'.[141]

Notes

1 H. Draper *Karl Marx's Theory of Revolution* Vol. 1 (New York, 1977), pp. 23–6; E. Hobsbawm 'Introduction' to K. Marx *Pre-Capitalist Economic Formations* (London, 1964), p. 53.
2 Gerry Cohen is Chichele Professor of social and political theory at Oxford University. Steve Rigby is a reader in history at the University of Manchester.
3 S. Rigby *Marxism and History* (Manchester, 1998 [1987]), pp. 2–3; G. A. Cohen *Karl Marx's Theory of History: A Defence* (Oxford, 2000 [1978]), p. ix.
4 Cohen *Karl Marx's Theory of History*, p. x. Rigby *Marxism and History*, p. 7.
5 Rigby *Marxism and History*, p. 10.
6 R. Dunayevskaya *Rosa Luxemburg, Women's Liberation and Marx's Philosophy of History* (Chicago, 1991), p. 120.
7 J. Ferraro *Freedom and Determination in History According to Marx and Engels* (New York, 1992), p. 86.
8 *Grundrisse*, p. 101.
9 Cohen *Karl Marx's Theory of History*, pp. 150–66.
10 A. Prinz 'The Background and Ulterior Motive of Marx's "Preface" of 1859', *Journal of the History of Ideas* 30, 1968. Croix *Class Struggle in the Ancient Greek World*, p. 47.
11 Draper *Marx's Theory of Revolution* Vol. 1, pp. 20–1.
12 E. Hobsbawm 'Introduction' to K. Marx and F. Engels *The Communist Manifesto* (London, 1998), p. 14. Cf Mészáros's claim that 'the first systematic presentation of historical materialism in *The German Ideology* contains all its principal defining characteristics': I. Mészáros 'The Nature of Historical Determination' *Critique* 30–1, 2000, p. 104; and Christopher Hills's claim that 'their fundamental ideas about history had . . . taken shape by 1848': C. Hill (1948) 'The English Civil War Interpreted by Marx and Engels' in B. Jessop and C. Malcolm-Brown eds *Karl Marx's Social and Political Thought: Critical Assessments* Vol. 3 (London, 1990), p. 643.
13 Colletti *From Rousseau to Lenin*, p. 13.
14 *The German Ideology*, pp. 62; 42; 46.
15 Ibid., p. 47.
16 Feuerbach is today famous primarily as the author of the phrase 'You are what you eat'.
17 *The German Ideology*, pp. 48–9.
18 N. Geras *Marx and Human Nature* (London, 1983).
19 *Capital*, Vol. 1, pp. 758–9. It is in light of this argument that Marx's famous sixth thesis on Feuerbach should be read: 'Feuerbach resolves the essence of religion into the essence of man. But the essence of man is no abstraction inherent in each single individual. In reality, it is the ensemble of the social relations. Feuerbach, who does not enter upon a criticism of this real essence is hence obliged: 1 To abstract from the historical process and to define the religious sentiment regarded by itself, and to presuppose an abstract – isolated – human individual. 2 The essence therefore can by him only be regarded as 'species', as an inner 'dumb' generality which unites many individuals only in a *natural* way' (cf. Geras *Marx and Human Nature*).

20 B. Southgate *History: What and Why?* (London, 2001), pp. 96–7; *The German Ideology*, p. 57.
21 M. Perry *Marxism and History* (London, 2002), p. 47.
22 *Capital* I, p. 286.
23 K. Marx 'Notes on Adolph Wagner' in *Karl Marx: Texts on Method*, ed. T. Carver (Oxford, 1975), p. 190.
24 *Grundrisse*, p. 85.
25 Ibid., p. 94.
26 Ibid., p. 99.
27 Ibid., p. 101.
28 Hobsbawm 'Introduction to Pre-Capitalist Economic Formations', pp. 17–18.
29 While empiricism is the dominant mode of research amongst contemporary historians, no one comes to the evidence naked so to speak. It is through the assumptions of practicing historians – about human nature or the naturalness of certain institutions etc. – that reductionism slips in through the backdoor of historical research. Nevertheless, the worst reductionists are not usually to be found amongst the historians – sociobiologists and evolutionary psychologists are the most prominent contemporary offenders. On these see H. Rose and S. Rose eds *Alas Poor Darwin* (London, 2000).
30 P. Vilar 'Marxist History, A History in the Making: Towards a Dialogue with Althusser' *New Left Review* 80, July–August 1973, p. 75.
31 *The German Ideology*, p. 48.
32 K. Marx *A Contribution to the Critique of Political Economy* (London, 1970 [1859]), p. 20.
33 Cohen *Karl Marx's Theory of History*, p. 32.
34 G. Therborn *Science, Class and Society* (London, 1976), p. 366; A. Callinicos *Making History* (Leidon, 2004 [1987]), p. 48; see also note 98, below.
35 Therborn *Science*, p. 366.
36 Cohen *Karl Marx's Theory of History*, pp. 29, 35.
37 *The German Ideology*, pp. 43, 51–2.
38 Ste. Croix *Class Struggle in the Ancient Greek World*, pp. 43–4. G. de Ste. Croix 'Class in Marx's Conception of History, Ancient and Modern' *New Left Review* no.146, July–August 1984, p. 100.
39 Ste. Croix *Class Struggle in the Ancient Greek World*, p. 90. Ste. Croix 'Class in Marx's Conception of History', p. 102.
40 K. Marx *Capital* Vol. 3 (London, 1981), p. 927.
41 Cf. C. Harman *Marxism and History* (London, 1998).
42 Hobsbawm 'Introduction to Pre-Capitalist Economic Formations', pp. 36, 38.
43 *The German Ideology*, p. 57.
44 Hobsbawm 'Introduction to Pre-Capitalist Economic Formations', pp. 49–50.
45 T. Shanin 'Late Marx: Gods and Craftsmen' in T. Shanin ed. *Late Marx and the Russian Road* (London, 1983), p. 7. This was no isolated event: for instance in 1854, when asked to write a short piece on Spain for the *New York Tribune*, Marx took his duties seriously enough to learn Spanish (Vilar 'Marxist History', p. 105). More generally, Marx's thoroughness was legend: for instance, Engels once complained regarding his delay in writing *Capital* that 'as long as you still have a book before you that you consider important, you do not get down to writing': quoted, Draper *Marx's Theory of Revolution* Vol. 1, p. 26.

46 *Capital* Vol. 1, p. 91.
47 Shanin 'Late Marx'; H. Wada 'Marx and Revolutionary Russia' in T. Shanin ed. *Late Marx and the Russian Road* (London, 1983); E. Kingston-Mann 'Deconstructing the Romance of the Bourgeoisie: A Russian Marxist Path Not Taken' *Review of International Political Economy* 10:1, 2003.
48 Kingston-Mann 'Deconstructing the Romance of the Bourgeoisie', p. 95.
49 P. Chattopadhyay 'Capital, the Progenitor of Socialism: Progress as the Dialectic of Negativity in the Critique of Political Economy' *Historical Materialism* (forthcoming).
50 Wada 'Marx and Revolutionary Russia', p. 70.
51 D. Sayer and P. Corrigan 'Late Marx: Continuity, Contradiction and Learning' in Shanin ed. *Late Marx and the Russian Road.*
52 Marx argued that if Russia was analysed in isolation from the rest of the world then the communes 'were feted to perish'. However, because Russia exited 'in a modern historical context', which included both a 'higher culture', and the 'world market in which capitalist production is predominant', then the communes might offer a vehicle for regeneration: K. Marx 'The Second Draft of a Reply to Zasulich' in Shanin ed. *Late Marx and the Russian Road*, p. 102. While Marx's global frame of reference prefigures Trotsky's theory of combined and uneven development, his theory is very different to Trotsky's, for whom socialism was on the agenda in Russia because of the growth of a modern proletariat, not because of the existence of a communal peasantry.
53 *The German Ideology*, p. 56
54 Rigby *Marxism and History*, p. 101.
55 A. MacIntyre 'Notes from the Moral Wilderness' in *The MacIntyre Reader*, ed. K. Knight (the essay was published originally in two parts in *New Reasoner*, nos. 7 and 8, 1958–59).
56 *Capital* Vol. 1, p. 284; cf. Ferraro *Freedom and Determination*, p. 41.
57 F. Engels *Anti-Dühring* (Moscow, 1947 [1877]), p. 140.
58 R. Dunayevskaya *Freedom and Revolution* (Columbia, 1988), p. 53; K. Marx 'Economic and Philosophic Manuscripts' in K. Marx *Early Writings* (London, 1975), p. 386.
59 A. MacIntyre 'Freedom and Revolution' *Labour Review*, February–March 1960.
60 *Capital*, Vol. 3, p. 959.
61 F. Wheen *Karl Marx* (London, 1999), p. 368.
62 *Capital* Vol. 1, p. 461.
63 Quoted, J. Bellamy Foster *Marx's Ecology* (New York, 2000), p. 197.
64 "The Part Played by Labour in the Transition from Ape to Man', in F. Engels *The Origin of the Family, Private Property and the State* (London, 1972). p. 251.
65 Ibid., p. 252. This formulation could be interpreted as evidence for Engels's supposed confusion of Darwinism and Lamarckianism: R. Weikart *Socialist Darwinism: Evolution in German Socialist Thought from Marx to Bernstein* (San Franscisco, 1998), p. 72. However, I do not think that Engels meant that culturally evolved characteristics could be inherited directly, and certainly his argument need not be interpreted in that way: see Foster *Marx's Ecology*, p. 206; and S. Jay Gould *An Urchin in the Storm* (London, 1987), p. 111. Rather he posits a dialectical relationship between cultural and natural evolution,

whereby an important part of the 'natural' environment within which humans compete for survival is culturally constructed, such that cultural structures will act as part of the context within which natural selection takes place.

66 'The Part Played by Labour in the Transition from Ape to Man', p. 253.
67 Ibid., p. 255.
68 Ibid., p. 259.
69 Ibid., p. 259. Gould points out that the fundamentals of Engels's case were shown to be correct with the discovery of *A. africanus* in the 1920s, but despite the evidence of the fossil record the alternative opinion has proved a long time dying: S. Jay Gould *The Panda's Thumb* (London, 1980), p. 110. The Darwinian thesis implies the existence of the famous 'missing link' – a big-brained monkey – which has never been found.
70 R. Weikart *Socialist Darwinism*, p. 72; and see T. Benton 'Social Darwinism and Socialist Darwinism in Germany 1860 to 1900' in P. Blackledge and G. Kirkpatrick eds *Historical Materialism and Social Evolution* (London, 2002), p. 68. Jean Lamarck argued both that characteristics acquired during an organism's lifetime could be inherited by its offspring and that the basic dynamic of evolutionary change occurred independently within each individual unit in a collection. In contrast to this *developmental* model of evolution Darwin held to a *variational* model, according to which 'there is no preordained ladder of life that living forms are inherently disposed to ascend': E. Sober *The Nature of Selection* (Chicago, 1984), p. 154.
71 See note 65.
72 F. Engels *The Origin of the Family, Private Property and the State* (London, 1972), p. 71.
73 Ibid., p. 87.
74 Ibid., p. 118.
75 Ibid., p. 221.
76 Ibid., p. 220.
77 Ibid., p. 121.
78 Ibid., p. 120.
79 Ibid., p. 224.
80 Ibid., pp. 229, 231.
81 E. Burke Leacock *Myths of Male Dominance* (New York, 1981), p. 25.
82 J. Mitchell *Psychoanalysis and Feminism* (London, 1974), p. 365.
83 J. Townsend *The Politics of Marxism* (London, 1996), p. 203.
84 L. Vogel 'Engels's Origin: Legacy, Burden and Vision' in C. J. Arthur ed. *Engels Today* (London, 1996), pp. 144–7; L. Vogel *Marxism and the Oppression of Women* (London, 1983), pp. 151ff.
85 L. German *Sex, Class and Socialism* (London, 1989), p. 66; *Origin of the Family*, p. 72.
86 W. Seccombe *A Millennium of Family Change* (London, 1992), pp. 35–6; cf. C. Harman 'Engels and the Origins of Human Society' *International Socialism* 65, 1994, p. 138.
87 *Origins of the Family*, p. 98.
88 R. Lewontin *Human Diversity* (New York, 1995), p. 149.
89 P. Anderson 'W. G. Runciman: A New Evolutionism' in P. Anderson *A Zone of Engagement* (London, 1992), p. 165.

90 Ibid., p. 167.
91 A. Callinicos *Social Theory* (Cambridge, 1999), p. 103. Sober calls Lamarckianism a 'developmental' type of evolutionary thinking, and points out that Lamarck posited two evolutionary forces: first, he saw a progressive tendency over time for organisms to evolve to an increasing state of perfection; while, second, variations in circumstance allowed for a degree of local differentiation within and between species: Sober *The Nature of Selection*, p. 148.
92 E. Said *Orientalism* (London, 1978), p. 153.
93 Ibid., p. 155.
94 A. Ahmad *In Theory* (London, 1992), p. 230.
95 K. Marx 'The Future Results of the British Rule in India' in K. Marx *Surveys from Exile* (London, 1973), p. 323.
96 Ahmad *In Theory*, p. 228
97 K. Marx 'Revolution in China and in Europe' in Marx *Surveys from Exile*, p. 325.
98 K. Marx *The Poverty of Philosophy* (Moscow, 1978 [1847]), p. 56.
99 F. Engels *The Peasant War in Germany* (Moscow, 1956 [1850]), pp. 138–9.
100 Ibid., p. 50.
101 *The German Ideology*, p. 56.
102 Rigby *Marxism and History*, p. 34.
103 T. Ball 'History: Critique and Irony' in T. Carver ed. *The Cambridge Companion to Marx* (Cambridge, 1991), p. 140.
104 R. Brenner, 'Bourgeois Revolution and the Transition to Capitalism' in A. L. Beier, D. Cannadine and J. M. Rosenheim eds, *The First Modern Society: Essays in English History in Honour of Lawrence Stone* (Cambridge, 1989), p. 279.
105 Ibid., p. 273.
106 *Capital* Vol. 1, p. 873.
107 *Capital* Vol. 3, pp. 317–75.
108 *Capital* Vol. 1, p. 876.
109 Ibid., pp. 926, 874.
110 Ibid., p. 878.
111 D. McNally *Against the Market* (London, 1993), p. 5.
112 J. Schlumbohm 'Relations of Production – Productive Forces – Crises in Proto-Industrialisation' in P. Kriedte *et al.* eds *Industrialisation Before Industrialisation* (Cambridge, 1981), p. 94.
113 *Capital* Vol. 3, p. 444; see K. Marx 'Economic Manuscripts of 1961–1863' in K. Marx and F. Engels *Collected Works* Vol. 30 (London, 1988), p. 38.
114 *Capital* Vol. 3, p. 449.
115 Ibid., p. 450.
116 Ibid., p. 452.
117 Ibid., p. 453.
118 *The German Ideology*, pp. 45, 66.
119 G. Comninel *Rethinking the French Revolution* (London, 1987), p. 205. A. Callinicos 'Bourgeois Revolutions and Historical Materialism' *International Socialism* 2:43, 1989, pp. 161–4.
120 Comninel *Rethinking*, p. 29.
121 K. Marx and F. Engels 'The Manifesto of the Communist Party' in K. Marx *The Revolutions of 1848* (London, 1973), p. 69.

122 E. Hobsbawm *Echoes of the Marseillaise* (London, 1990), p. 109.
123 M. Löwy '"The Poetry of the Past": Marx and the French Revolution' *New Left Review* 177, September–October 1989, p. 113.
124 Ibid., p. 115.
125 K. Marx 'The Eighteenth Brumaire of Louis Bonaparte' in Marx *Surveys From Exile*, pp. 146–50.
126 Callinicos *Making History*, pp. 239–54.
127 F. Engels *The Role of Force in History* (London, 1968 [1887–8]), p. 56.
128 Ibid., p. 80.
129 Ibid., pp. 86–7.
130 Ibid., pp. 69, 61, 89.
131 Ibid., pp. 97–8.
132 Ibid., p. 101.
133 *The Peasant War in Germany*, p. 22.
134 Ibid., pp. 18, 155.
135 Ibid., p. 29.
136 Comninel *Rethinking the French Revolution*, pp. 46–7; Callinicos 'Bourgeois Revolutions and Historical Materialism'.
137 F. Engels (1886) 'Ludwig Feuerbach and the End of Classical German Philosophy' in K. Marx and F. Engels *Selected Works in One Volume* (London, 1968), pp. 563, 583, 587.
138 For a perceptive analysis of Engels's *Peasant War in Germany* see E. R. Wolf 'The Peasant War in Germany: Friedrich Engels as Social Historian' *Science & Society* 51:1, spring 1987. Wolf (p. 85) points out that whereas Ranke explained the peasant uprising of 1525 as a 'convulsion of nature', Engels 'treated all of these strata, including the peasantry, as rational political actors, pursuing their interests within the determinate social and economic constraints of their time'; cf. J. Bak ed. *The German Peasant War of 1525* (London, 1976).
139 F. Engels (1892) 'The Mark' in *The Peasant War in Germany*, p. 162.
140 *Capital* Vol. 1, p. 491.
141 Hobsbawm 'Introduction to *The Communist Manifesto*', pp. 27–8.

3

Historical materialism: from the Second to the Third International

Introduction

The Second International of socialist parties was the undoubted custodian of Marxist 'orthodoxy' from its formation in 1889 until its *de facto* collapse at the outbreak of the First World War. While the German Social Democratic Party (SPD) was the organisational centre of the International, it would be a mistake to reductively explain its hegemony within the International as a simple function of its relative numerical strength; for Germany was also home to the International's most distinguished intellectual – Karl Kautsky – whose interpretation of Marxism is, for many commentators, synonymous with Second International Marxism.

Few intellectuals today would defend Kautsky's interpretation of historical materialism. Steve Rigby's critique of Kautskyism is in this respect typical: he argues that the fundamental weakness with Kautsky's thought was that it embraced 'a form of productive force determinism'. Likewise, Matt Perry argues that as Marx and Engels's 'influence on the Second International faded, a biologically or technologically deterministic version of historical materialism spread through the socialist parties of Europe'. A similar assessment of the Second International was made three decades ago by Lucio Colletti, who insisted that its political weaknesses were grounded in its 'fatalistic' and 'providential' faith in the automatic progress of economic evolution, which underpinned the certainty that its eventual rise to power would come about 'in a spontaneous, constant, and irresistible way, quite tranquilly like a natural process'.[1] Colletti suggested that this evolutionary interpretation of Marxism, which he likened unfavourably to the 'voluntarist' Marxism of the Third International, was born out of Engels's crude systemisation of Marx's thought and reached its zenith in Kautsky's theory of history. While Engels's part in this ossification of Marxism is still debated, Kautsky's thinking has long since been condemned to the dustbin of history, such that two recent assessments have agreed to write it off as a form of 'vulgar evolutionism'.[2]

This dismissive approach to Second International Marxism, generally, and Kautsky's thinking, more specifically, is unfortunate, for at the turn of the twentieth century Marxists operating within the International did produce some fascinating and influential historical works that repay re-reading today.[3] A more interesting approach to the Second International was suggested by Raphael Samuel, who made the simple but compelling point that this tendency in Marxism was far from homogenous.[4] Samuel is right: the Second International was an arena of contestation, where fierce political debates were informed by competing interpretations of history. Furthermore, if the histories written by Kautsky's European counterparts are not to be understood reductively as simple applications of his interpretation of historical materialism, then neither is his, or their, interpretations of Marxism adequately understood as reified totalities stretching over the decades between 1889 and 1914. Rather, various Second International thinkers, including Kautsky, produced historical and methodological works of varying quality in the years up to the First World War. Regrettably, considerations of space preclude a comprehensive discussion of these various contributions to historical materialism, so in this chapter I merely survey some of the more powerful methodological essays of Kautsky, Georgi Plekhanov and Antonio Labriola.[5] My reasons for choosing to examine the ideas of these thinkers will become evident in the text; but, briefly, Kautsky was undoubtedly the dominant intellectual within the Second International, while the works of Plekhanov and Labriola informed the best historiography produced by the succeeding generation of Marxists.

Whereas the Second International was, in part, a product of the period of relative social peace in the two or three decades leading up to the outbreak of the First World War, the Third, or Communist, International (Comintern) was a product of the period of war and revolution which erupted in 1914. Nevertheless, while this contrast between the pre- and post-1914 eras is useful, these two epochs were not hermetically sealed totalities, for while 'the global economic orchestra played in the major key of prosperity' prior to 1914, this was also an era when a number of intellectuals began to recognise the growing contradictions generated by capital's global dominance: social peace existed alongside an increasing sense of looming imperialist and class wars.[6] Perry Anderson has suggested that despite its superficial stability, the socio-political coordinates of this epoch included the 'imaginative proximity of social revolution'.[7] Nonetheless, while Second International thinkers spoke a language of revolution, the practice of many of their number became increasingly reformist in the first decade-and-a-half of the twentieth century, such that they conceived the coming 'revolution' as the culmination of a long process of peaceful evolutionary advance. It was obvious that this optimistic worldview could not withstand the shock of 1914, but as war brought revolution in its wake, it was less obvious that all socialist hope for the future of humanity was lost in the trenches. If the horrors of the First World War represented one extreme possibility for the realisation of the potential of modern industrial civilisation, the Bolshevik revolution of 1917 represented a radical alternative to this barbarism. Regrettably, the main theoreticians of the Second International, including Kautsky in Germany and Plekhanov in Russia, not only failed to embrace this new movement but actually tied their fortunes to the old system: after a lifetime of professed internationalism, both supported their own national states in the First World War, and opposed the October revolution. What is more, Kautsky's anti-Bolshevism cannot be explained as a simple corollary of his belief that Russia was economically too backward in 1917 to sustain a socialist revolution; from 1918 onwards, he opposed the revolutionary overthrow of the much more advanced German State, insisting that the priority for the German proletariat in 1918 was 'to exert its influence on the forms of economic recovery after the war within the framework of capitalism'.[8]

When, in 1914, he read reports of the German Social Democrats' support for the war, Lenin famously dismissed them as the product of a German government misinformation campaign. Once his shock at discovering that the reports were true was over, he immediately wrote that the Second International was dead, and called for it to be replaced by a new international of *revolutionary* workers' parties. In 1914 this demand was essentially propagandistic. Nevertheless, within three years, Lenin had the authority of a successful revolution to back up his call for a new international, and this, as the Comintern, was eventually launched in March 1919.

Like Lucio Colletti, Perry Anderson has interpreted the shift from Second to Third International Marxism as including a 'voluntaristic' break with 'fatalistim'.[9] Conversely, Steve Rigby has insisted that while this new organisation embodied a novel form of 'political practice' as compared to its predecessor, this practical change 'was not accompanied by any innovation in the realm of historical theory': Trotsky, Lenin, Stalin, and Bukharin – all leaders of the Bolshevik Party in 1917 – shared with Kautsky and Plekhanov 'a conception of historical materialism as a form of productive force determinism'.[10] In this chapter I argue that neither of these general approaches adequately explains the level either of change or of continuity between Second and Third International Marxisms. For the interpretation of historical materialism associated with the more sophisticated Second International thinkers in their best works was much more powerful that either Anderson or Rigby allow, and it was this power that informed some of the more influential historical analyses produced in the period of the Third International.

Superficially, Rigby's approach seems the more compelling. Indeed, Lenin, long after his split with Plekhanov, continued to advise young Bolsheviks: 'you cannot hope to become a real, intelligent Communist without making a study – and I mean study – of all of Plekhanov's philosophical writings, because nothing better has been written on Marxism anywhere in the world'.[11] This was no mere rhetorical comment: Lenin was so much a keen student of Kautsky's and Plekhanov's work that on his death in 1924 'his library contained more books by Kautsky than by any other author' – the majority of which had been published, officially, in Russia after 1917.[12]

Rigby is therefore right to stress the important level of continuity between Second and Third International Marxisms. However, his contention that all of these interpretations of historical materialism can adequately be characterised, and dismissed, as exemplars of productive force determinism is far too strong a claim. For instance, Trotsky's magisterial *History of the Russian Revolution*, which directly influenced C. L. R. James's classic *The Black Jacobins*,[13] alongside a host of more recent scholarly works, deserves a much more careful appraisal than is to be found on the pages of Rigby's book. Similarly, while the importance of the break between Stalinism and Trotskyism cannot be overestimated, the traditions of 'people's history' and 'history from below' which were inaugurated in their Marxist forms under the influence of the Stalinised Comintern in the 1930s, and which influenced, for instance, the great historians who came out of the Communist Party of Great Britain (CPGB) Historians' Group, cannot easily be reduced to examples of productive force determinism. Nevertheless, contra Colletti and Anderson, I argue that these powerful studies are best understood as evolving out of rather than simply breaking with the best elements of Second International Marxism

Kautsky's interpretation of historical materialism

Given the typical charge that Second International Marxism represented a type of vulgar and fatalistic social evolutionism, it is of some interest to enquire into the relationship between it and the theory of evolution as it was understood in the nineteenth century. Social Darwinists have, since the publication of *Origin of Species*, sought to utilise Darwinism to legitimise political programmes of one form or another.[14] Nonetheless, the exact mechanism through which Darwin's theory of natural selection was given a social spin depended to a large extent on national cultural traditions. America in the nineteenth century was, as Hofstadter points out, 'the Darwinian country' where the themes of the 'survival of the fittest' and the 'struggle for existence' appealed.[15] Precisely because of the hegemony of these ideas, American socialists defended their political beliefs in social Darwinian terms. Pittenger argues that 'in such a cultural milieu, thoughtful laymen who inclined toward socialism could hardly avoid addressing evolutionary ideas'.[16] A similar story has been told of Victorian Britain, where a dominant conservative social Darwinism existed alongside a minority socialist social Darwinism.[17] In stark contrast to the dominant conservative reading of Darwin in the Anglophone world, his ideas experienced a very different popular reception in Germany. Kelly claims that 'Darwinism became a kind of popular philosophy in Germany more than in any other country'. This, though, was not the laissez-faire Darwin of the USA:

> German popular Darwinism was a continuation of the old enlightenment tradition. German Darwinism sought to crush superstition, to inform, to liberate, and, indirectly, to democratise. In a narrower sense popular Darwinism may profitably be viewed as a cultural extension of the radical democratic spirit of 1848 – a spirit that was suppressed in the political arena but could live on in less threatening non-political guises.[18]

Ted Benton has shown how Germany's conservative academic establishment rejected Darwinism, compelling the country's most prestigious Darwinist Ernst Haeckel to accept a chair at a provincial university. Haeckel's liberal social Darwinism therefore never attained the level of hegemony associated with similar views in the elite discourses of either Britain or America. Instead, despite his own explicit rejection of the link between Darwinism and socialism, his ideas were taken up and radicalised inside Germany's socialist movement, which in turn infused German popular Darwinism with a much greater radical edge than was common elsewhere.[19]

Undoubtedly the most popular work of Darwinian Marxism produced in late nineteenth-century Germany – going through fifty-three editions in its author's lifetime – was August Bebel's *Women and Socialism*. Bebel (1840–1913), a cabinet-maker who, through his involvement in socialist politics and trade unionism, rose to lead the SPD, was widely respected within the international socialist movement for both his political and his theoretical contributions. Bebel argued that 'socialism was a logical consequence of Darwinian theory and that the Darwinists who were disputing this deduction . . . were influenced by class considerations, fear, or other base motives'.[20] Regardless of the undoubted political merits of Bebel's critique of the attempt to naturalise the inequality between men and women, theoretically his book was weak, such that Vogel noticed an implied, but unmistakable, 'polemic' by Engels against Bebel over the issue of women's oppression.[21]

While Bebel made the most overt link between Marxism and social Darwinism, Karl Kautsky is usually regarded as the most sophisticated proponent of a mechanical interpretation of Marxism, through 'a much more thorough synthesis of Marxism and biological evolution'.[22]

After an inauspicious early encounter with Marx, when the older man described his young epigone as a pedant,[23] Karl Kautsky's reputation as a Marxist theoretician rose to a peak in the first decade of the twentieth century, only to endure a dramatic reversal in the years after the outbreak of the First World War. Despite Marx's misgivings about this young 'mediocrity', Kautsky's early theoretical renown was placed on a sure footing when, in 1883, he launched and edited what was to become the Second International's most important journal of socialist theory: *Neue Zeit*. When, subsequently, first Engels set him to work editing Marx's *Theories of Surplus Value* in 1888, and then, after Engels's death, he was named as the editor of Marx's literary estate, Kautsky's pre-eminence among Marxist intellectuals was assured. It was from this position that he firmly stamped his imprint on the international socialist movement when, in 1891, he co-authored the German SPD's *Erfurt Programme*. In fact, so influential were Kautsky's ideas in the two decades between Engels's death and the outbreak of the First World War that he became, according to Steenson, 'the most important theorist of Marxism in the world', who 'did more to popularise Marxism in western Europe than any other intellectual'.[24] Such was Kautsky's status during this period that when one wiseacre described him the 'Pope of Marxism' the label stuck.

While it is beyond dispute that Kautsky had come to Marxism via Darwinism,[25] it is also the case that as early as the 1890s he understood that Darwin's ideas could not be equated with Marxism.[26] So, whereas in his magnum opus *The Materialist Conception of History* (1927) he defended an evolutionary interpretation of Marxism, he understood this theory of history, contra Stack's claim, in Lamarckian rather than Darwinian terms.[27] What is more, in the two decades leading up to the publication of *The Materialist Conception of History*, Kautsky's interpretation of Marxism took an increasingly mechanical turn. An interesting example of this shift can be seen if we compare one of the arguments defended in this book with that outlined in his 1906 essay 'The American Worker'. Commenting on the claim, made in the Preface to the first edition of *Capital*, that 'the country that is more developed industrially only shows, to the less developed, the image of its own future',[28] in 1927 Kautsky suggested that this statement 'remains valid', while in 1906 he replied that 'this assertion can be accepted only with great reservations'.[29] In 1906 Kautsky argued that while Marx's general thesis had been true in 1867, there no longer existed a 'classical model' of development, such as England had constituted forty years earlier. In fact, there were now two national states that represented extreme elements of the contemporary mode of production: America, where the capitalist class was disproportionately strong, and Russia, where the workers were excessively powerful. Meanwhile, or so he argued, Germany had an economy that 'is closest to the American model', but was politically 'closest to' Russia.[30] So, in contrast to the unilinearity of mythological 'Kautskyism', the real Kautsky, at least in 1906, argued that the complex developmental pattern of the contemporary world 'only contradicts that kind of historical materialism of which our opponents and critics accuse us, by which they understand a *ready-to-hand model*, and not a *method of inquiry*'.[31]

More generally, as Donald points out, Kautsky 'warned against the practice of invoking Marx's authority', and in 1896 he insisted that 'it would be quite un-Marxist to close one's eyes to facts and persevere with the old Marxist viewpoint'.[32] While the flexibility inherent in this approach is most evident in two essays published in 1906, 'The American Worker' and 'The Driving Force of the Russian Revolution and its Prospects',[33] it is also true of his historical studies of the early Church and Reformation communism.[34]

As I have argued elsewhere, in the period around the first Russian revolution of 1905 Kautsky made three significant contributions to historical materialism that undermine the simplistic claim that his work, at that juncture, can adequately be labelled either 'fatalistic' or a form of 'vulgar evolutionism'. First, in his essays on the early Church and on Reformation communism he broke with a crude model of historical progress. Second, in his brilliant comparative analyses of the American, English, German and Russian social formations he rejected unilinear models of historical development. Third, in the essays on Thomas More, America and Reformation communism he clearly stressed the causal significance of ideas in history. We can therefore agree with Paul Le Blanc that Kautsky's Marxism was at this time far more sophisticated than it later became.[35]

For instance, in 1905, Plekhanov asked of Kautsky, regarding the revolutionary ferment in Russia: 'are we facing a bourgeois or a socialist revolution . . . what should be [our] attitude . . . towards the bourgeois democratic parties, which are struggling in their own way for political liberty . . . what tactics should [we] . . . pursue in the Duma elections in order to utilise the strength of the bourgeois opposition parties?'.[36] The very structure of these questions, as Lenin pointed out in his Preface to Kautsky's reply, were loaded in such a way as to preclude the interpretations of Plekhanov's Russian critics.[37] In posing the question of the character of the coming revolution as a simple dichotomy between bourgeois or socialist, Plekhanov attempted to disqualify any suggestion that Russia might be moving towards either a new type of revolution or some combination of the two types he mentioned. Beyond this, he posed the questions of the relationship of the socialists to the liberals in such a way as to attempt to exclude any disagreement with his approach to this issue. If Plekhanov hoped that Kautsky's reply would aid his polemic against his opponents, he was sadly mistaken: for Kautsky wrote an analysis of the revolution that was embraced by both Lenin and Trotsky as a vindication of their analyses.[38] Without going into the details of Kautsky's arguments, which I have discussed at length elsewhere, it is enough, perhaps, to point out that in contrast to Plekhanov's mechanical reading of Russian history, Kautsky not only dismissed the claim that Marx's comments from *Capital* could be mechanically imposed on Russian history, but even insisted that 'we are approaching completely new situations and problems for which no earlier model is appropriate'.[39]

Plekhanov and Labriola: a synthetic theory of history

While Plekhanov's theoretical interventions after 1905 took an increasingly mechanical form, this shift was informed primarily by his political analysis of the rise of the Cadets, a bourgeois liberal party the emergence of which seemed to confound his earlier diagnosis of the weakness of the Russian middle class.[40] What is more, despite Plekhanov's deployment of mechanical concepts to justify this perspective from 1905 onwards, he had previously developed a much more fertile interpretation of historical materialism.

Unlike Kautsky, whose Marxism derived from his reading of Darwin, Plekhanov first read Hegel before he came to embrace historical materialism. Consequently, while his Marxism resembled the generality of nineteenth-century thinking in that it involved an evolutionary component, he criticised the one-sidedness of those interpretations of history which perceived the operation of social evolutionism in gradual terms. Against such models he insisted that 'leaps in the process of development' were inevitable.[41] So, while he argued that it is the development of the forces of production that underpinned social evolution, he maintained that this is an irregular and episodic process.[42] More generally he insisted that as history was made by men 'it is manifest that it is also made by 'great men'. But how did he understand the process through which great men make history? Plekhanov sought to escape from those superficial accounts of history which reduced it to the outcome of a clash between the wills of great individuals without losing sight of the fact that it is human actors who make history. To this end he aimed to look behind the individuals to the processes through which 'the activities of such men are determined'.[43] In formulating a method through which he might make sense of this problem, Plekhanov suggested that as great events had tended to call forth great actors through which they might be realised, then, or so he argued, the same forces that gave rise to the event might also be reasonably assumed to produce the actors necessary for their realisation:

> It has long been observed that great talents appear everywhere, whenever the social conditions favourable to their development exist. This means that every man of talent who actually appears, i.e. every man of talent who becomes a social force, is the product of social relations. Since this is the case, it is clear why talented people can change only individual features of events, but not their general trend: *they are themselves the product of this trend; were it not for that trend they would never have crossed the threshold that divides the potential from the real.*[44]

Plekhanov spelt out the practical consequences of this approach when he imagined the death of Robespierre in January 1793: 'His place would, of course, have been taken by somebody else, and although this person might have been inferior to him in every respect, nevertheless, events would have taken *the same course* as they did when Robespierre was alive.'[45]

Plekhanov's polemic was targeted at Russia's Narodniks, who aimed, through acts of individual terrorism, to overthrow tsarism and institute some form of peasant socialism, and against whom Plekhanov intended to develop a clearer materialist conceptualisation of the basis for revolutionary practice.[46] In particular he wanted to follow Hegel and Engels in their discussions of the relationship between freedom and necessity. He referred to Engels's discussion in *Anti-Dürhing* of Hegel's claim that 'necessity is blind only in so far as it is not understood'.[47] Commenting on this suggestion, Engels insisted that 'freedom consists in exercising "control over ourselves and over external nature, a control founded on knowledge of natural necessity".'[48] Following the logic of this argument, Plekhanov sought to comprehend the parameters of material necessity such that he might be able to outline a realistic strategic perspective for Russian socialists, and despite the obvious weaknesses with his discussion of Robespierre's role in the French revolution, he claimed that his method involved a break with 'fatalism'.[49]

Unfortunately, even in his own terms, the logic of Plekhanov's argument is faulty. In *Fundamental Problems of Marxism* he argues, rehearsing the claims he made in *The Role of the Individual in History*, that replacements for important individuals can always be found in the 'long run', as 'the 'average' axis of mankind's intellectual development [runs] parallel to that of its economic development'.[50] Yet, on any account, Robespierre was no average individual, and elsewhere Plekhanov talks of the role of either the 'genius' who 'grasps earlier than [his contemporaries] do the meaning of new social relations which are coming into existence'[51] or of the 'outstanding individual' whose strength is reflected 'in his contact with a class, with the masses, with the people'.[52] Those individuals, precisely because of their 'genius', cannot be reduced to the average type, and cannot easily be said to be replaceable. Moreover, the claim that individuals are always replaceable in the 'long run' contradicts a central dictum of Plekhanov's thought, which he repeated endlessly and which Lenin took up as a guiding motto: 'there is no abstract truth: truth is always concrete'.[53] Trotsky's discussion of the role of Lenin in 1917[54] supersedes Plekhanov's theorisation of the role of the individual in history, as I show below, precisely because he takes seriously the demand that theory rises to the level of practice, such that it is able to comprehend the concrete truth of history.

Trotsky's interpretation of historical materialism was, however, not simply marked by its break with Plekhaov's, but rather grew out of its best elements. In fact, Trotsky noted that his own interpretation of Russia's peculiar historical evolution was built on methodological foundations borrowed from Kautsky, Plekhanov and Labriola.[55] Trotsky was particularly impressed by Labriola's essay, because he believed that it provided the most sophisticated Marxist critique of the pluralist approach to the interpretation of historical causality: 'He made short work, and in marvellous style, of the theory of the multiple factors which were supposed to dwell on the Olympus of history and rule our fates from there.'[56] In his 1897 essay *The Materialist Conception of History*, Plekhanov was equally impressed by Labriola's 'replacement of the theory of factors . . . by a synthetic view of social life'.[57] What is more, in Labriola's essay and in Plekhanov's review we see the most sophisticated expressions of Second International Marxism, and they explode the myth that these thinkers merely 'vulgarised' Marxism.

Raymond Williams argued that 'in the transition from Marx to Marxism', the concepts of 'base', 'superstructure' and 'forces and relations of production', among others, 'were projected, first, as if they were precise concepts, and second, as if they were descriptive terms for observable "areas" of life'.[58] Ironically, given that Williams singled out Plekhanov for criticism in this respect, the Father of Russian Marxism had polemicised against much the same misrepresentation of historical materialism in his review of Labriola. In *Essays on the Materialist Conception of History* (1896), Labriola explicitly challenged bourgeois historiography's factoral approach to the explanation of historical causality.[59] This approach, he argued, separated history into its economic, political, legal, ideological, etc., components, therefore lending itself to a misrepresentation of Marxism as a type of economic determinism. In contrast, Labriola insisted, it was only because the critics of Marxism themselves held a reified conception of the economic that they could so misunderstand Marx's method. In an attempt to make Marx's method clear to these critics he proposed to rename it the 'organic conception of history'. This is not to suggest that Labriola sought to throw out the baby of Marx's concepts of base and superstructure, etc., along with the bathwater of the designation 'economic conception of history'. Rather, he sought to re-emphasise the dynamic nature of Marx's conception of productive base, which, at the level of the capital–wage labour relationship, 'is the whole inner essence of modern history'. With the young Marx, he insisted that history is at its heart an attempt by people to satisfy their needs through social productive activity; a process which, in turn, produces new needs and capabilities in an 'upward development'. While this conception obviously involved some evolutionary component, Labriola was keen to stress the gap between Marx's theory of social evolution and Darwin's model of natural evolution: he criticised the 'epidemic' of Darwinism that had recently 'invaded the minds of more than one thinker'.

Nonetheless, Labriola noted a real parallel between Marx's and Darwin's approach: both could be characterised by their method of enquiry, and neither included a 'vision of a great plan or of a design'. Labriola then compared Marx's method with the method of 'factors'. The latter, he argued, could not simply be dismissed as an erroneous approach to history, for it grew out of the desire on the part of historians, to make scientific sense of the myriad facts presented by history. Every historian, he argued, must proceed, first, by 'an act of elimination' through which she marks the delineation between her proposed area of enquiry and the surrounding general clamour of events and processes. Beyond this procedure, the narrator must organise into discrete groups those facts she considers pertinent to her argument. Unfortunately, while this is a necessary moment in the process of analysis, there exists a tendency inherent to this scientific procedure to move beyond this course of action and to begin to conceive of those groups of facts as 'independent categories'. The factoral approach consequently reflects not mere error, but a partial, reified, movement towards a scientific approach to history. Labriola therefore resisted the temptation to simply reject the factoral approach; he suggested, rather, that scientific historians must aim to 'overcome it, explain it and outgrow it'. He argued that the very process of writing history demands that historians develop a conception of 'reciprocal action' through which various factors interact. And, as this conception of 'reciprocal action' implies a move beyond the original abstractions through which the historian's materials were categorised, then it also implies something like Marx's 'organic conception of history'.

But why should such an 'organic conception of history' remain attached to concepts such as base and superstructure? Labriola's answer to this question relates to his humanist model of history, noted above. Because humans create and re-create themselves through an ongoing process of production by which they aim to satisfy their needs, then 'the only permanent and sure fact . . . is men grouped in a determined social form by means of determined connections' whose goal is to produce socially those things that they need. Such a conception of production offered a 'base' for a theory of history that moved beyond that provided by the inadequate – because ahistorical – traditional concept of human nature. Conversely, and in contrast to non-Marxist conceptions of the totality such as those which contrasted the factoral approach with some model of society as a 'social organism', Labriola insisted that social production – the economic understood in a non-reified way – determines the structure of the historical totality. He aimed to move beyond the limitations of the factoral approach, without losing sight of the fact that societies are hierarchically structured totalities. While politics and ideas, etc., could play a decisive role in history, they did not arise other than from the productive process on which they later reacted. As Labriola liked to insist against the factoral approach to history, and, by extension, against non-materialist conceptions of the social totality: 'ideas do not fall from heaven, nothing comes to us in a dream'. So while it was 'foolish' to conflate historical materialism with economic history, it was true that the social totality was constructed as a unity, in the modern world, 'by the working of the capitalist form of production', which determines, 'in the first place and directly', class struggle, law, morals and relations of power, and, 'in the second place . . . [and] in an indirect fashion, the objects of imagination and of thought in the production of art, religion and science'. Neither of these facts implied a predetermined pattern to history; rather, history refuses any 'preconceived' plans because 'struggle incessant among the nations, and struggles between the members of each nation', preclude such an easy comprehension of historical processes. So, while the productive process shaped the structure of social conflicts, it could not determine their outcome: the success or failure of revolution, while shaped by previous social evolution, could not be reduced to this latter process. While Labriola in this way outlined a rich and suggestive interpretation of historical materialism, he combined it with a typically weak Second International approach to politics: in stark contrast to the method outlined above, he continued to believe that the triumph of socialism was 'inevitable'. Nevertheless, it was Labriola's critique of the factoral approach to history that most impressed Plekhanov.

Plekhanov opened his review of Labriola's book with an enthusiastic reception of his critique of economic history, in particular, and factoral history, in general. Noting that 'the theory of factors' had emerged as a scientific attempt to make sense of the course of human history, he bemoaned the process through which this breakthrough had eventually become fettered, in part as a consequence of academic specialisation which tended to trap thinkers within a framework of unintegrated concepts: economists studied economic factors while political theorists studied political factors, for example. Plekhanov insisted that while all 'historico-social factors' are useful 'abstractions', they involve an inbuilt tendency towards reification:

> thanks to the process of abstraction, various sides of the social complex assume the form of separate categories, and the various manifestations and expressions of the activity of social man . . . are converted in our minds into separate forces which appear to give rise to and determine this activity and to be its ultimate cause.[60]

So, while he would have agreed with Raymond Williams that the metaphor of base and superstructure should not be taken too literally, he remained convinced of its utility as a model of social structures. Indeed, Plekhanov posited historical materialism as a 'synthetic view of social life', one which was free of a teleological component, and which involved a complex conception of society as a structured hierarchy. Social evolution, according to this model, occurred as a response to humanity's constant creation and re-creation of itself through its attempts to satisfy needs. As these needs were 'to a large extent . . . determined by . . . the state of his productive forces', Plekhanov was able to embrace the concepts of base and superstructure without reifying them.[61] It is with this model in mind that we should read his 'nutshell' overview of the five social levels of base and superstructure, as outlined in his *Fundamental Problems of Marxism*: 'the state of the productive forces'; 'economic relations'; the 'socio-political system'; the 'mentality of social man'; and 'various ideologies'.[62] Williams criticised this formulation for forgetting that each of these factors are 'not separate "areas" or "elements"'.[63] Ironically, that was exactly Plekhanov's point, with the proviso that while he understood social structures to be indissoluble totalities, he also insisted that there existed within those totalities a hierarchy of activities: as Engels said at Marx's graveside, 'mankind must first of all eat, drink, have shelter and clothing, before it can pursue politics, science, art, religion, etc.'.

So, while Plekhanov made some sharp criticisms of certain of Labriola's detailed arguments, the thrust of his review was positive: Labriola, he believed, had made a significant contribution to Marxism. In particular,

Labriola's critique of the factoral approach to history armed Marxists with a powerful reply both to the traditional methods of historical scholarship and to suggestions that historical materialism was a form of economic reductionism. Labriola had therefore added to a method which aimed to comprehend the dialectical relationship between freedom and necessity without reducing history to a 'fatalistic' process through which some iron laws worked themselves out.[64]

Lenin and Trotsky on the Russian revolution

While it is undoubtedly true that elements of Second International Marxism were mechanical and fatalistic, it is also the case that a layer of Second International thinkers laid the basis for a much more open interpretation of historical materialism. Prominent among those who forged this reinterpretation of Marx's theory of history was Trotsky, who, after reading Labriola in the 1890s, became convinced that Marxism was more than a 'narrow' and mechanical apology for the development of capitalism in Russia.[65] Trotsky went on to apply the method he developed from Second International influences both in his analysis of Russia's social evolution and in his monumental *History of the Russian Revolution* (1931–32). So powerful was this latter work that Perry Anderson has labelled Trotsky the first 'great Marxist *historian*':

> No other classical Marxist had so profound a sense of the changing tempers and creative capacities of the masses of working men and women, pushing at the foundations of an archaic social order 'from below' – while at the same time pre-eminently able to chart the complex shifts and organised political forces 'from above'.

Trotsky accordingly attempted the kind of total history to which most historians only aspire.[66]

Trotsky formulated two major contributions to historical materialism in the wake of the revolutions of 1905 and 1917; or rather, he made one fundamental contribution, and one seminal restatement of a truth that had been distorted within the Second International. His fundamental contribution was the law of combined development,[67] which underpinned his theory of permanent revolution, while his restatement was of the activist core of Marxism.

When Trotsky joined the Russian Social Democratic movement the broad shape of its strategic orientation had already been forged. At its heart was Plekhanov's argument, deepened by Lenin, that the Russian bourgeoisie constituted a structurally conservative class which would retreat from the kind of militant action necessary to realise the serious reforms required to unfetter capitalist development in Russia. In the 1880s and 1890s Plekhanov argued that while capitalist development in Russia was undermining her peasant communes, the Russian State was simultaneously fettering the further development of this process; that Russia was therefore ripe for a bourgeois, but not a socialist, revolution; and that, paradoxically, socialists, because of the weakness of the Russian middle classes, would be forced to lead this revolution.[68] Lenin opened his contribution to this literature, *The Development of Capitalism in Russia* (1899), with a methodological defence of his attempt to write total history. It was not enough, he argued, to choose facts that showed the 'formation and growth of a home market, for the objection might be raised that such facts had been selected arbitrarily'. He argued that without losing sight of the evidence – and his study was crammed with economic data – it was necessary to depict the development of capitalism in Russia 'in its entirety'. He was not unaware of the power of the criticism that such a project was 'beyond the powers of a single person', but believed that by confining his discussion to analyses of, first, the home market exclusively, second, the post-reform period, third, processes in the interior and, finally, the economic side of developments, he could begin to make some sense of Russia's developmental process as a totality.[69]

Against the Narodnik reading of Marx, from which the populists learned about the evils of capitalism and which informed their romantic anti-capitalism, Lenin's thesis showed that any attempt to move back to some mythological past was both utopian and reactionary. However, unlike Plekhanov, whose analysis of Russian capitalist development tended in the direction of apologetics for the 'objective' process of history, Lenin refused to shy away from criticisms of either the bourgeoisie or their system.[70] Furthermore, while Lenin mentioned the progressive character of capitalism, vis-à-vis Russia's feudal past, his arguments for so doing were thoroughly humanist:

> One has only to picture to oneself the amazing fragmentation of the small producers, an inevitable consequence of patriarchal agriculture, to become convinced of the progressiveness of capitalism, which is shattering the very foundations the ancient forms of economy and life of the peasants who vegetated behind their medieval partitions, and creating new social classes striving of necessity towards contact, unification, and active participation in the whole of the economic (and not only economic) life of the country, and of the whole world.[71]

So, while he used the characteristic Marxist short-hand of equating progress with increases in the productivity and socialisation of labour, he refused to reify these concepts,and lose sight of the human suffering that was the corollary of this process: 'Recognition of the progressiveness of this role is quite compatible . . . with the full recognition of the negative and dark sides of capitalism'.[72]

Lenin followed Marx's discussion of the role of merchant capital in the transition from feudalism to capitalism. As I noted in the previous chapter, Marx argued that it would be the greatest error to identify merchant capital specifically with capitalism more generally, but he also insisted that in specific circumstances merchant capital could foster the development of capitalism proper.[73] Lenin argued a similar case, quoting volume 3 of *Capital* to the effect that merchant capital does not in itself 'represent a sufficient premise for the rise of industrial capital', but that 'the formation of the latter "depends entirely upon the stage of historical development and attendant circumstances"'.[74] So, while Marx's analysis of the emergence of capitalism provided Lenin with the method through which he analysed Russian economic development, it did not provide him with the answers to the problems besetting Russian socialists. Rather, he insisted that the issue of whether or not the old mode of production had developed to the point where merchant capital could act to foster capitalist development was a 'question of fact'.[75] Lenin insisted that 'orthodoxy' in Marxism was characterised neither by 'simple interpretation of Marx' nor by 'taking things on trust'. On the contrary, orthodoxy implied 'developing the basic tenets of Marxism in accordance with the changing conditions and the local characteristics of the different countries'.[76]

Consequently, Lenin attempted a concrete application of Marx's method to Russian social history. Capitalism, he insisted, emerged from within the domestic economy, and it necessarily forced an increasing differentiation within the peasantry. This analysis entailed that the political perspectives of Narodism were both utopian, in the negative sense of being unrealisable, and reactionary, because they were so transfixed with capitalism's reactionary side that they were blinded to its liberating consequences. Lenin's arguments supported Plekhanov's general claim that there was no possibility of the development of socialism in Russia on the back of the old peasant communes. Likewise, as capitalist development had not yet fully matured, he agreed with Plekhanov that the coming revolution would be bourgeois. Nonetheless, he refused to reify the concept of bourgeois revolution, and was consequentially much more critical than was Plekhanov of the role of the bourgeoisie in the coming bourgeois revolution. In fact, while he accepted as fundamental the argument that the level of the development of the forces of production in Russia entailed that the only viable revolution in early twentieth-century Russia was a bourgeois revolution, his focus from that point onwards was centred on the problem of what would be the outcome of the coming bourgeois revolution: his aim was to ensure that the post-revolutionary regime would be as democratic as was practically possible, and he tended to label the coming revolution democratic rather than merely bourgeois to stress that characteristic.[77] And in an implicit swipe at Plekhanov's formulation of the role of individuals in history, he argued that it is 'pointless to speak of inevitability . . . It is not a question of whether it is easy or difficult to render the sweep of the revolution mighty and invincible, but of how to act so as to make that sweep more powerful.'[78]

In contrast to Lenin's outline of the domestic dynamics of Russian capital accumulation,[79] Trotsky located his discussion of Russia's transition to capitalism more securely within an international framework. He repeatedly insisted that a properly scientific examination of Russia's social formation could not be articulated if this analysis was undertaken from a one-sidedly national point of view.[80] Where Lenin had located the ancestry of Russian capitalism within its domestic structure, Trotsky stressed its international provenance,[81] and partially explained the weakness of Russian liberalism at the turn of the twentieth century by this fact: because the Russian bourgeoisie had not evolved spontaneously out of domestic conditions, they did not have the deep domestic roots of their European precursors.[82] Additionally, as European capitalists were investing in modern plant and equipment in Russia, the Russian working class had leapfrogged an entire epoch of social evolution which the European working class had had to endure. So, although it was relatively young, the Russian proletariat was organised in units that were comparable to, and in some cases even exceeded, those of the more advanced sections of the European working class.

In common with all sections of the Marxist movement in Russia, Trotsky insisted that a contradiction existed between the need for Russia's productive forces to develop and the inability of its archaic political superstructure to foster that growth: a contradiction which entailed that a bourgeois revolution was necessary if the fetters to capital accumulation were to be broken. Moreover, like Lenin and Kautsky, and in opposition to Plekhanov, he argued that the bourgeoisie would recoil from this coming revolution. Trotsky, following Kautsky, insisted that it would be a mistake to mechanically apply Marx's statement, in *Capital*, that the more backward states would follow the developmental course of the more advanced states: 'There could be no analogy' between capitalist development as it had occurred in England and as it was occurring in the 'colonies', 'but there does exist a profound inner connection between the two'.[83] Building on Marx's account of the increasingly conservative nature of the French bourgeoisie between 1789 and 1848, Trotsky insisted that after a further six decades of social evolution the bourgeoisie, nowhere, would be able to act as a revolutionary class. This conclusion obviously had some bearing on the concept of a Russian bourgeois revolution. It is at this point that the specificity of his analysis of the coming revolution is manifest: for while he agreed with Lenin that the backbone of the coming revolution would be provided by peasants in the countryside,[84] and following the German Marxist Parvus and in line with Marx's general analysis of peasant movements, he insisted that because modern revolutions are won and lost in the cities, the leadership of the coming revolution must necessarily fall to an urban class if it was to be successful.[85]

For Trotsky, because the bourgeoisie were a conservative class, only a workers-led revolution could realise the demands of the bourgeois revolution: 'the Russian revolution is a "bourgeois" revolution . . . But the principal driving force of the Russian Revolution is the proletariat.'[86] At this point Trotsky's analysis moved beyond that of Parvus as well as those of Lenin and

Kautsky: for he argued that a revolution led by the workers would necessarily give rise to demands that far exceeded the limitations of the bourgeois revolution. Therefore the contradictions that had generated the need for a bourgeois revolution would lead to the demand for workers' power, or socialism.[87]

This is the first element in Trotsky's theory of permanent revolution: the Russian bourgeois revolution would grow over into a socialist revolution. As this development was conceivable only because the structure of the Russian regime was deeply influenced by its position in the world capitalist economy, the sort of crisis that might be expected to trigger a revolution in Russia was also likely to trigger revolutionary upheavals in the West. And as the success of a Russian revolution was likely to magnify such a crisis, Russia's coming revolution could be expected to spread throughout the international capitalist system. The revolution would become permanent in a second, deeper, sense: its domestic success was predicated on the triumph of the international revolution.[88] As Russia's economic backwardness would act against the realisation of socialism, spreading the revolution abroad would 'become, for the Russian proletariat, a matter of class self-preservation'.[89] And, if the Russians succeeded in this attempt, then any 'theoretically "inevitable" stages can be compressed to zero by the dynamics of development'.[90]

This argument was predicated on two key insights: first, while the Russian social formation was obviously singular, its form was in large part structured by its position within the global mesh of capitalist production; and, second, Russia's *sui generis* structure could not be explained as an embryonic form of more developed capitalist states. Hence, while the events of 1905 had 'destroyed the myth of the "uniqueness" of Russia', they had, simultaneously, proved that 'the Russian revolution bore a character wholly peculiar to itself, a character which was the outcome of the special features of our entire social and historical development'.[91] In contrast to Krasso's claim that Trotsky tended to hypostatise social class and lose sight of the specificity of any particular social formation, Trotsky painted a picture of Russia as a distinct heterogeneous totality.[92]

Because Trotsky was concerned to outline 'the class dynamics of the Russian revolution',[93] he criticised both Lenin's and Plekhanov's analysis of the bourgeois character of the coming revolution, not because their discussions of the low level of the development of the forces of production in Russia was unimportant – he wrote that 'the development of the forces of production determines the social-historical process'[94] – but because their analyses failed adequately to cognise the dynamic forces of the coming revolution.[95]

According to mechanical interpretations of the traditional Marxist theory of uneven development, the capitalist mode of production would develop in a non-uniform way across the globe from its birthplace in North-West Europe, with late-comers replicating the general trajectory experienced by the first capitalist nations. Trotsky, by contrast, insisted that capitalism, through its uneven spread, would generate nationally and locally peculiar conditions the dynamic structure of which would not mechanically duplicate those of earlier capitalist social formations. In particular, in those countries where there had been such industrialisation as to create a modern proletariat, but whose growth remained constrained by feudal or semi-feudal superstructures, then the tasks of the bourgeois democratic revolution would fall to the working class because the petty bourgeoisie had become conservative. However, because the forms of power associated with workers' struggles tended to challenge capitalist social relations, then those struggles would, in effect, act to combine the demands of the bourgeois and the proletarian revolutions.

> The laws of history have nothing in common with a pedantic schematism. Unevenness, the most general law of the historic process, reveals itself most sharply and complexly in the destiny of the backward countries. Under the whip of external necessity their backward culture is compelled to make leaps. From the universal law of unevenness thus derives another law of combined development – by which we mean a drawing together of the different stages of the journey, a combining of separate steps, an amalgam of archaic with more contemporary forms.[96]

When the model of combined development was originally conceived, Trotsky understood by it a peculiarly Russian context. However, in the wake of the defeated Chinese revolution of 1927, he generalised it to account for the experiences of semi-modernised societies.[97] Beilharz argues that Trotsky, through this generalisation of the theory of permanent revolution, retreated from his nuanced analysis of Russian development to mechanically impose this model to *all* undeveloped states.[98] However, this critique is misplaced, for, as Mandel pointed out, Trotsky did not universalise the theory of permanent revolution; rather, he insisted that it was applicable only where there had been a degree of prior industrialisation.[99]

So, while Trotsky broke free of the mechanical politics characteristic of Second International Marxism, he did not reject Marx's materialist insight that it was the level of the development of the forces of production that set the parameters of the historically possible; on the contrary, he insisted that those forces must be conceived at an international, rather than a national, level. In his analysis of Trotsky's thought, Knei-Paz accepts and stresses both this point and the power of Trotsky's economic analysis of pre-revolutionary Russia. Nevertheless, he is very critical of the political conclusions which Trotsky drew from this analysis: 'It correctly identified the dynamics of economic change. But it was an exaggeration as far as social and political change was concerned.'[100] However, Trotsky's economic analysis cannot be so easily divorced from his political perspectives. As Molyneux has argued, Knei-Paz's critique of Trotsky's political analysis is unpersuasive because 'the existence of the Russian proletariat as "an independent, vital, revolutionary force" was, both in 1905 and 1917, a demonstrable fact'.[101]

While Knei-Paz's critique of Trotsky is unconvincing, there is a fundamental weakness in Trotsky's theory of permanent revolution, one which became evident after the Second World War. Molyneux argues that while this framework marked a 'major theoretical breakthrough because it challenged, in a number of ways, the dominant Marxism of the Second International', Trotsky unfortunately posed it as 'not only a strategy but also a prediction'.[102] This elision amounts to a special case of a form of fatalism that is a feature of a number of his weaker works.

Nevertheless, Trotsky was his own severest critic when he noticed this weakness. Thus, in 1928, he explained his decision not to join the Bolsheviks before 1917 as a consequence of his earlier fatalistic attitude to the class struggle.[103] He suggested that the central weakness with his earlier argument was that it was innocent of a sophisticated comprehension of the role of leadership in the socialist movement. After 1917 Trotsky came to understand the pivotal role that could be played by individuals at key junctures in history; and he theorised this most eloquently in *The History of the Russian Revolution*.

Trotsky's *History* is a monumental work within which he aimed to narrate the story of the Russian revolution from February to October 1917. Its guiding thread is signalled in its Preface: 'the most indubitable feature of a revolution is the direct interference of the masses in historic events . . . The history of the revolution is for us first of all a history of the forcible entrance of the masses into the realm of rulership over their own destiny.'[104] Through his attempt to map the popular participation in the revolution, Trotsky's *History* prefigures later attempts to practise history from below. Yet, the *History* is much more than a history from below: it is also deeply informed by his own analysis of the Russian social formation, and combines an insightful analysis of the trajectory of Russian workers and peasants with narrative accounts of the political machinations at a number of different levels in Russian society – within the pre and post-February regimes; within the armed forces; and within the bourgeois and workers' parties.

Nevertheless, despite its undoubted artistic power, Trotsky's *History* has been subjected to a number of important criticisms from those who would deny its status as a work of scientific history. However, the reasons given for the dismissal of Trotsky's scientific pretensions are far from uniform, and are sometimes even contradictory. Perhaps the strangest criticism is that outlined by Thatcher. He dismisses Trotsky's 'grand sounding' theory of uneven and combined development as 'just another instance of Trotsky responding to Stalin'; and he denigrates the entire structure of Trotsky's narrative of October as a story within which 'there was a hero (Lenin) and a villain (Stalin)'.[105] Conversely, despite both Trotsky's supposed myth-making and the teleological structure of his work, Thatcher points to the parallels between Trotsky's arguments and those of more recent scholarship. He claims that Waldron confirmed the generality of Trotsky's criticism of the tsarist regime's failure to modernise; while Figes confirmed Trotsky's suggestion that it was peasants returning from military service who acted as a radicalising force in the countryside; and Marot testified to the pivotal role of the Bolsheviks in making the October revolution. Even Richard Pipes occasionally 'relies upon *The History of the Russian Revolution* for a factual version of events'. So, Thatcher concludes, Trotsky's *History* remains 'essential reading' for the student of the Russian revolution.[106] Now it is hard to imagine how the *History* could be of any more than historical interest if Trotsky's method had not produced real insight: impossible if his was really only the story of how Lenin the hero overcame Stalin the villain; a narrative apparently uninformed by the theory of combined and uneven development.

Beilharz, in contrast to Thatcher, argues that not only is Trotsky's narrative 'excellent', but his 'sensitivity to the phenomenon of uneven development' is praiseworthy.[107] Yet, he argues, the *History* is peppered with 'worn out metaphors' which suggest a natural evolutionary, and a teleological, model of history.[108] While this criticism of Trotsky's supposed failure to break with Second International teleology has been widely repeated,[109] it sits uneasily with other criticisms of Trotsky's supposed voluntarist interpretation of historical materialism.[110] Knei-Paz has suggested that Trotsky's defence of the thesis that Lenin played an indispensable role in the October revolution can best be understood not as a voluntarist break with crude Marxism but as a subtle restatement of Marx's crude determinist framework. Knei-Paz combines a 'suspicion' that Trotsky 'equated "objective necessity" with success' with 'surprise' at Trotsky's claim that without Lenin the revolutionary opportunity 'might not have materialised', to conclude that, for Trotsky, while Lenin played an 'indispensable' role in the revolution his prior existence, and therefore his actions in the revolution, were 'inevitable'.[111] However, while Knei-Paz concludes that 'Trotsky did not write a "scientific history"',[112] he also points out that Trotsky's economic analysis is 'generally borne out by other sources'.[113]

Nonetheless, unless the congruence between Trotsky's analysis and later scholarship is merely fortuitous, then we must address seriously the scientific pretensions of Trotsky's work. For his part, Trotsky argued that 'the proof of scientific objectivism is not to be sought in the eyes of the historian or the tones of his voice, but in the inner logic of the narrative itself'. It was with an eye to this suggestion that he claimed that his book 'reveals the inevitability of October'.[114] So, while it is the 'first commandment' of historical narratives to be true to the facts,[115] Trotsky was well aware that the facts do not speak for themselves and must be interpreted. The concepts that he utilised for his interpretation began from the 'social structure', and moved through classes and parties to 'ideas and slogans' which are 'the small change of objective interests'.[116] The fruits of this method, as Trotsky himself argued, must be 'reckoned with' if the scientific status of the method itself is to be judged.[117] It would follow that if modern scholarship coheres with a good part of Trotsky's analysis, to dismiss his method as teleological without explaining either this peculiar coincidence or Trotsky's own rejection of teleology[118] seems somewhat implausible. In fact, Trotsky did not argue that the *success* of October was unavoidable, but that *October* was: Russia's historically constituted structure pointed to the inevitability of a revolutionary opportunity, which may or may not have been seized. This did not mean that Trotsky believed any conclusion to have been possible from this conjuncture: the parameters of possible outcomes of the revolution might have been broader than a preordained victory for Bolshevism, but they did not include the triumph of liberal democracy; his analysis of the insignificant social weight of the Russian bourgeoisie pointed to this conclusion, and was confirmed by the liberal Cadet Party's move to support General Kornilov's attempted military coup in 1917. If a stable liberal democracy was not therefore feasible, a counter-revolutionary dictatorship was. The choice, in late 1917, was between Lenin and Kornilov: a workers' revolution led by the Bolsheviks or a bourgeois dictatorship under the military.[119] But this remained a choice: history was not to decide for Lenin through the cunning of Reason. Trotsky therefore recognised the fundamental importance of the Bolsheviks for the realisation of the potential of socialism with which the old regime was pregnant.

Neither did Trotsky reduce the story of the revolution to that of Lenin's heroic rise to power. Rather, Lenin appears as the last link in a chain of events:

> Step by step we have tried to follow in this book the development of the October insurrection: the sharpening discontent of the worker masses, the coming over of the soviets to the Bolshevik banner, the indignation of the army, the campaign of the peasants against the landlords, the flood-tide of the national movement, the growing fear and distraction of the possessing and ruling classes, and finally the struggle for the insurrection within the Bolshevik party.[120]

It is Trotsky's analysis of this final struggle within the Bolshevik Party that has been the focus of much criticism of his general method. Beilharz asks how was it that 'Lenin was the only 'revolutionary' in the Bolshevik Party (Trotsky aside) after April 1917?';[121] while Deutscher, from a perspective that owes much to Plekhanov's interpretation of the role of the individual in history, suggests that Trotsky's 'grappling with the classical problem of personality in history' is the 'least successful' aspect of his thesis.[122] With reference to the discussion of the role of other key actors in the *History*, Knei-Paz claims that Trotsky's method is to deploy 'stereotypes', such that these actors are summoned onto the stage of the revolution merely to play some preordained role through which the *telos* of history is realised.[123]

Both elements of this criticism – the arguments that Trotsky overplays the genius of Lenin and underplays the scope for the creativity of non-Bolshevik actors – misunderstand Trotsky's method. For those two moments of his analysis are testimony to the fact that, while Trotsky broke with fatalism, his was not a voluntarist theory of history. To that end, Alasdair MacIntyre argued that Trotsky's Marxism is not reducible to Deutscher's Plekhanovite analysis, because Trotsky recognised that 'from time to time history presents us with real alternatives', such that our actions cannot be understood at such junctures as 'just part of an inevitable historical progress'.[124] Yet, the alternative courses of action from which we can choose are themselves constrained to a greater or lesser degree by our class location. In 1917 the political representatives of the Russian bourgeoisie – and in this we include all those who mechanically held to the bourgeois revolution paradigm – were constrained to a greater degree than were the representatives of the revolutionary proletariat. Trotsky explained this phenomenon by the lack of a social base from which liberal democracy could flourish. The choice between Lenin and Kornilov was a real one, which left those who wished to evade it looking helpless before the growing social polarisation. As MacIntyre argued, the power of Trotsky's analyses of the key participants in the political drama – 'the Shakespearean richness of character' – lies in his ability to differentiate between those actors who are replaceable representatives of social classes for which there is little scope for an alternative strategic practice and those, like Lenin, who cannot be so easily replaced because a crucial choice is at hand which alternative leaders were ill-positioned to make.[125]

This is not to suggest, as Beilharz does, that, according to Trotsky, he and Lenin were the only revolutionary Bolsheviks. Rather, Trotsky quotes Lenin repeatedly to the effect that the Russian working class in 1917 was more radical than the Bolshevik Party, while the party itself was more radical than the Central Committee. Lenin's success was premissed on his ability to appeal to ordinary workers and the rank and file members of the party against the more conservative Central Committee.[126] Lenin's decisive role in 1917 was, therefore, rooted in his comprehension of the dynamic movement of the class consciousness of the masses – a psychological ebb and flow that he aimed to understand, and which Trotsky aimed to record in his *History*.[127] Conversely, the conservatism of the bulk of the leadership of the Bolshevik Party was rooted, on the one hand, in their continued adherence to the old Bolshevik slogan of a 'Democratic Dictatorship of the Workers and Peasants' and, on the other, in the sociology of their position both within and against the old society: the obverse of their success in becoming embedded within the Russian labour movement was that they experienced a certain political inertia.[128]

Lenin's role, in this context, was to enter a 'chain of objective historic forces' in 1917, within which he acted as a 'great link', whose function it was to accelerate the learning process within the Bolshevik Party at a moment when time was at a premium, such that without him the revolutionary opportunity could have easily been missed.[129] However, Lenin was able to play this role in 1917 because he had built the Bolshevik Party in the years up to 1917: 'without the Party Lenin would have been as helpless as Newton and Darwin without collective scientific work'.[130] Nevertheless, the party was not a substitute for the activity of the proletariat; rather it acted like a piston-box to focus the energy of the working class: 'Without a guiding organization the energy of the masses would dissipate like steam in a piston-box. But nevertheless what moves things is not the piston or the box, but the steam.'[131]

More generally the October revolution was conceivable only as a workers' revolution, because of Russia's location within the international capitalist economy. This international framework was the bedrock of Trotsky's perspectives for the revolution, and became Lenin's after his studies for his book on imperialism at the beginning of the war: either the revolution would spread to Europe or it would perish.[132] Given this prognosis it seems strange that Beilharz should claim that Trotsky failed to account adequately for the rise of Stalin, and that Knei-Paz dismisses Trotsky's biography of Stalin as 'an exercise in demonology'.[133] For, despite suggestions that Trotsky held to a naïve vision of historical progress, the opposite is the case: the triumph of counter-revolution would, according to Trotsky, inevitably be the consequence of the failure of the revolution to spread abroad; for, in such circumstances, the material scarcity, stressed by those Marxists who continued to adhere to the bourgeois revolution paradigm, would act to fetter the socialist aspirations of the Government. Deploying a method that is reminiscent of Engels's suggestion that the seizure of power by the Anabaptists in sixteenth-century Münster was tragic because the time had not then been ripe for their rule,[134] in his biography of Stalin, Trotsky famously refers to the suppression of the Kronstadt rebellion of 1921 as a 'tragic necessity' which was ultimately caused by the relative economic backwardness of the revolutionary regime.[135] Similarly, his most considered analysis of Stalinism, *The Revolution Betrayed*, is predicated on Marx's claim that 'a development of the productive forces is the absolutely necessary practical premise' of communism. It was from this premiss that Trotsky concluded: 'the basis of bureaucratic rule is the poverty of society in objects of consumption, with the resulting struggle of each against all'.[136] Nevertheless, unlike Kautsky, who in 1919, from a framework that involved a much more mechanical application of Marx's productive force determinism than was evidenced in his writings from 1906, categorised the Soviet system as form of state capitalism,[137] Trotsky held a more open interpretation of Marxism, according to which the Stalinist bureaucracy did not represent the final form of 'bourgeois restoration', but merely the 'first stage' of that process. Trotsky also insisted that the only force which could counter this tendency was 'the victory of the proletariat in the West'.[138] In the wake of the defeat of the Western proletariat, and prior to the completion of the process of 'bourgeois restoration', he characterised the Stalinist bureaucracy as a 'gendarme' in the sphere of circulation: a parasitic growth the existence of which was necessitated by the relative economic backwardness of Russia, but whose nature could not be mechanically reduced to his structural constraint.[139]

Because the bureaucracy, according to Trotsky, had, at the level of production relations, evolved no antagonistic relationship to the working class, this layer could best be conceived as a bureaucratic caste that, while parasitic on the workers, was not *yet* a distinct social class.[140] Trotsky insisted, despite the many deformations of the Stalinist State, it remained, in some sense, a workers' state. In fact, he argued, rather unrealistically, that the bureaucracy continued 'to preserve state property only to the extent that it fears the proletariat'.[141] Segal criticises this argument, because in it Trotsky failed to recognise that Stalin's 'personal despotism' was incompatible with a conception of Russia as a workers' state.[142] Despite the obvious power of this suggestion, Segal mistakenly locates the problem with Trotsky's characterisation of the Russian State as a consequence of his crude productive force determinism.[143]

Unfortunately, this critique grasps neither the complexity of the novel situation with which Trotsky was grappling in the 1930s nor the real source of his failure to develop an adequate conceptualisation of Stalinism. In fact, Trotsky's answer to the question of how the working class could have been politically expropriated by its own state was far from unequivocal: he maintained that the Soviet regime was, in the 1930s, in a transitional phase, and that its final shape had yet to be decided.[144] We should not reify Trotsky's understanding of Stalinism, for his arguments, as MacIntyre suggests, were in a process of development throughout the 1930s.[145] This process can best be explained, first, by the very novelty of the Stalinist phenomenon: it was too much to expect of any one person that she or he adequately cognise its structure even as it took shape; while, second, it was not any residual productive force determinism that informed Trotsky's analysis. Rather, as MacIntyre argued, the root problem with Trotsky's analysis lay in his 'use of nationalised property as a criterion for socialism'.[146] Interestingly, in his book *1905* Trotsky had suggested that despotic *class* states could exist on the basis of nationalised property, an insight that can be traced back to Plekhanov's arguments noted above.[147] That Trotsky did not deploy this insight in his analysis of Stalinism is unfortunate, but it is not a ground on which we may condemn him as a crude economic reductionist; quite the reverse: Trotsky's discussion of the Stalinist State as a 'gendarme' in the sphere of circulation, whatever its analytical defects, cannot be said to be a mechanical reduction of the 'superstructure' to the 'base'.

Stalinist 'Marxism'

In July 1918, Lenin argued, in the wake of his studies for *Imperialism* (1915),[148] that 'we never harboured the illusion that the forces of the proletariat and the revolutionary people of one country, however heroic and however organised and disciplined they might be, could overthrow imperialism. That can be done only by the joint effort of the workers of the world', thus dovetailing with Trotsky's analysis of the dynamics of the Russian revolution; while in January of that year, he had insisted that 'the final victory of socialism in a single country is of course impossible'.[149] Unfortunately, while revolutionary upheavals did erupt outside Russia, these movements were universally defeated. Most significantly, by the autumn of 1923, the opportunity for a successful revolution in Germany had been lost.[150] It was in the wake of this defeat that the Soviet bureaucracy began to develop as a distinct social layer, a process the ideological corollary of which was the emergence, in 1924, of Stalin's dogma of socialism in one country.[151] As I have shown, while Trotsky recognised the emergence of this bureaucratic tendency, he rejected the idea that the bureaucracy had coalesced into a new ruling class. More realistically, Michal Reiman has convincingly argued that while 1924 marked an important watershed in Soviet politics, the key turning point was the period 1927–29: 'the Stalin of 1926 was not the Stalin of 1929'. Stalin, as we now know him, emerged out of a structural crisis which had been evolving throughout the 1920s to finally plunge Russia into chaos at the end of the decade. Stalinism developed out of this crisis to become a socio-political system that was 'diametrically opposed' to socialism.[152] So, in contrast to Lenin and Trotsky's strategy of fostering world revolution, from the late 1920s onwards Stalin sought to solve the problem of Russia's historical backwardness through a process of state-led industrialisation, one which differed from tsarist Prime Minister Witte's pre-revolutionary attempt to achieve the same mainly in its scope and ferocity.[153]

More than a decade earlier, the old Bolshevik Nikolai Bukharin, who moved from being Stalin's most trusted lieutenant in the 1920s to become one of his most renowned victims in the 1930s, laid the basis for a conceptualisation of this novel phenomenon. In his *Imperialism and World Economy*, written to explain the First World War, he concluded, through an analysis of contemporary economic trends, that '(as far as capitalism will retain its foothold) the future belongs to economic forms that are close to state capitalism'.[154] Elsewhere, Bukharin explained his use of the concept 'state capitalism' by arguing that the essence of capitalism could not adequately be grasped through the mere description of its phenomenal forms: rather he understood that capital evolved through a series of stages; mercantile; laissez-faire; and most recently imperialism, or state capitalism.[155] While Bukharin could imagine the abstract possibility of the Soviet regime degenerating into a form of state capitalism, it was left to others, notably Tony Cliff, to utilise his insights to make sense of the Stalinist regime's forced industrialisation programme as a form of bureaucratic state capitalism.[156] Nevertheless, while Stalinism was a clearly counter-revolutionary phenomenon, Stalin continued to deploy the – bastardised – language of Marxism.

There was some obvious utility in Stalin's deployment of socialist rhetoric to describe his regime: it legitimised the Soviet State by reference to the October revolution, while simultaneously robbing socialist opponents of the regime of the language of historical materialism. Stalin, however, faced a problem: the possibility remained that Marx's critical concepts could be brought to bear on Stalinist Russia itself. To mediate against the unappealing consequences of such a critique, Stalin sought to rob Marxism of some of the more obvious conceptual tools through which the regime might have been criticised. Most markedly, Trotsky's analysis of the regime's degeneration and Bukharin's work on the theory of state capitalism were suppressed; while at a more esoteric level, as I argue in chapter 4, Marx's concept of an Asiatic mode of production was dropped from Stalin's newly universalised interpretation of Marx's theory of history.[157] Marxism, for Stalin, became in effect simply an ideological weapon used to justify, *a posteriori*, the policies of the Soviet regime.[158] Nevertheless, even with all of the provisos mentioned above, the gap between theory and practice could easily become so strained that they could be justified only through increasingly bizarre intellectual rationalisations. To that end, as Edward Thompson wittily observed, Marx's historical and dialectical materialism was transformed in the hands of the Stalinists into 'hysterical and diabolical' materialism: the great virtue of the dialectic, thus conceived, became that nobody understood what it meant, and it could be utilised, therefore, to excuse almost any irrationality.[159]

Remarkably, despite this being a period when Stalin's crude distortion of Marxism, as plagiarised from Bukharin's weak interpretation in his *Historical Materialism* (1921), was taken as orthodoxy,[160] Marxism within the international communist movement continued to inspire creative work. If members of the CPGB Historians' Group were among the more influential historians to emerge from the Stalinist parties, they did so as students of a much more interesting interpretation of historical materialism which survived inside the communist movement despite Stalin's monolithic intents.

Boris Hessen's Newton

One minor piece of evidence which suggests that Stalin held a less than clear vision of the direction in which he was taking Russia during the period immediately after 1929 can be gleaned from his relations with Bukharin in the years between the latter's expulsion from the Central Committee and his murder in 1938. For rather than have this 'enemy of the people' immediately arrested, Stalin made him director of research under, first, the Supreme Economic Council, and then, after the dissolution of that body, under the Commissariat of Heavy Industry: positions from which Bukharin was able 'to play a leading role in the Academy of Sciences' and whence he led the highly influential Soviet delegation to the International Congress of the History of Science and Technology in London in 1931.[161] Stalin, at the last moment, had decided to send a large and intellectually formidable contingent, under Bukharin's leadership, to this conference. While Bukharin's presence in London created something of a scandal, it was the contribution to the conference of Boris Hessen, director of the Moscow Institute of Physics, that proved to be the most controversial and influential.[162] John Saville remarked to Raphael Samuel of the CPGB Historians' Group that 'we all cut our teeth on Hessen's' study of Newton's *Principia*'.[163]

In his path-breaking study *The Social and Economic Roots of Newton's Principia* Hessen aimed to demythologise the idea of Newton's genius by subjecting the real Newton to a historical materialist analysis. In contrast to our inherited conception of Newton, Hessen sought to situate his ideas within their historical, political and social context. However, Hessen's analysis was a far from a crude reduction of Newton to his time; rather, he persuasively argued that the problems to which Newton applied his undoubted genius were the problems of his age. Furthermore, and long before Keynes described Newton as the last of the magicians,[164] Hessen's argument was based on an examination of the totality of Newton's output as an alchemist, a Christian and a scientist.

Hessen insisted on separating the method of Newton's presentation of his ideas from the actual process through which he had formulated them: he sought to elucidate the 'low source of inspiration' for the 'abstract mathematical language'.[165] To that end, he drew a portrait of Newton as a master of the technology of his age; one who advised a young friend that the most profitable way to realise the potential of a trip to Europe would be to study the following: the mechanism of steering and the methods of navigating ships; the methods of fortress construction; the natural mineral riches of a country; the methods of metallurgy; the methods for obtaining gold from gold-bearing rivers; the methods used by the Dutch to protect their ships from rotting during long voyages; the glass-polishing methods used in Holland; the utility of pendulum clocks to the determination of longitude; and the methods of alchemy.[166] Far from eulogising abstract thinking for its own sake, Newton stressed the application of thought to the solution of practical problems. Similarly, Newton had excelled at solving not a set of transhistorical scientific conundra but the problems associated with a particular moment in the history of capitalism. Newton, Hessen argued, was a child of the epoch of mature merchant capital, just prior to its transformation into industrial capital: an epoch which had its own problems, namely, those associated most closely with communication, the mining industry and military affairs.[167] Without going into the detail of Hessen's analysis, the main thrust of his deliberations was that the technical problems associated with all of these fields in the couple of centuries prior to the publication of the *Principia* could best be understood as bearing on different aspects of the physics of mechanics.[168]

Over this period, a number of practical men had sought to break free of the fetters of medieval scholasticism to develop more or less coherent solutions to those problems. To that extent, Newton was not far from the truth when he famously said: 'If I have seen further than most men, it is because I stood on the shoulders of giants.' Nevertheless, while Hessen pointed out that it was the practical demands of the epoch of merchant capital which fundamentally shaped the structure of Newton's enterprise, he also insisted that it would be vulgar to reduce Newton's thought to a set of answers to economic questions. For Newton was a man of his time in a deeper sense: he shared the religion and ideology of his age; and his physics will not adequately be understood without recognising this context.[169] To that end, Hessen, as Fara rightly points out, situated Newton within the class struggle of his age, but, contra Fara, he did not reduce Newton's contribution to physics to the 'product of seventeenth-century class struggle':[170] rather, it was the development of the productive forces over the preceding centuries that framed the problems Newton answered, while the class struggle helped shape his answer. Hessen claimed that Newton was not only a child of the epoch of merchant capital, but the product of England's bourgeois revolution, understood broadly as lasting from 1640 to 1688. The bourgeoisie in this epoch, or so Hessen argued, found themselves repelled by philosophical materialism in both its Hobbesian and, more especially, its revolutionary form – as articulated in some of the works of Richard Overton.[171] Specifically, Hobbes's bleak materialism, because of its conservative overtones, held little appeal to the Puritans who had led the revolution: 'the "misanthropic" materialism of Hobbes was hateful to the bourgeoisie, not only because of its religious heresy but because of its aristocratic connections'. Meanwhile Overton's radical democracy had been defeated by Cromwell, and in any case his ideas were only those of an extreme group: 'the main struggle went on under the cloak of religion'.[172]

Newton, as a 'typical representative of' the bourgeoisie, shared that class's religious enthusiasm, such that the 'materialistic germs which were hidden in the *Principia* did not grow in Newton into a fully formed structure of mechanical materialism similar to the physics of Descartes, but intermingled with his idealistic and theological beliefs'.[173] The fundamental weakness of the *Principia* could be reduced to its 'basic idea' that two forces governed the movement of the planets, one gravity, and the other an initial impulse from God: 'The principle of pure mechanical causation leads to the understanding of the divine element.'[174] Thus God and religion exist at the centre of Newton's universe. Indeed, as Fara points out, the famous phrase, typically attributed to Newton, 'standing on the shoulders of giants' was not Newton's, but was a religious aphorism that dated from the twelfth century, and would have been understood as such by his contemporaries.[175] In fact, even Newton's alchemy was no mere idiosyncrasy: rather, 'the transformation of metals constituted an important technical problem, since the copper mines of the time were very few, and the war business and the casting of cannon demanded much copper'. Hence, when Newton was asked to work at the Royal Mint, it was in part because his 'knowledge of metals and metallurgy' were 'highly valued'.[176]

The power of Hessen's critique of the reified model of Newton the genius lies not simply in his exposition of the material and ideological roots of the

Principia, but perhaps more so in his elucidation of a missing piece of this great book. Interestingly, Hessen argued that while the law of the conservation of energy 'is a simple mathematical consequence of the central forces with which Newton deals', Newton himself had failed to make this extrapolation. But how could one who is revered by mathematicians as being among the greatest of their number have failed to make this 'simple' connection? Hessen answered this question through an historicisation of thermodynamics as an evolving field of scientific enquiry. He argued that it was only with the steam age, that is the period of industrial capitalism which immediately post-dates Newton's own era, that such practical problems emerged which demanded the new physics of thermodynamics as a pressing concern. Newton did not elucidate the law of energy conservation because the problems which demanded such a solution were not the problems of his time.[177]

Hessen drew some political conclusions from this analysis which appealed to some of Britain's finest scientists of that generation. He argued that as 'science develops out of production . . . those social forms which become fetters upon productive forces likewise become fetters upon science'.[178] Writing at the onset of the Great Depression, his concluding appeal to scientists to join the anti-capitalist effort should not be underestimated.[179] And, as Sheehan argues, the political reverberations set in motion by the conference were so great as to shape radical science in Britain for years to come.[180] Unfortunately, considerations of space prevent me from discussing the work in the history of science that was inspired by Hessen. Suffice to say that such giants in their fields as J. D. Bernal, J. B. S. Haldane, Hyman Levy, Joseph Needham and Lancelot Hogben were all influenced by Hessen;[181] and, among these, Bernal argued that Hessen's essay marked 'for England the starting point of a new evaluation of the history of science'.[182]

While the intellectual impact of Hessen's paper was immense, the fact that the Comintern was at the time in the throes of an extreme swing to the ultra-left meant that the scientists who had been drawn towards Marxism in 1931 remained isolated – the Communist Party was following Moscow in denouncing social democrats as social fascists. It was only when the Comintern shifted to embrace the Popular Front perspective a few years later that a new series of opportunities for 'anti-fascist' collaboration were opened to them. The Popular Front, announced by Dimitrov in 1935, also opened a space for a new kind of radical history – *people's history* – out of which were to emerge some of the greatest historians of the twentieth century, Marxist or otherwise. While the names of those historians who joined the CPGB at this time are now legendary – Thompson, Hobsbawm, Hill, etc., the 1930s–40s was a period when their mentors, most especially Maurice Dobb, Leslie Morton and Dona Torr, shaped a research paradigm which their more illustrious students were to extend in the post-war years; and, if we are to understand the history produced by the CPGB Historians' Group we must look to the work carried out by their teachers.

People's history

In his report to the Seventh World Congress of the Comintern in 1935, George Dimitrov, the new general secretary of that organisation, noted that across Europe fascists were writing national historical myths through which they hoped to justify their contemporary politics. In response to this development, it was imperative, or so Dimitrov argued, that communists should challenge those myths with their own histories of the progressive struggle for democracy experienced within each national state: 'to link up the present struggle with the people's revolutionary traditions and *past*'.[183]

Beyond the rhetoric, this new line had a basis in Stalinist *Realpolitik*. In the wake of Hitler's ascent to power in 1933, Stalin moved to attempt to negotiate alliances with Britain and France to help safeguard his borders against the rising threat from Germany – a process which culminated, in May 1935, in the signing of the 'mutual security pact' with France. Whatever the merits of the realist calculations that underpinned this move, they were hard to square with the French Communist Party's supposed revolutionary opposition to its national government. The Comintern's new Popular Front strategy is best understood, *primarily*, as an attempt to square this particular circle – Russia needed allies against Germany, and if that meant viewing the French and British bourgeois governments through rose-tinted spectacles, then so be it. Nevertheless, there was a democratic element to the new line: many Communists reacted against the sectarian isolation into which the Comintern had been plunged over the previous six or seven years, during the so called 'Third Period', and those individuals and groups welcomed the Popular Front strategy as a route through which they could once again make their politics relevant to the concerns of their countrymen. Unfortunately, the Comintern's swing to the right was so abrupt that any revolutionary potential inherent in this democratic movement was swiftly negated: the Popular Front essentially re-instituted the type of 'class-collaborationist' politics against which the Comintern had originally been formed in 1919.[184]

Irrespective of the political merits of this programme, historiographically it opened the door to a series of studies, from below, of movements which had sought to create and deepen democracy: 'We became', wrote CPGB historian James Klugmann, 'the inheritors of the Peasant's revolt, of the left of the English revolution, of the pre-Chartist movement, of the women's suffrage movement from the 1790s to today.'[185]

However much this innovation might have appealed to the CPGB's historians, the novelty of the imputation of the decidedly non-Marxist concept 'the people' into the Marxist lexicon cannot be overstated – like Stalin's earlier conceptual 'innovation' of socialism in one country, there was precious little to be found in the Marxist 'canon' that could be deployed to justify it. On the contrary, Marx's claim that 'the history of all hitherto existing society is the history of class struggles . . . oppressor and oppressed, stood in constant opposition to one another' would imply, even to the most cursory reader, that an undifferentiated conception of 'the people' was a concept about which Marxists would have traditionally been very critical.

Nevertheless, while the idea of people's history is difficult to square with Marx's insistence on the class-divided nature of historical societies, as Samuel has argued, this idea did provide 'the groundwork on which Marxist historians have built'.[186] And the structures constructed by the historians who inherited this tradition have been nothing short of stunning: from Dobb's *Studies in the Development of Capitalism*, Morton's *A People's History of England* and Dona Torr's *Tom Mann and His Times*, to the mature works of Hill, Hilton, Hobsbawm, Kiernan, Rude, Saville, Thompson *et al.*, the achievements of this group have been praised across the historical profession. Nonetheless, this work of construction involved the execution of a basic elision from the concept 'class' to the concept 'people'. This elision was made explicit by Christopher Hill, who wrote in 1948 that 'people, social classes, are the instrument through which social change is effected'.[187] Yet those Marxist historians who inherited the traditions of 1930s' communism did construct a great edifice, and they were able so to do, in part, because, despite the frame of reference which originated in Moscow, their understanding of Marxism could not be reduced to Stalin's vulgarisation of the same. To a degree, this was a consequence of their fortunate inheritance of Marx's general overview, in *Capital*, of the evolution of capitalism in Britain; all the same, that inheritance would have been worthless but for the independence of mind that was evident in the best Marxist historians of the period.[188]

The leading communist academic historian in this period, Maurice Dobb, was, ironically, not a professional historian at all, but a Cambridge economist who refused the ahistorical reifications of neo-classical economics. Dobb's most influential work was his 1946 *Studies in the Development of Capitalism*, which, as Hobsbawm wrote of the younger members of the post-war CPGB Historians' Group, 'formulated our main and central problem'.[189] Dobb, despite Schwarz's suggestion to the contrary,[190] rejected economic reductionism; and was roundly chastised on the pages of the *Daily Worker* for doing so. As Stuart Macintyre points out, in the seminal essay *On Marxism To-Day* (1932), Dobb criticised the 'abstract separation of events into "material" and "ideal", and maintained that the precise influence of the politics and morals of an epoch could only be determined by a careful examination of the social relations of that epoch'.[191] Similarly, in *Studies in the Development of Capitalism*, Dobb argued that

> the leading questions concerning economic *development* . . . cannot be answered at all unless one goes outside the bounds of that limited traditional type of economic analysis in which realism is so ruthlessly sacrificed to generality, and unless the existing frontier between what it is fashionable to label as 'economic factors' and as 'social factors' is abolished.[192]

Elsewhere, Dobb made the materialist, yet non-reductive, point that while ideas could play an important role in history, the 'two-way influence' between ideas and economic conditions was 'not symmetrical'; for 'events and conditions of life exercised a strongly selective and formative influence over ideas', while 'ideas could influence events only in certain ways and subject to definite limitations'.[193] Applying this method, Dobb's aim in *Studies in the Development of Capitalism* was to outline the historical development of British capitalism with a view to providing a basis from which those 'definite limitations' would become comprehensible. To that end, Kaye is correct to argue that while Dobb 'was far from writing "total history" . . . he pushed economic history beyond economics'.[194] It facilitated Dobb's endeavour that he took seriously Marx's historical model of capitalism as a distinct mode of production that was itself in a constant process of development;[195] and it was the resulting power of Dobb's economic history of British capitalism that lent itself to framing the research of the CPGB Historians' Group.

The group began to meet formally in 1946 with a view to aiding the production of a second edition of Leslie Morton's *A People's History of England*. Morton's book, the first edition of which had been published in 1938, was among the most significant intellectual products of the Popular Front period which, as Samuel argued, 'grew out of the "common sense" of British communism in [that] epoch'.[196] In many ways it was also a model of radical historical popularisation: written in beautiful prose with a keen eye for detailed micro-narratives which illuminated the grand narrative of the people's struggle for freedom, from the earliest settlers through the revolts against feudalism and the English revolution to the modern struggles of the industrial age, Morton wove a compelling synthetic 'history from below' of England. Furthermore, despite the fact that it is now dated in many ways, the book continues to inspire: no less an authority on the seventeenth century than Christopher Hill admitted that when he was pressed, in the late 1980s, to speak on the centenaries of both the glorious revolution and the defeat of the Spanish Armada, it was a re-reading of Morton – half a century after its first edition and four decades after its second – that provided him with the bones of his argument.[197] Unfortunately, despite the many strengths of this book, as a consequence of a combined distrust of Marxism, and because Morton, a journalist and schoolteacher, was not a professional academic, on publication it received very little attention within academia.

The same cannot be said of the work of Hill, whose essay 'The Norman Yoke' was, as Schwarz claims, the 'central text' of the Historians' Group. In this essay, first published in 1954, Hill traced the notion of the Norman yoke from the seventeenth century – though he suggests that the concept may have had roots going back to 1066 – through to the birth of the modern socialist movement. Interestingly, while Hill argued that Norman yoke theory – the idea that the oppressive institutions of the English State were imported at the time of the conquest, prior to which 'the Anglo-Saxon inhabitants of this country lived as free and equal citizens, governing themselves through representative institutions'[198] – became 'subsumed by theories of socialism',[199] he did not, as Schwarz implies, suggest a simple continuity between early popular struggles against absolutism and the contemporary socialist movement.[200] Rather, alongside his narrative of radical continuity, Hill stresses important moments of change: 'after 1832 (as after 1660) the theory of continuity became an anti-revolutionary theory . . . Paeans in praise of the ancient constitution suited those who wished to preserve the *status quo*.'[201] So while Hill undoubtedly traced a continuous trajectory of democratic struggle associated with the Norman yoke theory between the seventeenth and the nineteenth centuries, his was no simple model of upward evolutionary progress. For Hill was keen to stress the novel role played by the proletariat in the democratic struggle that developed from the nineteenth century onwards.

If Hill was the first to publish a powerful historical justification for this position, it was the inspirational Dona Torr who outlined the most sophisticated version of this perspective. Tragically Torr died before this project could be fully realised, and only the first volume, plus fragments of the second, of her study *Tom Mann and His Times* have been published – and, because of her illness, the central chapters of the first volume were written up from her notes by Hill and Morton. Torr is, in many ways, the lost genius of British Marxist historiography, who taught 'historical passion' to the young members of the CPGB Historians' Group, according to John Saville, Maurice Dobb, Christopher Hill and George Thomson; they suggested that Torr imbued her protégés with the idea that 'history was the sweat, blood, tears and triumphs of the common people, our people'.[202] Nevertheless, Torr did not allow her passions to cloud her historical judgements; on the contrary, her intense belief in the importance of history sharpened her insight. As Christopher Hill commented, 'she knew more, had thought more about history than any of us; moreover, she put her work, learning and wisdom at our disposal'.[203]

Torr argued that Tom Mann was a representative of the 'newfangled'[204] working class of the industrial age, a class that had inherited half a millennium of struggles for freedom: 'Our story of the struggle for freedom begins with the great Rebellion led by Wat Tyler and inspired by Ball's 20 years' preaching.'[205] She divided the 5 centuries of struggle from Tyler to Mann into 3 periods: first, feudalism; second, the rise of capitalism; and, third, the 'newfangled' industrial age. In the epoch of feudalism, individual rights were tied up in the community, while capitalism separated humanity into atomised individuals whose rights were envisaged in opposition to those of the community. It was only the new proletariat of the industrial age who, she argued, could conceive of restoring 'to the democratic movement some of its old ideas of community without rejecting what was best in the bourgeois conception of individual freedom'.[206] This, then, was the goal of the socialist movement, born in the late eighteenth century and growing to maturity, through a 'zig-zag line of advance', in the nineteenth century;[207] to realise the democratic goals of Tyler, the Levellers and the Chartists in a new world which created the potential for those demands to be actualised with a depth that would have been inconceivable to earlier democrats. For Torr, therefore, the hopes of the nation were embodied in the democratic struggles of the workers – the class which inherited the mantle and the struggles of 'the people' for the realisation of full democracy.

Conclusion

Communist historiography in England in the two decades from the mid-1930s to the mid-1950s inhabited a curiously ambivalent space. Politically, 'people's history' was a corollary of the Moscow-led break with revolutionary politics that was embraced by the CPGB during this period. At a theoretical level, the concept of a democratic revolution acted to elide over Lenin's argument that the capitalist state must be smashed if the transition to socialism was to be realised. The national frame of reference of this historiography also flew in the face of Lenin's analysis of imperialism. This reworking of Lenin's ideas easily lent itself to liberal conclusions. Nevertheless, the communist historians of this period did not reduce people's history to liberalism: for, while the concept of people's history is necessarily ambiguous, in the hands of these communists 'the people' were understood historically to evolve into the proletariat from earlier oppressed and exploited classes.[208] Like Lenin, these communists understood that it would be the proletariat who would be at the forefront of the democratic revolution. While such an approach to history did not impinge on the detailed strategic concerns of contemporary politics – so long as the historians did not analyse post-1917 history then the party machine did not interfere with their work – it did lend itself to a general justification of the politics of the Communist Party in this period. Unfortunately, because an examination of particular tactics and policy reversals of the Communist Party itself were out of bounds, this historiography included a divorce of theory from practice that is the very negation of Marx's method, and which ensured that it never rose to the level of political and historical synthesis that is to be found in Trotsky's *History*.

If Trotsky's *History* thus marks the high point of Marxist historiography in this period, the general method associated with his approach was best expressed in the works of Gramsci and Lukács. While Gramsci celebrated the Russian revolution as a manifestation of the victory of voluntarism over evolutionism,[209] as his Marxism matured he increasingly sought to integrate the subjective and objective moments of the historical process whereas a mechanistic reading of agency had tainted previous versions of evolutionism, Gramsci, in the *Prison Notebooks* (1929–35) insisted on the centrality of the role of subjective agency within history. So, in contrast to Plekhanov's suggestion that history would have produced another Robespierre had the original died before he was called to the centre of the historical stage, Gramsci argued that an 'organic crisis' could continue on indefinitely if the agency required to overcome it did not appear.[210] Similarly, he argued that while it is essential to map the material terrain – structural and conjunctural – on which socialists organised, it was absurd to make purely objective predictions.[211] In a direct criticism of Bukharin's *Historical Materialism*, he wrote: 'in reality one can "scientifically" foresee only the struggle, but not the concrete moments of the struggle, which cannot but be the results of opposing forces in continuous movement, which are never reducible to fixed quantities since within them quantity is continually becoming quality'.[212] Paralleling Gramsci's contribution to Marxism, Lukács argued in *History and Class Consciousness* (1923) that 'fatalism and voluntarism are only mutually contradictory to an undialectical and unhistorical mind'.[213] In respect of the evolution of capitalist society, Lukács argued, 'the blind power of the forces at work will only advance "automatically" to their goal of self-annihilation as long as the goal is not within reach'. He insisted that at a certain level of this development 'only the conscious will of the proletariat' could redirect these forces in a socialist direction: 'the objective economic evolution could do no more than create the position of the proletariat in the production process . . . Any transformation can only come about as the product of the – free – action of the proletariat itself.'[214]

At its best, as articulated in the histories of Trotsky and Hessen, Third International historians did produce history which synthesised structure and agency in ways suggested by Lukács; and even those historians on whom the malign influence of Stalinism can be felt, such as Dobb, Hill, Morton and Torr, produced historical studies that continue to repay re-reading, and which have inspired, as I show in the chapters following, some of the most important radical historiography of the last half century.

Notes

1 S. Rigby *Marxism and History*, p. 13; M. Perry *Marxism and History*, p. 22; L. Colletti *From Rousseau to Lenin*, p. 105.

2 D. Sassoon *One Hundred Years of Socialism* (London, 1996), p. 5; Callinicos *Social Theory*, p. 112.

3 Jean Jaures, whose history of the French revolution influenced all serious subsequent debate, would probably lead this list. I can only apologise for not discussing his contribution to historical materialism in this book and point the interested reader to two excellent essays by George Rudé: 'Interpretations of the French Revolution' in *The Face in the Crowd: Selected Essays of George Rudé*, ed. H. Kaye (Atlantic Highlands, 1988); and *The French Revolution* (London, 1988), pp. 12ff. I would have liked to write on William Morris who, in his later writings, 'got near the heart of Marx's view of history': D. Torr *Tom Mann and His Times* (London, 1956), p. 192; see also N. Salmon ed. *William Morris on*

History (Sheffield, 1996). More generally on Second International methodology see Karl Mehring *Karl Marx: The Story of His Life* (Ann Arbor, MI, 1962 [1918]); also Mehring's *Absolutism and Revolution in Germany 1525–1848* (London, 1975 [1892, 1897, 1910]) and *On Historical Materialism* (London, 1975 [1893]): all include weak formulations, but do so alongside others which offer insight to the historical method.

4 R. Samuel 'British Marxist Historians, I' *New Left Review* no. 120, March–April 1980, p. 23.

5 Labriola (1843–1904) was a Hegel scholar who became professor of moral philosophy and pedagogy at the University of Rome in 1874. At that time he was a liberal, but he moved to the left in the 1880s, becoming a Marxist in the 1890s. Plekhanov (1856–1918) had been a supporter of Russian populism prior to becoming a Marxist in the 1880s. Known thenceforth as the 'Father of Russian Marxism', Plekhanov moved to the right of the movement in the early years of the twentieth century when he stood against revolutionary agitation in the 1905 revolution, opposed the 1917 revolution and supported Russia in the First World War.

6 E. Hobsbawm *The Age of Empire* (London, 1987), pp. 46, 9.

7 P. Anderson *A Zone of Engagement* (London, 1992), p. 34.

8 M. Salvadori *Karl Kautsky and the Socialist Revolution* (London, 1979), p. 230.

9 P. Anderson *Arguments Within English Marxism* (London, 1980), p. 101.

10 Rigby *Marxism and History*, p. 62; cf. J. Molyneux *Leon Trotsky's Theory of Revolution* (Brighton, 1981), p. 196.

11 V. I. Lenin (1921) 'Once Again on the Trade Unions', available at www.marxists.org/archive/lenin/works/1921/jan/25.htm#fw03b.

12 M. Donald *Marxism and Revolution* (London, 1993), p. 247.

13 James argued that Trotsky's *History* was the 'greatest history book ever written . . . the climax of two thousand years of European writing and study of history': C. L. R. James 'Trotsky's Place in History' in *C. L. R. James and Revolutionary Marxism: Selected Writings of C. L. R. James, 1939–1949*, ed. S. McLemee and P. Le Blanc (New Jersey, 1994), p. 118.

14 M. Hawkins *Social Darwinism in European and American Thought, 1860–1945* (Cambridge, UK, 1997).

15 R. Hofstadter *Social Darwinism in American Thought* (Boston, MA, 1955), pp. 4–6.

16 M. Pittenger *American Socialists and Evolutionary Thought 1870–1920* (Madison, 1993), p. 26.

17 G. Jones *Social Darwinism and English Thought* (Brighton, 1980), pp. 8, 63.

18 A. Kelly *The Descent of Darwin: The Popularization of Darwinism in Germany, 1860–1914* (Chapel Hill, NC, 1981), pp. 5–7.

19 T. Benton 'Social Darwinism and Socialist Darwinism in Germany 1860 to 1900' in P. Blackledge and G. Kirkpatrick eds *Historical Materialism and Social Evolution* (London, 2002), pp. 36–75; R. Weikart *Socialist Darwinism: Evolution in German Socialist Thought from Marx to Bernstein* (San Francisco, CA, 1998), p. 104.

20 R. Weikart *Socialist Darwinism*, pp. 134–5.

21 L. Vogel *Marxism and the Oppression of Women* (London, 1983), p. 98.

22 Weikart, *Socialist Darwinism*, p. 152.
23 In the wake of their first meeting in 1881, Marx famously described Kautsky, in a letter to his daughter Jenny – 11 April 1881 – as 'a mediocrity with a small-minded outlook, super wise (only 26), very conceited, industrious in a certain sort of way, he busies himself a lot with statistics but does not read anything very clever out of them, belongs by nature to the tribe of the philistines but is otherwise a decent fellow in his own way'.
24 G. Steenson *Karl Kautsky, 1854–1938* (Pittsburgh, 1991), pp. 101, 3.
25 K. Kautsky *The Materialist Conception of History* (London, 1988 [1927]), p. 6; Salvadori *Karl Kautsky*, p. 23.
26 A. Kelly *The Descent of Darwin*, p. 125.
27 Kautsky *The Materialist Conception*, p. 520; cf. D. Stack *The First Darwinian Left* (Cheltenham, 2003), pp. 80–4.
28 *Capital*, Vol. 1, p. 91.
29 Kautsky *The Materialist Conception*, p . 418; K. Kautsky (1906) 'The American Worker' *Historical Materialism* 11:4, 2003, p. 15.
30 Kautsky 'The American Worker', p. 16.
31 Ibid.
32 M. Donald *Marxism and Revolution*, pp. 83–4.
33 K. Kautsky (1906) 'The Driving Forces of the Russian Revolution and its Prospects' in N. Harding ed. *Marxism in Russia: Key Documents 1879–1906* (Cambridge, 1983).
34 P. Blackledge 'Karl Kautsky and Marxist Historiography' *Science and Society*, forthcoming.
35 P. Le Blanc 'The Absence of Socialism in the United States: Contextualising Kautsky's "American Worker" *Historical Materialism* 11:4, 2003, p. 134.
36 Plekhanov quoted in ibid., p. 370.
37 V. Lenin [1906] 'Preface to Kautsky's 'The Driving Forces of the Russian Revolution and its Prospects' in N. Harding ed. *Marxism in Russia: Key Documents 1879–1906* in N. Harding ed. *Marxism in Russia*, p. 355.
38 Ibid.; L. Trotsky 'Results and Prospects' in L. Trotsky *The Permanent Revolution and Results and Prospects* (New York, 1969 [1906]), pp. 33–4; and *1905* (London, 1973 [1907]), p. 10.
39 Kautsky 'The American Worker', pp. 15–16; and 'The Driving Forces of the Russian Revolution', p. 371; cf. Blackledge 'Karl Kautsky and Marxist Historiography'.
40 N. Harding 'Introduction' in N. Harding ed. *Marxism in Russia: Key Documents 1879–1906* (Cambridge, 1983), p. 35.
41 G. Plekhanov *Fundamental Problems of Marxism* (Moscow, 1962 [1908]), p. 38.
42 Ibid., p. 41.
43 Ibid., p. 70.
44 G. Plekhanov *The Role of the Individual in History* (London, 1940 [1898]), p. 53.
45 Ibid., p. 46.
46 Ibid., p. 61.
47 *Anti-Dühring*, p. 140.
48 Plekhanov *Fundamental Problems*, p. 83.

49 Plekhanov *The Development of the Monist View of History*, p. 74.
50 Plekhanov *Fundamental Problems*, pp. 70–1.
51 Plekhanov *The Development of the Monist View of History*, pp. 191–2.
52 Plekhanov *The Role of the Individual in History*, p. 7.
53 Plekhanov *The Development of the Monist View of History*, p. 240.
54 L. Trotsky *The History of the Russian Revolution* (London, 1977 [1931–32]), p. 343.
55 L. Trotsky *My Life* (London, 1970 [1930]), p. 123; *1905*, pp. 10 and 347; and 'Results and Prospects', pp. 33–4.
56 Trotsky *My Life*, p. 123.
57 G. Plekhanov *The Materialist Conception of History* (London, 1946 [1897]), p. 13.
58 R. Williams *Marxism and Literature* (London, 1977), pp. 77, 80.
59 A. Labriola *Essays on the Materialist Conception of History* (1896) available at www.marxists.org/archive/labriola/index.htm.
60 Plekhanov *The Materialist Conception*, p. 11.
61 Ibid., p. 13.
62 Plekhanov *Fundamental Problems*, p. 73.
63 Williams *Marxism and Literature*, p. 80.
64 Plekhanov *Fundamental Problems*, p. 90.
65 Trotsky *My Life*, pp. 123, 102; B. Knei-Paz *The Social and Political Thought of Leon Trotsky* (Oxford, 1978), p. 11.
66 Anderson *Arguments*, p. 154.
67 As Knei-Paz points out this phrase is not used by Trotsky before the 1930s, but is implicit in his analysis from 1905 onwards: *Social and Political Thought of Leon Trotsky*, p. 89.
68 G. Plekhanov *Socialism and the Political Struggle 1883* at www.marxists.org/archive/plekhanov/1883/struggle/index.htm.
69 V. Lenin *The Development of Capitalism in Russia* (Moscow, 1964 [1899]), p. 25.
70 T. Cliff *Lenin: Building the Party* (London, 1975), pp. 36–7.
71 Lenin *The Development of Capitalism in Russia*, pp. 386–7.
72 Ibid., pp. 602–3, 322.
73 *Capital* Vol. 3, p. 449.
74 Lenin *The Development of Capitalism in Russia*, p. 187.
75 Ibid.
76 Ibid., pp. 639, 623.
77 V. Lenin (1905) 'Two Tactics of Social Democracy in the Democratic Revolution' in V. Lenin *Selected Works* (Moscow, 1968), p. 78.
78 Ibid., pp. 92, 117.
79 N. Harding *Lenin's Political Thought* Vols 1 and 2 (London 1983), p. 87.
80 Trotsky *History of the Russian Revolution*, pp. 38, 991, 1219ff.
81 Trotsky 'Results and Prospects', p. 49; M. Löwy *The Politics of Combined and Uneven Development* (London, 1981), p. 48.
82 Trotsky *1905*, p. 37. Trotsky believed that 'Tsarism represents an intermediate form between European absolutism and Asian despotism, being possibly closer to the latter of these two': *1905*, p. 26. This model, as Sawer has argued, was based on his suggestion that the Russian cities were 'non-Western' in nature;

they did not evolve spontaneously with a strong urban petty bourgeoisie which could act as a revolutionary alternative to Tsarism: M. Sawer *Marxism and the Question of the Asiatic Mode of Production* (The Hague, 1977), p. 182.

83 Trotsky *1905*, p. 67.
84 Ibid., p. 50.
85 Knei-Paz *Social and Political Thought of Leon Trotsky*, p. 18; Trotsky *My Life*, p. 172; I. Deutscher *Trotsky: The Prophet Armed* (Oxford, 1954), pp. 104–5; Knei-Paz *Social and Political Thought of Leon Trotsky*, p. 21.
86 Trotsky *1905*, p. 66.
87 Ibid., p. 73.
88 Molyneux *Leon Trotsky's Theory of Revolution*, pp. 21–9.
89 Trotsky *1905*, p. 333.
90 Trotsky 'Results and Prospects', p. 241.
91 Trotsky *1905*, p. 21.
92 N. Krasso 'Trotsky's Marxism' *New Left Review* no. 44, 1967, p. 72; Trotsky *1905*, p. 53. For critiques of Krasso see E. Mandel 'Trotsky's Marxism: An Anti-Critique' *New Left Review* no. 47, 1968, p. 37, and Lowy *The Politics of Combined and Uneven Development*, p. 49.
93 Trotsky *1905*, p. 317
94 Trotsky 'Results and Prospects', p. 37
95 Trotsky *1905*, pp. 321, 328.
96 Trotsky *History of the Russian Revolution*, p. 27.
97 Molyneux *Leon Trotsky's Theory of Revolution*, p. 42.
98 P. Beilharz 'Trotsky as Historian', *History Workshop Journal*, 20:1, 1985, p. 38.
99 E. Mandel *Trotsky: A Study in the Dynamic of His Thought* (London, 1979), p. 20.
100 Knei-Paz *Social and Political Thought of Leon Trotsky*, p. 105.
101 Molyneux *Leon Trotsky's Theory of Revolution*, p. 39.
102 Ibid., pp. 40, 43.
103 Trotsky *Permanent Revolution*, p. 173.
104 Trotsky *History of the Russian Revolution*, p. 17.
105 I. Thatcher *Trotsky* (London. 2003), p. 182.
106 Ibid., pp. 185–7.
107 Beilharz 'Trotsky as Historian', p. 40.
108 Ibid.
109 G. Eley 'Marxist Historiography' in S. Berger, H. Feldner and K. Passmore eds *Writing History* (London, 2003), p. 70. W. Thompson *Postmodernism and History* (London, 2004), pp. 63–4.
110 Anderson *Arguments*, p. 101.
111 Knei-Paz *Social and Political Thought of Leon Trotsky*, p. 510.
112 Ibid., p. 501.
113 Ibid., p. 75.
114 Trotsky *History of the Russian Revolution*, p. 509
115 Trotsky 'What Is Historical Objectivity?' in L. Trotsky *Writings of Leon Trotsky* (New York, 1972), p. 187; Trotsky *History of the Russian Revolution*, p. 316.
116 Trotsky, *History of the Russian Revolution.*, p. 509.
117 Trotsky 'What Is Historical Objectivity?', p. 184.

118 Trotsky *History of the Russian Revolution*, p. 1192.
119 Ibid.,pp. 468, 575, 642.
120 Ibid., p. 1079.
121 Beilharz 'Trotsky as Historian', p. 43.
122 I Deutscher *Trotsky: The Prophet Outcast* (Oxford, 1963), p. 241.
123 Knei-Paz *Social and Political Thought of Leon Trotsky*, p. 509.
124 A. MacIntyre 'Trotsky in Exile' in A. MacIntyre *Against the Self-Images of the Age* (London, 1971), p. 59.
125 Ibid.
126 Trotsky *History of the Russian Revolution*, p. 994.
127 Ibid., p. 18.
128 Ibid., pp. 989, 1015–16.
129 Ibid., p. 343.
130 L. Trotsky *Stalin* (London, 1947 [1940]), p. 205.
131 Trotsky *History of the Russian Revolution*, p. 19.
132 Ibid., p. 1227.
133 Beilarz 'Trotsky as Historian', p. 47; Knei-Paz *Social and Political Thought of Leon Trotsky*, p. 529.
134 Engels *The Peasant War in Germany*, pp. 138–9.
135 Trotsky *Stalin*, p. 337.
136 L. Trotsky [1936] *The Revolution Betrayed* (New York, Pathfinder 1972), pp. 56; 112.
137 Donald *Marxism and Revolution*, p. 240
138 Trotsky *Stalin*, pp. 429, 433.
139 Trotsky *The Revolution Betrayed*, pp. 52–6.
140 Ibid., p. 248.
141 Ibid., p. 251.
142 R. Segal *The Tragedy of Leon Trotsky* (London, 1979), p. 386.
143 Ibid., p. 387.
144 Trotsky *Revolution Betrayed*, p. 249.
145 MacIntyre 'Trotsky in Exile', p. 54.
146 Ibid., p. 57.
147 Trotsky *1905*, p. 27.
148 Neil Harding points out that with the outbreak of war in 1914 it became apparent to Lenin that his old national frame of analysis was no longer adequate to the international problems facing the labour movement. Therefore, 'just as capitalism in its imperialist phase could be appraised only on a global basis, so too the balance of class forces had to be assessed on a similarly international plane': N. Harding *Lenin's Political Thought*, p. 6.
149 D. Hallas *The Comintern* (London, 1985), p. 7.
150 C. Harman *Germany: The Lost Revolution* (London, 1982). P. Broue *The German Revolution* (Leiden, 2005 [1971]).
151 Trotsky *Revolution Betrayed*, p. 32.
152 M. Reiman *The Birth of Stalinism* (London, 1987), pp. 119, 122.
153 M. Haynes *Nikolai Bukharin and the Transition from Capitalism to Socialism* (London, 1985), p. 110.
154 N. Bukharin *Imperialism and the World Economy* (London, 2003 [1915]), p. 167.

155 N. Bukharin (1915) 'Towards a Theory of the Imperialist State' in N. Bukharin *Selected Writings on the State and the Transition to Socialism* (London, 1982), p. 16.
156 T. Cliff 'The Nature of Stalinist Russia' in T. Cliff *Marxist Theory After Trotsky* (London, 2003 [1948]).
157 J. Stalin *Dialectical and Historical Materialism* (1938) available at www.marxists.org/reference/archive/stalin/works/1938/09.htm.
158 N. Harris *Beliefs in Society* (London, 1968), p. 152.
159 Ibid., p. 162.
160 P. Blackledge 'Historical Materialism: From Social Evolution to Revolutionary Politics' in Blackledge and Kirkpatrick *Historical Materialism and Social Evolution*, p. 19.
161 S. Cohen *Bukharin and the Bolshevik Revolution* (Oxford, 1980), p. 352.
162 P. Fara *Newton* (London, 2002), p. 262; E. Hobsbawm 'Preface' B. Swann and F. Aprahamian eds *J. D. Bernal: A Life in Science* (London, 1999), p. xvii; H. Rose and S. Rose 'Red Scientist: Two Strands from a Life in Three Colours' in ibid., p. 143. Later in the 1930s Hessen became one of the many victims of Stalin's purges.
163 Samuel 'British Marxist History', p. 80.
164 Fara *Newton*, p. 273.
165 B. Hessen 'The Social and Economic Roots of Newton's "Principia"' in N. Bukharin ed. *Science at the Crossroads* (London, 1931), p. 171.
166 Ibid., p. 172.
167 Ibid., pp. 155, 157.
168 Ibid, p. 165.
169 Ibid., p. 177.
170 Fara *Newton*, p. 262.
171 Hessen *Newton*, p. 181.
172 Ibid., p. 182.
173 Ibid., p. 183.
174 Ibid., p. 184.
175 Fara *Newton*, p. 207.
176 Hessen *Newton*, p. 173.
177 Ibid., p. 203.
178 Ibid., p. 210.
179 E. Roberts *The Anglo-Marxists* (Oxford, 1997), pp. 150ff.
180 H. Sheenan *Marxism and the Philosophy of Science* (New Jersey, 1993), pp. 306ff.
181 Ibid., pp. 304–36; Roberts *Anglo-Marxists*, pp. 143–208.
182 J. D. Bernal *The Social Function of Science* (London, 1964), p. 406.
183 G. Dimitrov The Fascist Offensive and the Tasks of the Communist International in the Struggle of the Working Class against Fascism (1935) available at www.marxists.org/reference/archive/dimitrov/works/1935/08_02.htm#s18.
184 F. Claudin *The Communist Movement: From Comintern to Cominform* (London, 1975), pp. 171–99; Hallas *The Comintern*, pp. 139–42.
185 B. Schwarz "The People' in History: The Communist Party Historians' Group, 1946–1956' in R. Johnson, G. McLennan, B. Schwarz, and D. Sutton eds *Making Histories: Studies in History-Writing and Politics* (Minnesota, 1982), p. 56.

186 Ibid., p. 71; Samuel 'British Marxist History', p. 37.
187 C. Hill (1948) 'Marxism and History' in J. Tosh ed. *Historians on History* (London, 200), p. 89.
188 Samuel 'British Marxist History', p. 64.
189 E. Hobsbawm 'The Historians' Group of the Communist Party' in M. Cornforth ed. *Rebels and Their Causes* (London, 1978), p. 23.
190 Schwarz '"The People" in History', pp. 46–53.
191 S. Macintyre *A Proletarian Science* (London, 1986), p. 121; H. Kaye *The British Marxist Historians* (London, 1995), pp. 27–8.
192 M. Dobb *Studies in the Development of Capitalism* (London, 1963), pp. 32, 281.
193 M. Dobb (1951) 'Historical Materialism and the Role of the Economic Factor' in M. Dobb *On Economic Theory and Socialism* (London, 1955), p. 228.
194 Kaye *British Marxist Historians*, p. 67.
195 Dobb *Studies in the Development of Capitalism*, pp. 7ff.
196 R. Samuel 'A Rebel and His Lineage' in M. Heinemann and W. Thompson eds *History and the Imagination: Selected Writings of A. L. Morton* (London, 1990), p. 23.
197 C. Hill 'A People's Historian' in Heinemann and Thompson eds *History and the Imagination*, p. 13.
198 C. Hill (1954) 'The Norman Yoke' in C. Hill *Puritanism and Revolution* (London, 1958), p. 64.
199 Ibid., p. 119.
200 Schwarz '"The People" in History', p. 70.
201 Hill 'The Norman Yoke', pp. 117–19.
202 J. Saville *et al.* 'Foreword' in J. Saville ed. *Democracy and the Labour Movement: Essays in Honour of Dona Torr* (London, 1954), p. 8.
203 C. Hill quoted in Kaye *The British Marxist Historians*, p. 14.
204 This phrase is taken from Marx's 1856 'Speech at the Anniversary of the People's Paper': Marx *Surveys from Exile*, p. 300.
205 Torr *Tom Mann*, p. 98.
206 Ibid., pp. 100–1.
207 Ibid., p. 175.
208 W. Thompson *What Happened to History?* (London, 2000), p. 29.
209 A. Gramsci (1917) 'The Revolution Against "Capital"' in A. Gramsci *Selections from Political Writings 1910–1920* (London, 1977), pp. 34–5.
210 A. Gramsci *Selections from the Prison Notebooks* (London, 1971 [1929–35]), p. 178.
211 Ibid., p. 171.
212 Ibid., p. 438.
213 G. Lukács *History and Class Consciousness* (London, 1971 [1923]), p. 4.
214 Ibid., pp. 70, 208–9; see G. Lukács *Tailism and the Dialectic* (London, 2000 [1925–26]), p. 54; J. Rees *The Algebra of Revolution* (London, 1998), pp. 202–62.

4

Modes of production and social transitions

Introduction

One of historiography's fundamental problems is that of periodisation: the question of how, if at all, it is possible scientifically to delineate between various epochs in history. It has been argued that modern sociology in general, and Marxism in particular, evolved in part to explain one such perceived transition between two distinct historical epochs: the emergence of modern capitalist society out of its pre-modern, pre-capitalist, precursor.[1] The Marxist variant of this controversy, the debate over the nature of the transition from feudalism to capitalism, has been articulated most famously in two influential exchanges: that between Dobb, Sweezy and others in the 1950s; and in the so called Brenner debate that flared up some two decades later. Given that Marxism evolved, centrally, as an attempt to understand the laws of motion of capitalism, it was only natural that Marxist historiography tended, from *Capital* onwards, to focus on this issue. Accordingly, it is with a discussion of the various contributions to this debate that this chapter focuses. Nonetheless, the transition from feudalism to capitalism itself occurred at the end of a long process in which humanity had experienced a number of similar epochal transitions. While the transition from feudalism to capitalism has dominated Marxist debates on historical periodisation, Marxists have also attempted to analyse a series of similar epochal transitions between various modes of production. As the debate on the transition to capitalism can be illuminated through a discussion of this broader literature, in this chapter I survey the competing Marxist interpretations of some of those earlier transitions.

In his Preface to *A Contribution to the Critique of Political Economy*, Marx commented that with the socialist solution to the contradictions between capitalist forces and relations of production, 'the prehistory of human society . . . closes'. Earlier in that text he had sketched humanity's prehistory as including, 'in broad outline, the Asiatic, ancient, feudal and modern bourgeois modes of production'.[2] As this schema was but one of many outlined by Marx and Engels throughout their lifetimes, Chris

Wickham has justifiably argued that to accept as definitive any particular variant of this list would be 'absurd'.[3] Nevertheless, the general sense of Marx's argument, both here and elsewhere, is undeniable: human history has passed through a series of epochs, each defined by the mode of production dominant within it. Moreover, each of these modes of production could be characterised, or so Marx suggested, by a specific combination of forces and relations of production, the contradictions between which generated a series of revolutionary upheavals out of which emerged the next mode of production. Obviously, if we are to model the entirety of human history along these lines, then to Marx's pre-capitalist modes of production noted above must be added, at a minimum, a further mode of production which preceded the original emergence of class societies. Two issues immediately spring to mind when confronted by this schema: first, could Marx's theory of history account for the multiplicity of transitional moments throughout the history of class society; and, second, could this model account for the prior emergence of class society?

In this chapter, I survey a small part of the considerable literature that relates to these questions to give the reader a flavour of the power of historical materialism. I begin with an overview of the contribution of V. Gordon Childe, perhaps the twentieth century's most influential archaeologist, who was deeply influenced by Marx. Childe introduced the concepts of 'neolithic' and 'urban' revolutions, which have since become a commonplace within the academic literature. He also deployed the concept of the Asiatic mode of production to explain certain features of the societies that emerged out of the urban revolution. More recently, this concept has come under sustained criticism from Marxists, and, reflecting this development, I move on from a discussion of Childe's work to an examination of later Marxist attempts to explain some of the historical processes analysed by Childe. I outline some of the Marxist contributions to the explanation of the decline of classical antiquity, including the accounts of Perry Anderson, Geoffrey de Ste. Croix, Chris Wickham and Ellen Wood. I then move to discuss the debates on the nature of pre-capitalist peasant societies. These debates have centred on the applicability to various societies of several modes mentioned by Marx and Engels at various points in their lives, including the feudal, the Asiatic and the tributary. I discuss these debates with particular reference to the contributions made by Samir Amin, Halil Berktay, Maurice Godelier, John Haldon, Chris Harman and Chris Wickham. Finally, I discuss the debates on the transition from feudalism to capitalism generally, and the concept of bourgeois revolution specifically, particularly the contributions made to this literature by Perry Anderson, Christopher Hill, Eric Hobsbawm and Edward Thompson. It will become clear that Marxism includes a rich, and fiercely contested, series of explanations of these transitions.

Gordon Childe: revolutions in archaeology[4]

As I noted in chapter 2, Engels, following Morgan, had differentiated three stages in humanity's movement from pre-history to history: savagery; barbarism; and civilisation itself. While Engels had given Morgan's findings a materialist spin by more securely locating the economic distinction between food-gathering savagery and food-producing barbarism,[5] it was V. Gordon Childe (1892–1957),[6] the man described by Patterson as 'the most influential archaeologist of the twentieth century',[7] who placed Marxist categories at the centre of archaeological thought.[8] And while much of the detail of Childe's arguments has been superseded by later developments within the field – a prospect that he himself predicted[9] – two of his more important contributions to the understanding of archaeological data, the concepts of neolithic and urban revolution, have withstood the test of time.[10] In addition to these fundamental contributions to archaeology, Childe's schematic analysis of the rise and fall of antiquity has informed subsequent debates within Marxist historiography.[11]

Childe, himself, wrote overtly as a non-dogmatic Marxist. In a letter (1938) to the British communist R. Palme Dutt he argued: 'To me Marxism means effectively a way of approach to and a methodological device for the interpretation of archaeological and historical material and I accept it because and in so far as it *works*.'[12] The pragmatic approach to theory that is embraced in these lines helped immunise Childe from the more absurd of Stalin's distortions of Marxism. While Childe, in his book *History* (1947), referred positively to the contribution made to Marxism by Stalin in *Dialectical and Historical Materialism*,[13] he did so in such a way as to justify his own non-reductionist, and therefore implicitly anti-Stalinist, methodology.

In *Dialectical and Historical Materialism* (1938), Stalin had suggested a unilinear model of social evolution, according to which humanity moved through a series of stages from primitive communist to slave, to feudal, to capitalist and, finally, to the socialist mode of production. As McGuire points out, these stages were 'dogmatised' in Russia in the 1930s, such that, for instance, the Stalinists excluded Marx's concept of an Asiatic mode of production from scholarly debate.[14] Moreover, in this essay, Stalin reasserted a mechanically fatalistic interpretation of Marxism within which 'revolutions made by oppressed classes are a quite natural and inevitable phenomenon'. Despite the overt respect for Stalin noted above, Childe implicitly challenged this framework of analysis.

Methodologically, as Patterson points out, Childe started not from Stalin's crude economistic analysis of society, but from an examination of social formations as totalities.[15] Following from the best of Second International historiography, Childe held that productive processes and relations existed at the heart of such totalities, but that the social whole could not be reduced mechanically to its productive core. In the first chapter of *Man Makes Himself* (1936), Childe attempted to outline a Marxist alternative to traditional political history. While political history was, he claimed, an inadequate approach to the explanation of even recent historical processes, it was doubly blind when it came to the study of prehistory, as the archaeological traces left from that period contain scant direct evidence of politics or ideologies. In contrast to traditional political history, he argued, Marxism offered a scientific basis from which to study humanity's past: 'Marx insisted on the prime importance of economic conditions, of the social forces of production, and of applications of science as factors in historical change.'[16] Childe, it seems, had been attracted to Marxism since his youth; but it was in 1935, on a trip to Russia, that he was finally convinced of the power of Marx's attempt to conceptualise technological change 'in a social and political context'.[17] While it was unfortunate for him that he gravitated towards Marxism at just the moment when Stalin was attempting to rob it of its critical faculties, Childe's own theoretical instincts, reinforced by his reading of Marx and Engels, acted to immunise his thought against Stalin's crudities, such that his Marxism tended to much more open interpretation.

Childe equated Marx's method with a form of 'cultural history', implicitly breaking with both bourgeois political history and Stalinist economic reductionism.[18] It was from this perspective that, in *Archaeology and Anthropology* (1946), he criticised 'technological determinist' interpretations of Marx's base and superstructure metaphor.[19] While this criticism was aimed at the American archaeologist Leslie White, it could just as easily have been deployed against Stalin, who, in 1938, had proselytised an extreme form of technological determinism: 'First the productive forces of society change and develop, and then, *depending* on these changes and *in conformity with them*, men's relations of production, their economic relations, change.' In stark contrast to this crude caricature of historical materialism, Childe, as Trigger points out, insisted that the Marxist concept of determination could not be equated with the concept of causality, for while forces of production might determine the parameters of viable alternate relations of production, and the economic base might determine the parameters of viable alternate political and ideological superstructures, the superstructure could not be read off mechanically from the base.[20] In the same text in which he positively refers to Stalin's interpretation of historical materialism, Childe wrote that 'adjustments between the ideological superstructure and the relations of production is . . . by no means automatic', and insisted that while Marx and Engels might have believed that revolutions were 'desirable or essential' if social contradictions were to be overcome, this did not imply that they believed that such revolutions would be 'inevitable'.[21] As Trigger points out, Childe's framework was a powerful, if implicit, critique of Stalin's inevitabalist schema: social relations of production could so act on the forces of production to 'indefinitely' halt social progress.[22]

On a similar note Childe made light of simplistic models of the relationship of the superstructure to the base in *Man Makes Himself*: 'the precise forms of the English constitution and of English Protestantism in the nineteenth century', he commented sardonically, 'cannot be deduced from the capitalist system'.[23] Correspondingly, neolithic civilisation was not a uniform totality whose characteristics could simply be read off from the tools used therein, but, rather, existed only as a 'multitude of different concrete applications'.[24] While Childe distanced himself from crude forms of economic reductionism, he did not reject the concept of economic determination. Rather, he insisted that if Marx's materialist method was understood in a complex and mediated way it retained its explanatory power.

Childe argued that there were two pivotal moments in the evolution of class societies: the neolithic and the urban revolution. Patterson describes Childe's view thus: in the wake of the last ice age, while many food-gathering cultures 'disappeared because of their inability to cope with waning resources and new conditions', other groups 'succeeded in domesticating plants with edible seeds or fruits and animals'.[25] It was this 'neolithic revolution', based on a shift from hunting and gathering to food production, that created the basis, after the later urban revolution, for civilisation. Childe insisted that these revolutions were not inevitable: they were made in 'specific societies, each with its own distinctive history'. Moreover, the various cultural trajectories of these societies up to the epoch of revolutionary transformation included the development of diverse technological innovations – innovations which informed the abilities of each of these groups to succeed in the new environment.[26] In fact, Childe was keen to stress the scientific and technological creativity of the pre-class societies; and, as Trigger points out, he predicated the success of the neolithic and urban revolutions on these prior developments: 'Childe saw both the Neolithic and Urban revolutions as being brought about by the application of a series of interlocking discoveries of varied origins that were brought together as a result of a widespread network of contacts.'[27] Childe argued that it was egalitarian nature of the pre-class societies that helped foster technological and scientific innovation. In the period between the two revolutions, he suggested, it was perhaps 'the very absence of rigid ideologies and deeply-rooted institutions that permitted the rapid progress from self-sufficing villages to industrial and commercial cities in less than 2000 years'.[28] Furthermore, in sharp contrast to much of the racist discourse that polluted archaeology in the 1930s, Childe argued against the idea of distinct ethnic cultural traditions to maintain that there had been a continuous process of cultural diffusion between various pre-class societies, through which both artefacts and cultural traditions were pooled over generations.[29]

It was on the technological and cultural foundations laid by this process that the shift towards a life of food production could emerge as a response to the environmental transformation after the last ice age. The shift from the palaeolithic to the neolithic period involved a revolution in humanity's relationship to the natural world, which was a progressive step when measured by human population growth: 'It was only after the first revolution – but immediately thereafter – that our species really began to multiply at all fast.'[30] Childe insisted that population growth, and the related increase in life expectancy, were the only objective criteria from which general judgements about human progress could be made.[31]

This neolithic revolution marked the point at which (certain elements of) humanity made itself, or at least it marked the point at which humanity constructed the basis from which it would later create itself in the urban revolution; in the sense that humans transformed their relationship to nature from a parasitic connection to a constructive one, and made the move from natural to social history.[32] This final movement into history culminated in a *second* urban revolution which 'transformed some tiny villages of self-sufficing farmers into populous cities, nourished by secondary industries and foreign trade, and regularly organised as States'.[33] This second revolution was necessary, argued Childe, if neolithic communities were to overcome two contradictions which beset their lives. First, as these communities produced a surplus, and as population growth could be realised only through expansion, they were susceptible to wars which were potentially catastrophic. Second, the small size of these communities meant that they were particularly susceptible to natural disasters such as floods. Both problems could be alleviated, to some extent at least, by the growth in size of the community units, characteristic of the urban revolution.[34]

Following arguments articulated by Marx, Engels, Plekhanov and others, suggesting that the areas where this breakthrough occurred required collective efforts to control alluvial plains,[35] Childe argued that the states thus created did not act merely to protect the interests of a new ruling class but played a functional role of organising the mass labour needed to control flood waters.[36] The productive role executed by the new states had a decisive consequence for the future developments of all of the new social formations on the Nile, Indus and Euphrates. While the new organising and controlling functions of these states informed the emergence of writing, mathematics and other sciences, which themselves were rooted in the prior cultural developments, the two millennia after the urban revolution 'produced few contributions of anything like comparable importance to human progress'. In fact, Childe noted only four contributions over that period: 'decimal notation'; 'an economic method for smelting iron'; 'truly alphabetic scripts'; and 'aqueducts for supplying water to cities'.[37] The poverty of the innovative record of the great civilisations is in fact worse than this list would imply, for alphabets and iron-smelting were developed in states on the fringes of these empires.[38] Childe gave three reasons for this 'disappointing' record: first, the vast inequalities of those empires; second, the endemic warfare of this period; and, finally, the conservative magico-religious ideology of the ruling class. The first of these factors left the masses too degraded economically to innovate, while the wealthy ruling classes were under little pressure to compel innovation. The second ensured that economic surpluses, when they were made, were often squandered on warfare. Finally, the priest rulers, who had little actual understanding of the underlying structure of the natural forces that these civilisations sought to control, acted to stifle innovative approaches to the problems of production lest they place the empires in conflict with just those gods who had previously ensured their success.[39] To explain the broad historical convergence of these trajectories Childe deployed Marx's concept of an Asiatic mode of production. This application of Marx's concept is interesting, as Stalin had, from 1931, 'virtually banned' the concept of an Asiatic mode of production.[40] What is more, Childe utilised the concept to explain the process of forced retardation which he had located at various historical junctures; a process which Stalin's model of historical materialism explicitly denied.[41]

Childe outlined a contrast between innovative egalitarian societies and conservative inegalitarian societies in his discussion of ancient Greece. He insisted that the birth of a recognisably modern science in Greece occurred, interestingly, not in the so-called 'golden age', but rather 'when the Greeks were just emerging from the dark age after the fall of Minoan–Mycenaean civilisation'. It was at this point that 'the scientific traditions of the Orient were transformed by a new spirit'.[42] This argument is of crucial significance to the theses of both *Man Makes Himself* and Childe's later book *What Happened in History* (1942). In this latter book, Childe takes the story of human history beyond the neolithic and urban revolutions to give a general survey of history up to the collapse of classical antiquity.

In *What Happened in History*, Childe develops his critique of the paralysing structural contradictions of the Oriental or the Asiatic states in an attempt to explain the rise and fall of the new slave mode of production associated with various states including Athens and Rome. Already, in *Man Makes Himself*, Childe had noted that the endemic warfare of the Asiatic states had opened up the possibility that people could be productively enslaved.[43] In *What Happened in History* he explained how a new mode of production, built on slavery, generated the contradictions that would eventually doom it.

Childe suggested that the discovery of an efficient and cheap process for the smelting of iron 'democratised agriculture and industry and warfare too'.[44] Nonetheless, while iron weapons allowed barbarian armies to meet the Asiatic empires on a more than equal footing and, eventually, to destroy them, the new barbarian states did not then build civilisation on virgin soil. Rather, while the so-called dark age involved a collapse in the cultural level of the elite, the innovations of the previous epoch were not forgotten among the mass of the population, so that decline was far from absolute. In fact, the barbarian invasions, 'in the most favourable instances, particularly in Greece itself . . . just swept away top-heavy superstructures to make room for more progressive additions to a fundamentally healthy building'.[45] When viewed from the bottom up, the dark ages does not appear to be quite as dark as it does to traditional political historians.

Nevertheless, while the new social formations were able to overcome some of the worst contradictions of the *totalitarian* political structure of the Asiatic states, they did so only by creating new contradictions of their own. Specifically, the institution of slavery acted as a brake on technical innovation. This Childe explained as a consequence of several factors: first, rich slave-owners had no incentive to develop labour-saving devices when slaves were relatively cheap; second, because slaves received little more than their necessary sustenance they were limited as a consumer market for commodities; and, third, the very existence of slavery effectively degraded industrial production.[46] Childe deployed this understanding of the conservative function of slavery to explain a paradox of Greek history: while the period between around 600–450 BCE marked an effervescence of 'amazing' scientific progress, this theoretical advancement did not, outside its use in warfare, 'find expression in technical inventions'.[47] Even in the period after Alexander's conquests, when Hellenistic science 'brought forth a crop of mechanical inventions', those inventions 'found little application in practice – save in warfare – during the Hellenistic age'.[48] Similarly, despite its superficial grandeur, Rome neither contributed any significant scientific hypotheses to the stock of human knowledge, nor did it originate a 'single major invention'.[49]

One consequence of this was that transport remained extremely difficult, both on land and by sea. This was true even after the Romans built their famous roads, such that it remained rational for producers to relocate themselves to the market rather than to send goods to and from it.[50] This process fed into a *de facto* fragmentation of the Roman empire from within. Once the classical economy reached the limitations of its extensive growth – from around 150 CE, then its internal contradictions, which had limited intensive growth for the previous seven centuries, began to act as a contracting force on the empire.[51] Once the supply of new slaves acquired in military victories began to dry up, then it became rational for – indeed incumbent on – sections of the Roman ruling class, in an effort to maintain their wealth, to move from the exploitation of slave–cultivators to the exploitation of peasants. This new form of agricultural production was not carried out by 'free peasants such as had formed the backbone of classical Greece and early Italy, but by tenants dependent on the landlord for seed and equipment and paying rent'.[52] Childe argued that in the three-and-a-half centuries after 150 CE consecutive Roman emperors attempted to re-create, atop this productive base, states along the old Oriental lines. However, the economic demands of the imperial state, which could be met while the empire expanded, increasingly acted as a burden once that expansion came to an end.[53] The state, from here on in, could guarantee the revenues needed for its reproduction only if society itself was increasingly militarised, a process that included the transformation of tenants into serfs.[54] Nevertheless, Childe did not believe that the new Roman system was a mere replica of the old Oriental states, for the technological innovations of the early iron age were not forgotten, but were applied across Europe in the fragmentary cluster of small states that replaced Rome, once it fell.[55]

Rome's decline and fall was a consequence of the working out of the contradictions of the slave mode of production. But if the collapse of the slave mode of production did not lead to a reversion to the old Oriental structures, what was created in Europe? Childe only 'hinted' at an answer: the new feudalism involved progress from the old systems of both the Orient and Rome. Unfortunately, he did not discuss feudalism's positive characteristics; nor did he examine its differences from the old Asiatic societies' system.[56] Other Marxists have said much about the detail of this transition.

From antiquity to feudalism

While Childe only touched on the classical Marxist interpretation of the transition from antiquity to feudalism, in the years since his death in 1957 Marxists have attempted to extend, develop and – less frequently – wholly reject his analysis. Perhaps the most innovative of those Marxists who have been critical of the *orthodox* argument of theorists such as Childe has been by Ellen Meiksins Wood,[57] who writes as a leading member of the school of 'political Marxism',[58] which is associated most closely with Robert Brenner's analysis of the rise of capitalism in Europe. Without prejudging my analysis of Brenner's interpretation of this transition, I note that, for him, capitalism is a uniquely innovative mode of production, which can usefully be distinguished from *all* pre-capitalist modes of production by the manner in which it alone systematically fosters increases in the productivity of labour.[59]

Generalising from this approach, Wood argues that historians have misunderstood the reason for the relative paucity of technological innovation in Greece and Rome. Systematic innovation is not a common characteristic of human history, but is rather a novel product of modern capitalism:

> there seems to be nothing remarkable about the 'technological stagnation' of the Graeco-Roman world . . . The period of economic growth that began in early modern Europe, and specifically in England, is distinctive precisely because it broke the pattern of 'stagnation' punctuated by sporadic innovation typical of earlier ages.[60]

According to this line of argument, the relative technological stagnation of the Roman and Greek social formations is no more shocking than is the similarly sluggish rate of technological innovation associated with other pre-capitalist modes of production. While Wood argues that Greek and Roman slavery helped to limit technological advance, she insists that the large units of production characteristic of the Roman *latifundia* also created the conditions for the 'application of technical innovations'.[61]

According to Wood, it was peasant production, not slavery, that has acted throughout human history to preclude technological innovation: 'it can perhaps be stated as a general rule that small peasant property is not fertile ground for large-scale technological innovation'.[62] To illuminate this argument, she repeats the story, first told by Bloch and later deployed by Dockes, of peasant resistance to the application of the water-mill in medieval Europe; a resistance that was forcibly overcome by Europe's lordly class. Wood comments that the large units of production associated with Roman slavery had facilitated the development, if not the widespread diffusion, of the water-mill; while the medieval peasantry acted as a conservative opposition to its use, because they saw in its introduction a method through which the level of exploitation could only be increased.[63]

Wood explained the peasants' resistance to the introduction of the water-mill as a rational attempt to maintain their standard of living against lordly attempts to increase the rate of exploitation. Nevertheless, the main theme of her book is not an attempt to denigrate the peasantry as a conservative class; rather, she aims to challenge the reactionary myth that Athenian democracy was the democracy of an 'idle mob' who collectively exploited a mass of slaves.[64] Interestingly, this argument is informed by Wood's break with the traditional Marxist categorisation of classical Athens as a variant of the slave mode of production. She insists that the concept of a '"slave mode of production" is rooted in the myth of the idle mob'.[65] In this respect Wood is particularly critical of Engels, who accepted, she argues, 'that not only industry but agriculture was mainly carried on by slaves in the "heyday of Greece"'.[66]

While Engels seems to have been mistaken in his belief that the mass of agricultural production was carried out by slaves, later Marxists have developed a much more subtle and sophisticated model of the position and function of slavery in classical antiquity. Prime among these is Geoffrey de Ste. Croix (1910–2000),[67] whose *The Class Struggle in the Ancient Greek World* (1981) must be numbered among the greatest works of twentieth-century Marxist historiography. It is in respect of the power of this 'great book' that Perry Anderson commends it not only for Ste. Croix's mastery of the sources ranging over a 1,400-year period from 'Archaic Greece to the Arab Conquests', nor simply for its 'prose of exhilarating sharpness', but perhaps most of all because throughout it Ste. Croix exhibited a grasp of Marxist theory and concepts that was quite extraordinary for a practising historian: it 'is one of the most strenuously theoretical works of history ever to have been produced in this country'.[68]

In effect, Ste. Croix refined the Marxist concept of the slave mode of production in the light of two potential empirical anomalies: the evidence of the widespread deployment of free labour on the land; and the widespread use of non-slave modes of unfree labour in antiquity. To that end, Ste. Croix, first, reasserted one central theme of Marxist theory, while, second, he contributed a novel conception of the slave mode of production itself. With regard to his powerful reassertion of a theme from Marx, Ste. Croix argued that Marx 'implied' that modes of production should be delineated according to 'not so much *how the bulk of the labour of production is done*, as *how the dominant propertied classes*, controlling the conditions of production, *ensure the extraction of the surplus which makes their own leisured existence possible*'. It is perfectly possible, according to this model, to view classical Athens as a 'slave economy', even if, as is probably the case, a mass of free peasants produced the bulk of its agricultural yield; because it was from slaves or, more generally, unfree labour that the Athenian aristocracy received the bulk of the surplus that facilitated its social and historical reproduction.[69]

Second, Ste. Croix argued that the classification of the Athenian and Roman states as 'slave economies' is not dependent on the bulk of the surplus consumed by the ruling class having been produced by slaves in the narrow sense of the term. Rather, he stressed that 'slave economies' were characterised by unfree labour as the dominant form of labour from which the ruling class exploited a surplus: Ste. Croix defined unfree labour broadly to include those workers, alongside slaves proper, who were in debt bondage or who were, in effect, serfs. So while Ste. Croix suggested that it 'would not be technically correct to call the Greek (and Roman) world "a slave economy"', he slyly commented that he would 'not raise any strong objection if anyone else wished to use that expression'. The point that he was making, following a suggestion from Marx's *Grundrisse*, was that 'direct forced labour is the foundation of the ancient world'.[70] More precisely, he argued that slavery was the 'dominant form of ancient "unfree labour", not in the quantitative sense . . . but in the sense that slavery . . . was *the archetypal form of unfree labour* throughout Graeco-Roman antiquity'. Even in periods, for instance after around 300 CE, when *de facto* serfdom became the dominant quantitative form of unfree labour across Rome, the fact that the Romans had no notion of states that were transitional between freedom and slavery meant that the idea of slavery remained 'omnipresent in the psychology of all classes'.[71] Ste. Croix argued that as the Romans developed a terminology through which they might express the institution of serfdom – *coloni* was the word used in the late empire – they were driven, by the dominance of the idea of slavery in their culture, to apply to the *coloni* 'all but the strictly technical terms of slavery'.[72]

This novel defence of the idea that antiquity was defined, primarily, as a 'slave economy' has proved to be quite controversial. Ellen Wood, especially, has taken issue with Ste. Croix's thesis as applied to classical Greece. While Wood accepts that Greece was a 'slave society', she criticises the empirical grounds for Ste. Croix's claim that agricultural production in Greece was carried out by slaves, pointing out that he deploys little hard evidence to substantiate this argument, but rather relies on a few literary sources.[73] As I have noted, Wood suggests that the concept of a slave mode of production, which Ste. Croix qualifies but does not reject, can best be understood as a Marxist transposition of the traditional aristocratic criticism of Greek democracy as the rule of the idle mob. Wood's attempt to refute Ste. Croix's argument has been challenged by other Marxists. Empirically, Alex Callinicos points out an irony in Wood's rejection of Ste. Croix's thesis: she supports her argument on this issue by reference to the authority of Moses Finley, while Finley's arguments on this issue cohere with those of Ste. Croix.[74] At a more conceptual level, Perry Anderson argues that Wood's claim that the bulk of slaves in classical Athens worked in domestic service 'leaves unexplained' just how such a huge unproductive workforce could be sustained if slaves did not also work in agriculture.[75]

The beauty of Ste. Croix's position on this question is that he relates democracy to slavery in a neat dialectical combination. He argues that it was because Athenian democracy acted to mediate against the exploitation of the peasantry, and because foreigners – *metics* – could always leave the city if tax levels became exorbitant, then the only course of action that remained open to the Athenian aristocracy if they wished to maintain their wealth was to increase the rate of exploitation of slaves.[76]

The obvious question to ask when referring to this seemingly arcane debate on nomenclature is: does it matter? According to these Marxists it does, because the concepts deployed are used in the hope that they will explain historical processes. Anderson points out that the whole infrastructure of Ste. Croix's book was designed to offer much more than a description of the rise and fall of antiquity: Ste. Croix aimed instead to *explain* this process.[77] It was to this end that he rejected the Weberian conceptualisation of social stratification, because, or so he argued, Weber's concept of class is ahistorical, and therefore 'hardly helps us to understand or explain anything except in the most trite and innocuous way'.[78] Because it is so 'vague' and 'purely descriptive', when Moses Finley applied Weber's concept of class to antiquity he was quite incapable of analysing the dynamic nature of that society.[79]

In contrast to Finley's Weberian approach, Ste. Croix aimed to explain the decline and fall of classical antiquity along lines to similar Childe's, while deploying the most up to date research – he recommended Childe's sober analysis of cultural and technological continuity after the fall of Rome against the pessimism of more elitist historians, for whom the decline of antiquity was an unmitigated disaster.[80] Like Childe, Ste. Croix argued that it was the structural limitations of slavery that ultimately caused the fall of Rome. He deepened this analysis both through a rigorous discussion of the exact process through which slavery declined and via an analysis of the ways in which the suppression of Greek democracy helped facilitate the eventual outcome of the Rome's fall.

Democracy, Ste. Croix suggested, 'could play an important role by protecting the lower classes to some extent against exploitation and oppression by the powerful'. In fact, it was precisely because it could play this role that the class struggle between rich and poor Athenians came to be focused on the democratic structures of the Athenian State throughout the period of democracy: the rich aimed to suppress democracy, while the poor aimed to strengthen it.[81] From the late fourth century BCE, Ste. Croix argued, the attacks by the rich became increasingly successful until, eventually, the Macedonian and Roman conquerors slowly castrated Athenian democracy, so that by the third century of the Christian era the last vestiges of democracy had been suppressed. This process robbed the Athenian peasants, and peasants in lesser democracies across the Mediterranean, of a key mechanism through which they might defend themselves against increased exploitation. This defeat need not have heralded a long-term decline in the conditions of life of the Greek peasantry had not the slaves, the main source of surplus from which the Roman ruling class amassed its wealth, become scarcer during this period.[82]

As the expansionary wars, which had previously acted to provide a cheap and plentiful supply of new slaves, decreased in number from the inception of the Christian era, slave imports began slowly to dry up. To maintain a viable working population, Ste. Croix argued, 'slaves now had to be bred far more extensively than before'.[83] To breed slaves necessarily entailed that at least some of them be allowed a better quality of life than they had previously known; for they required time, at least, to raise children, which required that they became a long-term investment, rather than a cheap, and easily disposable, commodity. Unfortunately for the peasantry, this development meant that the ruling class, if it desired to maintain the wealth to which it had become accustomed, needed to find new sources of surplus; and the free peasantry could obviously be targeted, if only their traditional rights were suppressed. Ste. Croix suggests that 'it was because slavery was not now producing as great a surplus as it did in Rome's palmist days that the propertied classes needed to put more pressure on the free poor'.[84] In an inversion of the situation in Athens, where democracy mediated against the increased exploitation of the peasantry, providing a rationale for the greater use of slaves, once the last vestiges of democracy had been suppressed, and in conditions where slaves had become increasingly scarce, the Roman State came to look increasingly at the peasantry as a source of surplus.

The core of Ste. Croix's book is an explanation of precisely how that process developed, such that, on the one hand, the situation of the slaves slowly improved while, on the other, the peasantry's conditions of life slowly deteriorated, until the two groups eventually merged as the new class of serfs. Nevertheless, Ste. Croix was keen to insist that the fall of Rome was not, as has been suggested by a number of commentators since Gibbon, 'automatic'. Rather, the empire lost the tacit support of the peasantry in its wars against the barbarians, because the peasants had become increasingly alienated from *their* exploitative state – Ste. Croix uses the metaphor of the 'vampire bat' to describe the function of the late Roman empire. While this condition generated few peasant revolts – the military machine was too powerful for such revolts to occur often, and when they did occur they were 'never successful' – it did ensure that the peasantry did not support the empire when it came under military threat from the Germanic tribes. Ste. Croix therefore explains the decline and fall of Rome, primarily, through the destructive consequences of the Roman ruling class's creation of a highly exploitative and expensive state to which the peasantry afforded little affection.[85]

Additionally, Ste. Croix argues that, prior to the emergence of widespread serfdom, slave revolts were difficult in the Greek world because slaves were 'heterogeneous in character . . . sharing no common language or culture'.[86] Unfortunately, as Anderson points out, despite the overwhelming power of Ste. Croix's book, this argument suffered from a deficient sense of historical development. While Anderson welcomed Ste. Croix's critique of subjective models of class, in which – for instance, in the work of Edward Thompson – there exists a tendency to equate the concepts of class and class consciousness, he suggested that Ste. Croix had perhaps gone too far in the opposite direction in his history: he said very little, ironically, about actual class struggles in antiquity, despite the title of his book. This, Anderson posited, was because he had noticed in fact that 'the real mechanism' that accounted for the rise and fall of antiquity was not class struggle *per se* but the developing contradiction between 'forces and relations of production'. However, in stressing these blind forces, Ste. Croix had underplayed the conscious element of *agency* that existed even in antiquity. Anderson agreed with Ste. Croix that slavery was slowly undermined as the geographical limitations of the Roman empire were reached and the source of slaves, as the spoils of war, began to dry up. He suggested, however, that Ste. Croix had ignored the gradual weakening of Rome's ideological hold over slaves, as previously heterogeneous groups of slaves were brought together and thereafter were able to develop a common culture of resistance to the empire.[87]

Anderson developed this critical line of argument in his discussion of Ste. Croix's analysis of the fall of Athenian democracy. Ste. Croix failed to integrate into his account of the decline of Athens either the fact that the Macedonians, in a sense, had been created by the Greeks themselves, in as far as they had become militarised in opposition to the Greek states, or that Athenian democracy itself, because of its 'radically direct character', 'could never transcend municipal size without contradicting itself'.[88] With this argument, Anderson reiterated a theme that he had developed in his own analysis of this transition, as outlined in his *Passages from Antiquity to Feudalism* (1974): the democratic colonies created by Athens could not be fully integrated into the mother state, and Athens became trapped in a contradiction between her democratic ideals and her imperial aims.[89]

Beyond that argument, Anderson's book contains what is perhaps one of the strongest defences of the concept of the slave mode of production. That mode, he argued, was based on 'slave labour in the countryside', which, 'in the absence of municipal industry', was the 'condition of possibility' of antiquity's 'metropolitan grandeur'.[90] He argued that this mode, at its height, lasted from the fifth and fourth centuries BCE in Greece to the second century CE in Rome.[91] In *Passages from Antiquity to Feudalism* Anderson argued that with the fall of Rome the slave mode merged with the 'Germanic' mode over the next few centuries to create the feudal mode of production, and that 'by the death of Charlemagne, the central institutions of feudalism were thus already present'.[92] Central to Anderson's thesis is the claim that the feudal mode could not, as many previous Marxists had suggested, be equated with serfdom, and therefore that neither the late Roman empire nor any other state characterised by serf-like production could be categorised adequately as *feudal*. In this sense, Anderson's arguments dovetailed with those of Ste. Croix, who deployed Anderson's definition of feudalism to support his argument that the widespread use of serfs in the later Roman empire did not mean that the empire had become feudal.[93]

While Ste. Croix's rejection of the label 'feudal' to describe the late Roman empire is widely accepted, his suggestion that the late empire could best be understood as a 'slave economy' because of the extensive use of unfree labour, and the nature of slavery as the archetypical type of unfree labour, has proved to be a much more contentious argument. Chris Wickham,[94] for instance, has argued that a more nuanced analysis of the later Roman mode of production is necessary – one which disposes with the concept of the slave mode. Wickham actually agrees with the evidence cited by Ste. Croix – that feudalism evolved out of the fusion of slaves and tenants into a new class of serfs – but denies that this transitional state can adequately be described using the concept of a 'slave economy'.[95]

Going back to Marx's concept of an ancient mode within which towns first controlled and later exploited their surrounding countryside through a system of land taxation, Wickham suggests that, while elements of feudalism, alongside elements of slavery, existed in the late empire, the dominant mode of production in this period reverted back to the earlier ancient mode.[96] In fact, Wickham argues that the ancient mode of the late Roman State was a variant of what Samir Amin calls the 'tributary' mode of production. According to Wickham, this mode differed from feudalism not in the form in which surplus labour was pumped from the primary producers, but by the fact that the tributary social relations were 'aligned not with the interests of the landlords but with those of the state'.[97] Whereas in the feudal mode, the exploitation of peasant surpluses was carried out through the medium of rent controlled by landlords, in the tributary mode the State taxed both peasants and landowners.

These divergent structures required divergent social dynamics: the tributary ruling class was less close to the point of production than were the feudal lords, and were therefore less likely to directly intervene to increase productivity; while, the private interests of the landowners in the tributary mode were, as opposed to their position under feudalism, 'in contradiction with their interests as rulers and clients of the state'.[98] It was this latter conflict that informed the divergence of Wickham's interpretation of Rome's fall from Ste. Croix's more orthodox reading; for while Wickham's model was similar to Ste. Croix's, it differed in a key respect. Both men agreed that the fall of Rome was aided by the lack of popular military support for the empire against the barbarians in the late imperial period; however, where, Ste. Croix explained this as a consequence of the hidden class struggle of the peasantry against the empire, Wickham adds to the explanation the contention that a class struggle between the landowners and the empire existed which informed even elite indifference to the collapse of Rome's imperial power. While this application to the late Roman empire of Marx's aphorism that the history of all hitherto existing societies is the history of class struggle seems to subvert the intent of Marx's model, Wickham insists that it actually supports Marx's general claim: while 'tax-evading aristocrats are not the most instantly sympathetic heroes' of the class struggle, they were no less its protagonists for that.[99]

The feudalism debate[100]

One minor consequence of the Stalinist counter-revolution, as I noted in chapter 3, was the suppression in the Soviet Union, and by extension in the international communist movement, from around 1931 until the mid-1960s, of Marx's concept of the Asiatic mode of production, such that, certainly after the publication of Stalin's *Dialectical and Historical Materialism* in 1938, it became Marxist 'orthodoxy' to reject this concept. The reason for this apparently bizarre development had little to do with the theoretical power or consistency of Marx's concept, but was rather informed by political expediency.[101] In fact, the concept of the Asiatic mode was dropped as part of the fall-out from the Comintern debate on its Chinese policy in the 1920s. The Comintern leadership, at this point Stalin and Bukharin, argued that China was a feudal state, ripe for a bourgeois revolution. Additionally, they insisted that as China had been carved up by the imperialist powers, the bourgeois revolution would take the form of a national liberation movement. The Soviet leadership believed that these combined circumstances meant that both China's bourgeoisie and its peasantry would be compelled towards imminent revolutionary action, which the proletariat must support. Consequently, the Soviets argued that the Chinese Communist Party should subordinate itself to China's bourgeois Nationalist Party: the *Kuomintang*.[102] While this policy proved to be disastrous – Shanghai in 1927 was witness to the bloody suppression of the communists by the Kuomintang;[103] Stalin did not react to this defeat by rethinking his ideas; rather, he made the feudalistic Chinese economy a shibboleth and denounced as Trotskyists all who criticised this argument.

Given that 'Trotskyist' academics had contributed little to the Russian academic debate on the Asiatic mode in the late 1920s and early 1930s, the material foundations of Stalin's accusation were very slim.[104] Trotsky, though, in his political criticisms of the Comintern leadership, had made some remarks on China's social structure which did relate to the debate. In 1929, he argued that China's bourgeoisie was too tied up with both imperialism and land-ownership to act as a revolutionary class:

> at the bottom, in the agrarian bases of the Chinese economy, the bourgeoisie is organically and unbreakably linked with feudal forms of exploitation, [while], at the top it is just as organically and unbreakably linked with world finance capital. The Chinese bourgeoisie cannot on its own break free either from agrarian feudalism or from foreign imperialism.

If, with this argument, Trotsky posed testing questions of Stalin's political project, he had previously challenged the theoretical architecture of the dictator's perspectives: 'Unless one is playing with words, there is no feudalism in China. In the Chinese village there are serf–owner relations which are crowned, however, not by feudal, but by bourgeois property forms and a bourgeois socio-political order.'[105] So, while Trotsky said nothing that directly pertained to the issue of the Asiatic mode of production in China, his belief that China's social dynamic could not be explained using the category of feudalism helped ensure that those academic critics of the concept of Chinese feudalism were found guilty by association and their ideas suppressed by Stalin. From this moment on, as Hal Draper argues, Russian scholars researching Chinese history were required to reach conclusions that would help to justify Stalin's policy and to invalidate Trotsky's.[106]

A corollary of the insistence that the Chinese mode of production was feudal was the rejection, within the communist movement, of Marx's concept of an Asiatic mode of production. As this concept had been used by Marx to suggest a multilinear model of social evolution, its rejection by the Stalinists entailed that 'orthodox' Marxism, in the middle years of the twentieth century, embraced a unilinear model of historical development, according to which all societies moved mechanically through a series of stages towards a predetermined conclusion: primitive communist; ancient; slave; feudal; capitalist; and finally socialist. While the gap between this schema and the actual course of history may not have worried Stalin – for whom 'Marxism' became a mere talisman which he deployed to justify, *a posteriori*, the policy twists and turns of his regime[107] – it did trouble those historians who wanted to use Marx to aid their own critical investigations into history and politics. This issue came to a head in the debate on the transition from feudalism to capitalism; for when that debate was extended globally, one question was repeated: why had capitalism emerged independently only in Europe?

As I discussed in the last chapter, students of English history found in Marx's *Capital* a rich source of historical material relating to the development of capitalism in England; while students of French history could find equally stimulating material in Marx's various analyses of the revolutions of 1789, 1848 and 1871.[108] Building on those foundations, these two groups of historians would make a profound impact on their chosen fields in the twentieth century. Marx also articulated an explanation of the failure of capitalism to emerge in those societies, primarily in the Middle East, India and China, which had, but a few centuries prior to the capitalist breakthrough in the West, attained levels of economic and cultural development that far outstripped those known to the Europeans. Marx's answer to the conundrum posed by this comparison was framed by his articulation of the concept of the Asiatic mode of production; a mode which he characterised by a lack of private property in land, self-sufficient village communities and a state that collected tribute from the community as a whole.[109] Marx understood the Asiatic mode to have a universal rather than a peculiar geographic reference – paralleling the way that, for instance, nineteenth-century anthropology understood the term 'Peking Man' to have a universal reference.[110] Nevertheless, while this mode was universal, it had *fossilised* in some areas.[111] Marx aimed to comprehend these differential historical trajectories with a view to informing his historical understanding of the emergence of capitalism.

While the Stalinists had rejected the concept of the Asiatic mode of production, other Marxists, writing in the wake of the birth of a new generation of critical anti-Stalinist Marxism in the 1950s and 1960s, also tended, with much greater integrity, to resist embracing Marx's concept. One, minor, reason for this development was the peculiar resurfacing, in the late 1950s and early 1960s, of the concept of the Asiatic mode. In 1957 Karl Wittfogel, an ex-communist turned Cold-War warrior, published *Oriental Despotism*, in which he developed Marx's concept to explain the structures of states as diverse as Pharonic Egypt and Stalinist Russia. Wittfogel's was primarily a political text which aimed to prove that the Soviet Union was a new form of oriental despotism, a society characterised by 'bureaucratic state slavery', against which the West should act boldly lest it too be dragged into the totalitarian morass.[112] Unfortunately, any insights that may have been gleaned from Wittfogel's book were lost between his pro-Western rhetoric and his method of ahistorical amalgamation. Perry Anderson justifiably called the book a 'vulgar charivari'.[113] Nevertheless, despite his open hostility to Marxism, Wittfogel's crude Cold War polemic did compel some Marxists to re-examine the debates that Stalin had attempted to silence in the 1930s.

Perhaps the most sophisticated re-engagement with the concept of the Asiatic mode to be made by a Marxist in the 1960s was that offered by

Maurice Godelier.[114] Building on Childe's contribution, Godelier claimed: 'Marx, without having been completely aware of it, described a form of social organisation specific to the transition from classless to class society.'[115] He suggested that the actual reasons for the emergence of class societies may have varied in different places and at different times – for instance in some places the need for large-scale public works provided the impetus, while in others it was indirect intervention in the productive process by an elite that was the mechanism.[116] There was, though, a common feature to all of these forms: an aristocracy had emerged in each case that exercised 'state power and [was] consolidating the bases of its class exploitation by appropriating a part of the produce of the communities', and in doing so facilitated the development of society's productive forces.[117] In opposition to some of Marx's suggestions to the contrary, the Asiatic mode was not static: because there was a 'coincidence of community structures and class structures', Asiatic social formations would tend to develop, through their own internal contradictions, 'towards forms of class societies in which community-based (communal) relations have less and less reality because of the development of private property'.[118] This tendency could lead to 'at least' two possible outcomes, including the emergence of the slave mode 'via the ancient mode' or a movement towards 'feudalism'.[119] According to Godelier, the typical trajectory was the latter. Exceptionally, European historical evolution arrived at the feudal mode only through the medium of the slave mode. Europe, according to this model, should therefore be judged unique not by its feudal heritage, but by the path it took through the slave mode to feudalism. This trajectory, he argued, helped combine feudal private property with commodity production, which, in turn, informed the expansion of the forces of production in feudal Europe such that capitalism might emerge.[120]

Despite the power of Godelier's argument, the 1970s was not a good decade for the Asiatic mode. Perhaps the key factor in this conceptual eclipse was the publication of Perry Anderson's scholarly critique of Marx's use of the concept. Anderson argued that the concept of the Asiatic mode of production was essentially inherited by Marx from a long-standing Western tradition which compared the East negatively with the West; and Marx, in following this tradition, failed to outline a 'consistent or systematic account' of that mode.[121] Interestingly, Anderson commented that, despite Godelier's near universalisation of the concept of feudalism being 'untenable', his analysis of the 'different phases and forms of transition of tribal social formations towards centralised State structures is extremely illuminating'. Anderson's dismissal of Godelier's broader theoretical claims was based on his belief that this thesis obscured the unique dynamic of European feudalism.[122]

Anderson's main aim in his two-volume history of the European state system, from classical antiquity to the epoch of the bourgeois revolutions, was to locate the basis for the emergence, uniquely in Europe, of capitalism. His criticism of those Marxists who were influenced by Stalin's demand that

China, etc., be labelled *feudal* was that in defining feudalism as, in essence, 'landlordism', 'all privilege to Western European development is thereby held to disappear'.[123]

In an attempt to make sense of Europe's unique character, and following what he believed was Marx's method as articulated in the *Grundrisse*, Anderson argued that 'pre-capitalist modes of production cannot be defined except via their political, legal and ideological superstructures, since these are what determine the type of extra-economic coercion that specifies them'.[124] Since the key institution of extra-economic coercion was the state, Anderson essentially delineated pre-capitalist modes of production along lines set by their differential state structures.

Anderson defined feudalism as a mode of production characterised by a 'natural economy, dominated by the land', in which 'neither labour nor the products of labour were commodities'. The peasant was bound to the earth, legally defined as serfdom, which was 'owned' by the lord but in 'degree only'. The corollary of this was that the lord was required to use extra-economic means to extract surplus. These forces of extra-economic coercion ensured that sovereignty was devolved downwards from the state proper to the lords. However, nowhere did the lords exercise absolute property rights. Sovereignty was, in effect, parcellized, and was combined with 'scalar private property in land'.[125]

Even when defined in such a detailed manner, Anderson concluded that while feudalism was more restricted in its geographical spread than previous Marxists had believed, it was not coterminous with medieval Europe: specifically, pre-Meiji Japan bore all the hallmarks of the feudal mode of production.[126] Given that Japan had neither witnessed an endogenous transition to capitalism, nor had it begun a spontaneous movement towards *absolutism*, this implied to Anderson that the structure of feudalism *per se* could not explain the emergence of the capitalist mode of production.[127] Something else beyond this structure was necessary for capitalism to take hold in Europe. Anderson argued that the specificity of Western European feudalism lay in the nature of its foundation.[128] Born of a fusion between Rome and the Germanic tribes, the uniqueness of the West was rooted in its Roman heritage. In particular, Roman law supplied a legal framework which both underpinned 'Absolutist public authority' and 'absolute private property'. This dual role of Roman law provided Western Europe with its *differentia specifica*. Additionally, Roman law facilitated both the development, after the Renaissance, of absolutism, and, co-temporally but distinctly, facilitated the development of capitalism.[129]

Unfortunately, as Hirst has pointed out, Anderson's history is marked by a form of 'speculative empiricism',[130] which can be related to his failure to develop a general model of modes of production. According to Hirst, Anderson defined different modes of production variously 'by the socio-legal status of the labourer [slavery], by the form of division of state power [feudalism], and by a set of technical conditions of production [nomadic] . . . None of these usages is argued for or defended theoretically.'[131] As Anderson incorporated superstructural elements into his definition of pre-capitalist modes of production, he necessarily concluded that 'the form of the state is constitutive of the social relations of production, hence modes of production are identified with and by differences in state constitutions as revealed in empirical history'.[132] Anderson, in his analysis of pre-capitalist modes of production, therefore tended to reduce various modes of production to particular social formations.[133] Fulbrook and Skocpol have made a similar criticism of Anderson's method: they argue that there is a resemblance between Anderson's concepts and Weber's ideal types, but because 'Anderson's concepts refer to concrete sociohistoric complexes . . . [they] run the danger of being nothing more than economical devices for description'.[134]

An understandable consequence of the structure of his thesis, this weakness is less evident in Anderson's work than it might have otherwise been. For, beyond his discussion of Japanese feudalism, and other than pointing out that some of the social formations labelled 'Asiatic' by Marx were very different both from each other and from his model of the Asiatic mode, Anderson made few positive statements about non-European social formations. Nonetheless, his method implied that there existed as many non-European modes of production as there were non-European states. As a consequence of his failure to discuss the social dynamic of those states, he did not answer adequately the question: could any of these modes have moved independently towards capitalism?[135] Moreover, his discussion of the specificity of European feudalism is also to be doubted. David Parker has argued that Roman law did not 'engender a clear sense of absolute property rights',[136] and as Anderson did not discuss the actual 'reception and application of Roman law'[137] it would seem that Anderson's positive claims for the uniqueness of European feudalism are themselves highly suspect. In fact, Parker argues that Roman law 'had very little relevance to these issues'.[138] The problem of comprehending, in Marxist terms, Europe's unique path to capitalism therefore appears to have survived Anderson's attempted solution.

An alternative approach was posited by Samir Amin, and developed by Chris Wickham. Amin, in *Unequal Development* (1973), sought to clarify the meaning of Marx's concept of an Asiatic mode with a view to explaining, first, the relative social stability of those states, such as China and Pharonic Egypt, which Marx had labelled Asiatic and, second, the emergence of capitalism in Europe. Amin argued that while Marx's concept of the Asiatic mode 'showed very deep insight', his detailed arguments, necessarily, had to be updated in line with new archaeological evidence. Further, Amin rejected Marx's nomenclature, noting that what 'inaccurately has been called the "Asiatic" mode has existed in four continents'.[139] Amin re-labelled this mode of production the 'tribute-paying' or tributary mode, and argued that this was the mode that 'most normally succeeds the communal mode'.[140] He then argued that the tributary mode had five key characteristics; or at least that the two central variants of this mode, China and Egypt, did. First, these states were 'truly central', in terms of their populations relative to their surrounding civilisations. Second, the village communities in each state 'quickly weakened and almost disappeared as state authority became more powerful'. Third, the ruling state classes of these social formations were not 'particularly "despotic"'. Fourth, tribute-paying, in the form of taxes, was the dominant form of surplus extraction within these states. Finally, the social structure of the states was 'compatible with a wide range of levels of development of the productive forces'. This final point, argued Amin, meant that 'the conflict between productive forces and production relations makes its appearance only when the capitalist mode has been introduced from the outside. The historical duration of the fully developed tribute-paying mode was thus, in principle, very long.'[141]

It was in contrast to this model of tributary stability that Amin counterposed his conception of feudalism. He argued that feudalism was an 'incomplete form' of the tributary mode, within which the central state was weak and where therefore the local lordly class was relatively powerful. Consequentially, the main source of surplus for the ruling class was not extracted as tax by the state but as rent by landowners. The relative 'backwardness' of feudalism meant that the 'commercial sectors possessed greater independence' than was typical in other tributary states. This in turn meant that they had greater freedom to engage in 'long distance trade' than did their counterparts in the East. The ensuing trade led to an influx of new wealth and luxury goods, which, if the feudal lords were to afford them, they were compelled to 'modernise their methods of exploitation, extracting a larger surplus and converting this into money'; a process which would hasten 'the breakup of feudal relations'.[142] While Amin's detailed discussion of the logic of the feudal dynamic is unpersuasive; his comparison of feudalism and the tributary mode along a rent–tax axis is insightful. It also coheres with Marx's delineation, outlined in the third volume of *Capital*, between feudalism and the Asiatic mode.[143]

Amin's general understanding of the distinction between feudalism and the tributary mode has been developed by Chris Wickham. In two important essays, 'The Other Transition' and 'The Uniqueness of the East', first published in *Past and Present* (1984) and the *Journal of Peasant Studies* (1985), Wickham argued, as I noted in the preceding section, that it was Rome's transformation into a tributary state, from around the second century CE, that informed the growth of class conflicts between state and landowners, the consequence of which, in the context of barbarian invasions, was imperial collapse. Wickham therefore inverted the old Marxist delineation between the Asiatic and feudal modes. Where, for Marx, the former was a static mode and the latter dynamic, for Wickham the tributary mode, characterised by a single landowner, the state, was dynamic, while feudalism, characterised by a complex relationship between the central authority and the local landowner, was relatively static. He insisted that it is the contradiction between local landowners and the state, characteristic of the tributary mode, which explained the social evolution of particular tributary social formations.[144] While Wickham therefore rejected the detail of Amin's account of tributary stability, he accepted his general model of the tributary mode as characterised by surplus extraction through taxation.[145]

According to Wickham, 'in most traditional state societies' the tributary mode typically existed alongside and dominated the rent-based feudal mode.[146] Likewise, as the tributary mode was, like the feudal mode, based on the extraction of surplus from peasants, the 'existential' feel to the peasantry of exploitation through either tax or rent in these two modes of production would be more or less identical.[147] The distinction between taxation and rent, though, could be deployed to explain the differential historical trajectories of tributary and feudal states. Specifically, in states dominated by the feudal mode there would exist a 'structural' involvement on the part of the lordly class 'in production itself', which would be largely absent in states in which the tributary mode dominated.[148] Following the thesis developed by Rodney Hilton (noted below), Wickam argued that the structural involvement of the lords in the productive process would manifest itself as a class struggle between lords and peasants over control of that process; the outcome of which could range from total proletarianisation of the peasantry, at one extreme, or socialist revolution at the other.[149]

Wickham's essay 'The Uniqueness of the East' was originally published in 1985 in a special issue of the *Journal of Peasant Studies* entitled 'Feudalism and Non-European Societies'.[150] Among the more powerful contributions to this debate was that of Halil Berktay, who argued that while Wickham had made an authoritative contribution to Marxist theory, his attempt to distinguish between the tributary and feudal modes was unconvincing. Berktay suggested that Wickham had failed to show that his tributary and feudal modes actually produced two distinct 'class structures'. In fact, Berktay insisted, Wickham's approach led him, in effect, to follow Anderson in differentiating pre-capitalist modes of production according to their peculiar superstructural forms, particularly by the form taken by the state in each mode. Wickham, like Anderson, is led in this direction by his desire to explain the unique emergence of capitalism from European feudalism. By contrast, Berktay argues, Europe's distinct trajectory need not be reduced to an epiphenomenon of its distinct mode of production, but can be explained by the relatively weaker state form in Europe than was the usual case in non-European feudal societies. Accordingly, a universal feudal mode could generate multilinear historical patterns.[151]

John Haldon[152] has produced a more comprehensive version of this argument. He insists, following Berktay and Ste. Croix, that if a mode of production can best be categorised by the dominant mechanism through which the ruling class extracts surplus from the direct producers, then the feudal and tributary modes, based respectively on rent and tax, are in fact variations of one mode of production.[153] Feudalism, cognised as a synonym for the tributary mode, can be 'understood as the basic and universal pre-capitalist mode of production in class societies'.[154] But if that is so, then what of Europe's specificity? Haldon opens his answer to this problem with a theoretical claim as to the concept of a mode of production. Each mode of production, he argues, 'is not an ontologically real system of relations, but a conceptualisation of an ideal type', the structure of which 'is reached through theoretical abstraction from historical data collated by examining all those social formations corresponding approximately to the same state in the development of the productive forces'.[155] Feudalism, he continues, following Berktay, is the mode that 'corresponds to and is determined by that level of productive forces which roughly speaking emerged with the Neolithic revolution, and comprises field cultivation based on organic energy plus hand implements'.[156] More generally, he argues that because modes of production are ideal types, they 'do not develop' at all; it is only 'social formations that change'.[157] With respect to Wickham's claim that the feudal–tributary distinction allowed him to explain European feudalism's unique dynamic, Haldon counters, first, that Wickham does not provide a systematic account of why feudal landlords intervene thus and tributary states do not, and, second, that the actual 'prime mover' of the feudal mode was not lords intervening in the productive process, but the class struggle between lords and peasants for control of production.[158]

Interestingly, Haldon's comment on the central role of the class struggle in determining feudal society's dynamic coheres with Wickham's own conclusion, noted above; and despite Wickham's focus on the role of lords in increasing labour productivity, the implication of his analysis is that the development of the productive forces was not a prerequisite for the transitions either to capitalism or to socialism.[159] While this conclusion might have been politically informed by Wickham's rather absurd belief that Enver Hoxha's Albania was a socialist state,[160] its theoretical basis can be traced to an understandable Marxist reaction to Stalin's crude productive force determinism. Many Marxists have rejected the notion of the primacy of the productive forces altogether, and replaced it with an argument for the explanatory primacy of the relations of production in history. This perspective was most coherently articulated by Paul Hirst and Barry Hindess in *Pre-Capitalist Modes of Production* (1975), which Berktay, Haldon and Wickham commend.[161] Despite this admiration, Hindess and Hirst inspired little actual historical research after they famously dismissed all historical work as empiricist.[162] Others Marxist historians have, however, attempted to explain transitions from one mode of production to a second without reference to the development of the forces of production. Prime among them is Robert Brenner, whose reinterpretation of the transition from feudalism to capitalism provoked a heated debate on the pages of *Past and Present* in the 1970s and 1980s.

From feudalism to capitalism

In a review of Maurice Dobb's analysis of the transition from feudalism to capitalism, Robert Brenner argued that Dobb's thesis 'continues to be a starting point for discussion of European economic development'.[163] Whatever the accuracy of this claim, it is certainly true that Brenner's own analysis of the transition was written, in part, as an attempt to overcome some weaknesses in Dobb's argument.[164]

Brenner opened his review of Dobb's *Studies in the Development of Capitalism* by commending the author's break with the 'transhistoric' musings of the classical and neo-classical economists, for whom the peculiar ethos of modern capitalism is naturalised as a fundamental attribute of human nature.[165] Accordingly Dobb analysed the emergence of capitalism in terms of a revolutionary break between two distinct modes of production – modes which had fostered distinct ways of life. Rather than attempt an explicit defence of this framework of analysis, Dobb argued that 'the justification of any definition must ultimately rest on its successful employment in illuminating the actual process of historical development'.[166] Like Trotsky, he aimed to vindicate Marx's method by showing that its potential for powerful deployment could be actualised in historiography to provide an explanation of the transition that was more powerful than competing accounts.

Dobb argued that no real economic system is ever 'found in [its] pure form'. Rather, a historical period is 'moulded under the preponderating influence of a single, more or less homogeneous, economic form, and is to be characterised according to the nature of this predominant type of socio-economic relationship'.[167] Dobb actually defined the two main modes at the centre of his analysis, feudalism and capitalism, according to the relationship between the direct producer and the exploiter in each: he equated feudalism with 'serfdom' and capitalism with wage-labour.[168] He also argued that modes of production evolved over time, and the rise of capitalism could best be explained in terms of the internal dynamic of feudalism.[169]

While Dobb insisted that the prerequisites for the transition to capitalism included an increase in the productivity of labour such that the change from serfdom to wage-labour would became economically viable, he did not explain how such a productivity increase could develop systematically within feudalism.[170] Similarly, he argued that the story of the destructive influence of commerce on feudal society 'can largely be identified with the rise of towns', but went on to suggest that 'it would be wrong to regard [towns] as being, at this stage, microcosms of capitalism'.[171] Furthermore, he failed to integrate his analysis of the rise of towns in the medieval world into a model of the internal dynamic of feudalism. He noted several explanations for the rise of towns – as survivals of Roman cities, as a consequence of increasing rural population, as settlements of merchants or out of the growth of feudal right to sanctuary – but did not attempt to integrate these insights into a rounded theory.[172]

One point Dobb did insist on was that the rise of merchant capital, in and of itself, was not a sufficient cause for the disintegration of feudalism; although once serfdom had begun to give way to wage-labour, merchant capital could then act to accelerate this process.[173] Despite playing this role, merchants were not the prime movers in the transition. Following Marx's discussion of the two roads to capitalism – the first, 'really revolutionary way', involving a section of producers becoming capital accumulators; the second involving merchants taking 'possession directly of production' – Dobb argued that while merchants might play a revolutionary role in creating a wage-labour economy from one based on serfdom, this was a secondary process predicated on the 'really revolutionary way'; albeit that the two ways tended to 'merge' and 'intersect' over time.[174]

The argument that the growth of commerce in general and merchant capital in particular did not act as the prime cause of the disintegration of feudalism has become something of an accepted fact in Marxist circles in the wake of Dobb's engagement with Paul Sweezy over the issue in the 1950s. Sweezy (1910–2004)[175] argued that Dobb's equation of feudalism with serfdom was 'too general', and that feudalism would be better defined as a 'system of production for use'.[176] Hence, Sweezy insisted that in searching for the prime mover in the transition from feudalism to capitalism, historians should look for that force which shifted the goal of production away from the direct use of the peasants and lords. He argued that it was the rise of commerce from the tenth century onwards which facilitated the rise of capitalism: the 'important conflict' was that which emerged between 'production for the market and production for use'.[177] From that point onwards, first, 'the inefficiency of the manorial organisation of production . . . was now clearly revealed'; while, second, 'the very existence of exchange value as a massive economic fact tends to transform the attitude of producers'; third, the 'tastes of the feudal ruling class' were transformed; and, finally, towns re-emerged and acted as magnets that opened the possibility of the peasantry's 'flight from the land' – one of the 'decisive factors', Sweezy agreed with Dobb, 'in the decline of feudalism'.[178] By integrating the rise towns into his model of the transition, Sweezy pointed to an important gap in Dobb's argument. As Giuliano Procacci argued, Dobb's critique of the thesis that the rise of commerce was the prime mover in the transition was something of a negative success; for Dobb failed to reconstruct his own positive account of 'the internal dynamic of feudalism'.[179]

According to Dobb, capitalism emerged from within the ranks of the direct producers, after which certain merchant interests accelerated its development, while other merchants, more closely tied to the royal court, acted as a conservative break on this process. Dobb deployed this framework to explain the English revolution as a bourgeois revolution, within which the divisions between king and Parliament 'followed fairly closely along economic and social lines'. There was, though, no simple juxtaposition between the bourgeoisie and the feudal elements in this model of England's bourgeois revolution, as the interests of sections of the bourgeoisie intersected with those of the monarchy in myriad ways. Nevertheless, the nation divided in the 1640s along socio-economic lines such that 'the rivalry between industrial or semi-industrial interests in the provinces and the more privileged trading capital of the metropolis was no doubt an important element in the antagonism . . . between Presbyterian and Independent'. A key division within the bourgeoisie was that which existed between those involved in industry and those farthest removed from this interest.[180] Dobb was also well aware that a typical feature of bourgeois revolutions was that 'large sections of the bourgeoisie', despite the fact that they required radical forces to push through their demands, ran scared of these radical forces once they were released. The bourgeoisie typically plays, at best, but a timid role in its revolution.[181] Nevertheless, irrespective of the class composition of the revolutionaries, the revolution itself broke the fetters that feudalism had placed on capital accumulation. Dobb therefore defined the English revolution as a bourgeois revolution, not because of the role played in it by the bourgeoisie, but by the consequences of its success: 'In its economic policy the Commonwealth introduced a number of changes that were of substantial importance to the development of capitalism.' Among the Acts implemented were the Navigation Act, the abolition of feudal tenures and, half-a-century later, the Bill of Rights.[182]

Despite the power of this argument, Dobb's discussion of the class character of the pre-revolutionary regime did not seem to justify his claim that a bourgeois revolution acted to sweep away the old feudal superstructure. As Brenner points out, if feudalism is equated with serfdom, as it was in Dobb's thesis, and if serfdom was superseded from around the fifteenth century, as Dobb suggested, then surely feudalism was likewise 'dead' long before the upheavals of the 1640s. Consequently, the concept of a bourgeois revolution in the seventeenth century is thrown into question.[183]

Indeed, Dobb's analysis of the transitional phase in England from the fifteenth to the seventeenth centuries, as one dominated by a distinct 'petty mode of production', seems to undermine the idea that a revolution was necessary if feudalism was to be replaced by capitalism in England.[184] Dobb insisted that the petty mode was not 'capitalistic', but represented a 'form of simple commodity production, of a non-class, peasant type . . . which differed from the crafts undertaken on a feudal estate only to the extent that the craftsman was making his wares for sale on a market and not making them as an obligation of service for a lord'.[185] He located the basis for the emergence of this mode of production, which he argued grew into capitalism, in the conflictual relations, under the feudal mode, between lords and serfs. Commenting on the class struggles generated by those relations, he suggested that while the peasant revolts of the fourteenth century had been defeated, their mediated 'ghost', in the form of peasant flight, continued to haunt the landowners such that they were compelled to concede reforms to the peasants. But if peasants had ceased to be serfs, and if the petty mode grew into capitalism, then the very concept of a bourgeois revolution, in the traditional Marxist sense as a necessary step through which capital accumulation was to be unfettered, appeared to be unnecessary. This was the direction in which Brenner took Dobb's analysis.

In his essay 'Agrarian Class Structure and Economic Development in Pre-Industrial Europe' (1976) Brenner[186] argued that capitalism originated as an unintended consequence of the class struggle under feudalism:

> the breakthrough from 'traditional economy' to relative self-sustaining economic development was predicated upon the emergence of a specific set of class or social-property relations in the countryside – that is, capitalist class relations. This outcome depended, in turn, upon the previous success of a two-sided process of class development and class conflict: on the one hand, the destruction of serfdom; on the other, the short-circuiting of the emerging predominance of small peasant property.

In France serfdom was destroyed by the class struggle between peasants and lords, but the process went beyond that needed for the development of capitalism, leading instead to the widespread establishment of small peasant property. In Eastern Europe the peasants were defeated, leading to the reintroduction of serfdom. Only in England did conditions evolve that were optimal for the evolution of agrarian capitalism.[187] Capitalist development in England, and as a corollary in Europe and the world, did not emerge as a consequence of a victory of the peasantry over the feudal nobility in the class struggle, and still less the product of a rising bourgeoisie. Rather, capitalism evolved as an unintended outcome to the class struggle in the English countryside.

In the debate that followed on the publication of his paper, Brenner was widely criticised for his deviation from Marxist orthodoxy. Most pointedly, Guy Bois argued that Brenner's thesis 'amounts to a voluntarist vision of history in which the class struggle is divorced from all other objective contingencies and, in the first place, from such laws of development as may be peculiar to a specific mode of production'.[188] In defence of his revisionism, Brenner argued, in 'Bourgeois Revolution and the Transition to Capitalism', that Marx's works of the 1840s, particularly *The Communist Manifesto*, *The German Ideology* and *The Poverty of Philosophy*, had at their heart a defective model of the transition from feudalism to capitalism that was inherited from Adam Smith. Brenner suggested that Marxists should begin to remodel their account of the transition, not from these early works, but from Marx's later works, particularly *Capital* and *Grundrisse*; for while

Adam Smith developed a powerful account of the nature of capitalism, he built this account on a highly questionable thesis as to capitalism's origins.[189] In effect, Smith assumed the universality of capitalist rationality, and therefore in his analysis of the transition from feudalism to capitalism he looked for fetters to capitalist development within feudalism rather than to forces that could facilitate the evolution of rational capitalist individuals. Brenner argued that this is an unsustainable position, given the lack of historical evidence for capitalist behavioural patterns in pre-modern societies.

Brenner suggested that the model of the transition offered in Marx's earlier writings paralleled Smith's approach. One key effect of this methodology is that the young Marx, like Smith, failed to develop a theory of societal transformation; his model of the transition

> appears peculiar, for in neither town nor country is anything amounting to a transformation from one type of society to another actually envisaged. As for the urban economy, it is, from its origin, entirely bourgeois . . . As to rural development, feudalism . . . has no positive role . . . Finally . . . the bourgeoisie's rise to power is quasi-automatic.[190]

Brenner argues that

> if England was, in fact, essentially a feudal society . . . it was necessary to explain why the rise of trade should have led to capitalist development rather than the reproduction of the old feudal order . . . On the other hand, if English feudalism was on its way to dissolution . . . rural society was already well on its way to capitalism, and it was necessary to explain why its landlords were anything but capitalist.[191]

Brenner concludes this exploratory essay with the argument that a social interpretation of the transition was still necessary, but that – and this position is merely implied – the old Marxist concept of a bourgeois revolution should be rejected.[192]

Brenner's historical methodology is framed around a polemic against that which he considers to be an ahistorical approach to the issue of the development of capitalist rationality. With respect to English history, he argues that the pattern of class struggle up to and after the period of the Black Death, around 1350, created exceptional conditions whereby 'the English lords' inability either to re-enserf the peasants or to move in the direction of absolutism . . . forced them in the long run to seek what turned out to be novel ways out of their revenue crisis'.[193] This new path led towards agrarian capitalism. In this system, large landowners rented out their land to tenant farmers, and this social relationship underpinned the move towards a self-expanding economy: only in these exceptional conditions could 'Smithian "normal" development take place'.[194]

In developing his thesis, Brenner outlined a devastating critique of Malthusian explanations of the transition. He did this, not by contradicting the evidence presented by the Malthusians, but by showing that in different parts of Europe similar demographic trends led in differing directions.[195] Moreover, he argues that these consequences of the various class struggles across Europe were independent of the economic growth of towns.[196] It is in this sense that Brenner most clearly distinguishes his arguments from those of both Smith and Marx.

This is not to suggest that Brenner ignores the role of towns in the transition. For, on the one hand, he argues that his model of the transition from feudalism to capitalism is premissed on the 'necessary precondition' of the development of merchant capitalism in the medieval period:[197] though he insists that feudal property relations prevented the capitalist potential of this context from being realised before the breakthrough.[198] On the other hand, in 1993 he published the 700-page monograph *Merchants and Revolution*, on the English revolution, in which he placed London's merchant community at the centre of his analysis. In an eighty-page 'Postscript' to the book Brenner argued that the 'traditional social interpretation' of the transition was untenable,[199] because 'by the era of the Civil War, it is very difficult to specify anything amounting to a class distinction of any sort within the category of large holders of land, since most were of the same class'.[200] The available evidence could not sustain the idea of a rising bourgeoisie confronting a feudal aristocracy. Nevertheless, he remained convinced that the revisionist challenge to the old social interpretation was even less compelling, for the revisionists had reduced the Civil War to a conflict over particular individual and group interests within a general ideological consensus. Against this position, Brenner pointed out that 'analogous political conflicts over essentially similar constitutional and religious issues broke out on a whole series of occasions in the pre-Civil War period'.[201] Brenner maintained that although the traditional Marxist account of the revolution is untenable, a social account of the Civil War is indispensable. He suggested that while the landowners as a whole had been transformed into a capitalist class in the previous centuries, the monarchy maintained its position at the head of the State via a medieval legacy: monarchs, he argued, 'were no mere executives, but were great patrimonial lords'.[202] Moreover, 'the king was largely politically isolated from the landed class as a whole until the autumn of 1641'.[203] The fundamental conflict at the heart of the English revolution was between the bulk of the landowning class and this 'patrimonial group', which derived its wealth from politically constituted property rights.

The conflict between Brenner's capitalist landlords and the monarchy was, at its heart, a struggle over the nature and role of the State. Because the landlords had moved towards the production of a social surplus through capitalist exploitation, they no longer required extra-economic forms of surplus extraction. Rather they required a state with a minimal, but national, role to protect absolute private property.[204] The aristocracy was therefore more than happy to see the centralisation of state power in the hands of the monarchy, while the monarchy was happy to begin the movement towards absolutism, based on politically constituted property.[205] These differing bases for the evolving consensus on the direction of the development of state power could act along the same vector only up to a point: specifically, conflict arose when the 'monarchs tended to undertake specific wars – and pursue particular foreign policies – of which the parliamentary classes could not approve'.[206] Brenner argues that

> whereas capitalism and landlordism developed more or less symbiotically, capitalist development helped precipitate the emergence of a new form of state, to which the relationship of capitalist landlords and of the patrimonial monarchy were essentially ambiguous and ambivalent and ultimately the source of immanent fundamental conflict.[207]

However, immediately after arguing that the conflict was of a fundamental character, Brenner shifted to the weaker formulation that the difference between private property and the patrimonial monarchy was merely 'immanently problematic'.[208] This slippage towards the possibility of an early-modern compromise between the monarchy and the capitalist aristocracy is finally embraced when Brenner suggested that the differing policy objectives of the landlords and monarchy were 'almost obligatory': 'It cannot, of course, be concluded that it was inherently impossible for the patrimonial monarchy and the parliamentary classes to reach agreement, or that conflict was inevitable.'[209] As John Morrill has noted, this formulation allows Brenner to move from talking of the social causes of the Civil War towards discussing its social interpretation.[210] If Brenner is therefore talking of the social context within which the war was fought, then Morrill makes the point that this is not at all methodologically distinct from the type of interpretation of the war that the revisionists have themselves developed.

In effect Brenner's narrative of the revolution is the story of how a certain group of 'new merchants' came into conflict with the monarchy to the point of igniting open conflict. Traditionally, Brenner argues, England's merchants shared 'a profound dependence on the Crown-sanctioned commercial corporations that provided the foundation for their protected trade'.[211] Despite the arbitrary taxes imposed on this group by the crown in the 1620s, this relationship ensured that these merchants played a conservative role in the revolution.[212] Conversely, from the early seventeenth century a new group of merchants arose that had a much more contradictory relationship with the crown. These 'new merchants' were not 'mere merchants', as were their traditional counterparts, but were also actively involved in the process of production itself.[213] They were so involved because as poorer types, relative to the mere merchants, they could not enter into the enclosed world of the chartered merchant associations. This new group in effect could thrive only where the traditional merchants had failed, for it was there that markets were open. As members of London's burgeoning capitalist community, they had the experience to apply themselves practically to the production process in situations where the traditional merchants, who were merely interested in buying cheap and selling dear, could not exploit existing producers.[214] This new merchant group did not benefit from the elite merchants' relationship with the crown. Moreover, the 'new merchants' did not share in any of the protectionist benefits of the traditional merchant groups, but they did feel all of the burdens of arbitrary taxation. It was in response to the arbitrary actions of the crown that, in the period 1640–42, this group took up leading positions within the revolutionary ferment.[215] This narrative could be interpreted as one facet of a broader and irreconcilable contradiction between the middling sort of people and the Crown. However, it can just as easily be read in a revisionist manner: the revolution was caused by the foolish actions of the king. As Morrill argues, Brenner's evidence can be interpreted to support the revisionist account which suggests that had Charles's older and wiser brother survived the smallpox then the whole affair may have been averted.[216]

While Perry Anderson believes that Brenner has produced the 'most powerful social explanation for the breakdown of the Caroline monarchy we now possess', he also, and rather ironically, suggests that Brenner provides 'no plausible answer' to the question of 'why did most of the countryside in the North and West rally to the King, in the South and East to Parliament?'[217] On this point, Anderson criticises Brenner's utilisation of Weber's concept of 'patrimonial' to describe the Stuart monarchy as a 'self-contained household' against which the revolution was fought. Such a concept is a necessary component of Brenner's schema because he rejects the view that the monarchy rested on feudal forms of exploitation, which fettered the expansion of capitalist relations of production. While Anderson agrees with Brenner's general characterisation of the dominant relations of production in early seventeenth-century England, he suggests that Brenner's account of the process of revolution might be strengthened if he accepted that feudal property relations could be constituted both politically and 'ideologically'. He argues, citing the authority of Brian Manning, that the monarchy could be understood to be feudal given the 'ideological role' it had played up to the revolution.[218] While agreeing with Brenner's fundamental argument that the aristocracy was a capitalist class, Anderson thus sought to strengthen Brenner's thesis by attaching to it the added complexity that the monarchy could be understood through the feudal role it played at the ideological level.

Anderson's citing of Brian Manning as authority for this argument is somewhat disingenuous. For while Manning did argue that when Charles fled to York in 1642, 'the monarchy was reduced to its bare essence – the sentiment of loyalty to the person of the king', he went on to suggest that 'the monarchy was seen to rest, not upon the love of the people, but upon the interests of a class': specifically, the 'nobility and greater gentry'.[219] Additionally, Manning points out that 'as the war went on parliamentarians increasingly came to see the conflict, not so much as a struggle against the king, as a struggle against the aristocracy'.[220] Developing this argument in a later study, Manning followed Hill in pointing to the divisions within the gentry. Against older social interpretations, which related the revolution either to the rise or to the fall of the gentry, Hill and Manning pointed out that 'the gentry' was a status group, not a class, and that various of its members experienced the emergence of capitalism in the countryside very differently.[221] Moreover, Manning argued that while the 'wealth of the peers and gentry rested on the ownership of land', there was 'an important distinction in the type of income: in the upper levels the main part of income came from the rents of tenants, but for many in the lower levels it came from the sale of agricultural produce'.[222] Manning specifically criticised Brenner's account both for ignoring the growth of industry in the decades leading up to 1640, and for over-emphasising the growth of capitalist farming among the aristocracy before the revolution.[223] Interestingly, Manning did write that Brenner's empirical findings, relating to the role of merchants in the revolution, cohere with his own much more classical thesis that it was the 'middling sort' who were the driving force behind the revolution. He suggested that the growing importance of this group needs to be related to the development of industry; and because Dobb stressed this development, his model was better able than Brenner's to explain why 'industrial districts – not all of them – provided a main base for the parliamentarian and revolutionary parties'.[224] According to Manning, the English revolution can best be understood, as it had been by the classical Marxists, as a bourgeois revolution located within a framework dominated by 'the rise of capitalism'.[225]

Bourgeois revolutions

In his discussion of the Marxist concept of bourgeois revolution, Brenner made a peculiar admission: while rejecting what he claimed was the 'traditional social interpretation', he acknowledged that 'neither Stone nor Hill' –authors of supposedly traditional social interpretations – 'would today adhere to this synthesis'.[226] For Brenner, the traditional social interpretation of England's bourgeois revolution involved a 'rising bourgeoisie' coming into conflict with, and ultimately overthrowing, the 'old aristocracy'.[227] This normative model bears little relationship to either Hill's mature interpretation or to previous classical interpretations of the concept.[228] I have noted in previous chapters the comments of Marx and Engels on this concept, especially Engels's analysis of Bismarck's bourgeois revolution from above, and Lenin and Trotsky's radicalisation of it with regard to Russian history. In his discussion of the concept, Hill referred to the authority of Isaac Deutscher, although he could have equally cited Dobb's similar arguments, noted above, when in 1974 he defined bourgeois revolutions by their consequences – creating the 'conditions in which bourgeois property can flourish'– rather than by the agency, bourgeois or otherwise, by which they were made.[229] Hill therefore rejected the caricature of the Marxist interpretation of the English revolution as a conflict involving a mechanical juxtaposition of a rising bourgeoisie, on the one side, against a declining feudal order, on the other.[230] Nevertheless, Hill did insist upon locating the revolution in the context of the uneven emergence of capitalist relations of production in the English countryside in the centuries before 1640.

Perhaps Hill's most developed analysis of the background to the English revolution is to be found in his *Economic Problems of the Church* (1956). In this book he argued that the peculiar superstructural roles of the crown and the Church meant that, though each institution was, in effect, a great landowner in an economy in which production was increasingly directed towards the market, neither could be allowed, for political and ideological reasons, to fail in the marketplace. This policy obviously created an uneven playing field, which would tend to antagonise those landowners whose survival was less important to the old order. Beyond this cause of antipathy, Archbishop Laud's attempt to ensure the prosperity of the Church in the years prior to the revolution, alongside the State's attempts to control industrial profits, brought both the Church and the crown into an ever-more conflictual relationship with those who had grown increasingly wealthy in the century before the revolution: Hill explained the actions of James I in the early seventeenth century as an attempt to 'protect both the church and the aristocracy against the new levelling power of money'.[231] Hill sought to explain the causes of the revolution – religious, constitutional, economic, etc. – as a totality, rooted in the growth of capitalism in England in the centuries before 1640.[232] Nevertheless, he refused to embrace the crude model of a rising bourgeoisie facing an increasingly conservative old order. Rather, he explained the revolution as a consequence of the emerging contradictions between the old way of running society and the new, progressively more capitalist, context in which the old order attempted to reproduce itself. He demonstrated, for instance, that the old method through which the Church taxed the community – the tithe – had become increasingly obsolescent as the market expanded: where previously 10 per cent of a peasant's product was relatively easily determined, in the new monetary economy the profits of businessmen were much more ambivalent phenomena which lent themselves more readily to contested interpretation.[233]

One avenue through which the Church came into conflict with elements of the bourgeoisie was its attempt to maintain tax revenue from them. This process of contestation was uneven, as businessmen of greater power were, then as today, in stronger positions than their poorer counterparts to negotiate better deals on their taxes.[234] Hill rejected the idea that the revolution involved a rising gentry coming into conflict with the old order on the grounds that, with the rise of a monetary economy, elements of the gentry variously rose and fell.[235] Hill premissed his account of the revolution on a model of the prior development of capitalism and the growth of a monetary economy to which the old institutions of crown and Church were ill- adapted.

It was in this context that the ideological slogan 'No Popery' could help unite popular discontent with the economic attempts by the Church hierarchy to increase the tax burden on the poor, with oligarchic attempts at tax avoidance.[236] This complex context informed the manner in which sixteenth-century Protestantism combined elements of popular – 'democratic' – protest, alongside 'oligarchic' themes associated with traditional attempts by the landed class to 'plunder the church'.[237]

The response of the Church and the State to the growth of capitalism was not to radically reform themselves in line with the realities of the new situation, but to attempt a 'patch up' job, by which they hoped to maintain their pre-eminent positions in society.[238] This project increasingly faltered, such that Archbishop Laud came to believe that the only way by which the old order could be maintained would be a 'revolutionary' attempt to drag England back into the 'middle-ages'.[239] By 'making reform impossible [Laud] precipitated revolution'.[240] The Civil War unleashed by the growing conflicts in English society could, according to Hill, be characterised as a bourgeois revolution because in breaking the state structures under which the old order had sheltered, it led not merely to a change in the personnel at the top of society, but to a radical reform of the old order such that 'feudal tenures' and monopolies – of ideas as well as of production – went, while a new class for whom 'public credit, trade, and the colonies were more important than the ceremonies of the church or the wealth and dignity of clerics'.[241]

More recently, Hill has reiterated his insistence that the concept of bourgeois revolution 'does *not* mean a revolution made by or consciously willed by the bourgeoisie'. Commenting on his earlier reference to Deutscher in this regard, Hill pointed out that he quoted him 'as a respected and representative Marxist, not as an innovator'.[242] Elsewhere Hill has argued that the monarchy, the biggest landowner in the pre-revolutionary era, derived much of its wealth in a feudal manner through tenures, and that it is only if we understand the political importance of this fact that we can develop a materialist understanding the revolution itself. Hill reiterated his suggestion that the abolition of feudal tenures during the English revolution underpinned the agricultural revolution of the next century.[243] The abolition of feudal tenures occurred in 1646 in the wake of the first Civil War, was confirmed in 1656, and its acceptance was, according to Hill, 'one of the unspoken conditions of the Restoration'.[244] So, while it was true that the capitalist nature of much of English agriculture in many respects pre-dated the revolution, it was also true that the capitalist elements in English society developed slowly and at an uneven pace across the country,[245] and that they found it necessary to win a revolution in order to fully realise the potential of the new system which they had nurtured.

Brian Manning's major contribution to our understanding of the revolution relates directly to this point. He criticised Hill for downplaying bourgeois agency in the revolution, and insisted that an adequate account of the revolutionary dynamic required that the independent role of the 'middling sort' of people be recognised.[246]

Manning agreed with the traditional political interpretation, that the revolution began as a split within the ruling class in the period 1640–42. Indeed, Manning argued that Charles had become so distrusted by large sections of the aristocracy in the previous decade, that even when he bowed to their wishes and impeached his two key ministers, Laud and Safford, the trust of this class could not be regained, while Charles himself merely grew to hate those who forced him to execute Stafford.[247] However, Manning went beyond the traditional political interpretation of the revolution to argue that whereas Charles was all but isolated within his own class in 1640, by 1642 there had emerged a considerable royalist party which included the majority of the lords and a substantial minority of the commons. Manning explained this development by showing that the independent actions of the London crowd created a fear within the ruling class that acted to bring the bulk of that class into line behind the king: 'The genesis of the royalist party arose from dislike of popular tumults: it was less the party of Episcopalians or Staffordians than the party of order.'[248] Conversely, ruling-class parliamentarians came to believe that the only force that stood between them and the king's wrath was the London crowd.[249]

However, the crowd was no mere plaything of the parliamentary leadership to be deployed against the king at their whim; for it had interests of its own, and had begun to fight for them in the space created by the divisions within the ruling class. At its heart, the independence of this group was rooted in the growing economic independence of the 'middle sort of people' in the century leading up to the conflict.[250] Moreover, the middle sort of people not only acted independently, but developed a form of 'class-consciousness' which was expressed in their shared identity as the godly section of the community.[251]

Manning argued that the middling sort was not a class in the modern sense, but was rather a social layer which was beginning to bifurcate between, on the one hand, those who were moving up to the bourgeoisie, and, on the other hand, those who were being pushed down to the proletariat.[252] Nevertheless, this process was very much in its infancy in the early part of the seventeenth century, such that these 'independent small producers' could, in the early 1640s, be readily distinguished from both the 'class of rentiers . . . and financiers' above them and the 'class of wage-earners' below.[253]

According to Manning is was this social grouping that provided the leadership for, and shaped the trajectory of, the revolution. While the revolution had begun, therefore, as a quarrel within the ruling class, the intervention of the middling sort ensured that it deepened into something much more. Manning's analysis of the middling sort thus followed and deepened both Dobb's general argument that English capitalism emerged from within the ranks of the direct producers and his specific insistence, as I noted above, that the nation divided along socio-economic lines between 1640 and 1642. More generally, Manning shared with Hill and Dobb the belief that the revolution could best be understood as a specific manifestation of a general European crisis.[254]

Hill located his analysis of the English revolution within the context of 'analogous conflicts in other European countries'.[255] To substantiate this point, he referred to Eric Hobsbawm's famous analysis of the 'general crisis' of feudalism in the seventeenth century. In his introduction to the debate provoked by Hobsbawm's article, first published in the journal *Past and Present* in the 1950s and 1960s, Hill commented that this general European crisis gave rise to various national solutions.[256] For his part, Hobsbawm had argued that the crisis represented a general need to 'revolutionise' Europe's feudal structures, which had entered a period of crisis from around 1300, after which various parts of Europe 'trembled on the brink of capitalism'. Nevertheless, it was only in the seventeenth century that the revolutionary break between feudalism and capitalism acquired real potential.[257] While one solution to this crisis was the emergence of absolutism, 'the most decisive product of the seventeenth century crisis' was England's bourgeois revolution.[258] It was this revolution, Hobsbawm suggested, that finally allowed England to overcome the contradictions that beset feudal society.

The state that emerged out of England's seventeenth-century revolution did not, according to Robin Blackburn, 'invent capitalism but, rather, assured the further development of an already-existing agrarian and mercantile–manufacturing capitalist complex'. And it did so, in part at least, through its violent exploitation of slaves: 'the pace of capitalist industrialisation in Britain was decisively advanced by its success in creating a regime of extended primitive accumulation and battening upon the super-exploitation of slaves in the Americas'.[259]

While Hobsbawm shared Hill's general conceptualisation of bourgeois revolutions as events best understood through their outcomes rather than by the agents through which they were executed, other Marxists have attempted to formulate a more normative model of bourgeois revolutions. Perhaps Perry Anderson has produced the classic statement of this argument. Anderson wrote a schematic history of England, 'Origins of the Present Crisis' (1964), with the aim of informing contemporary socialist politics. This essay included a history of the failure of the British bourgeoisie fully to modernise the British State, and, as a corollary of this, it was a history of the aristocracy's successful struggle to maintain its control over the levers of state power.[260] England, Anderson famously wrote, 'had the first, most mediated, and least pure bourgeois revolution of any major European country'. Furthermore, this revolution represented not the triumph of a new bourgeoisie, but rather the victory of one segment of the landowning aristocracy over another. The Civil War was fought 'primarily . . . within and not between classes'; and while the parliamentary landlords were capitalists, they did not constitute a bourgeoisie. So while the revolution broke the obstacles to capitalist advance, it did so without altering England's 'social structure', such that, as a consequence, a pre-capitalist ideology remained hegemonic: 'The ideological legacy of the revolution was almost nil . . . Puritanism was a useless passion'.[261]

Edward Thompson produced a spirited polemical assault on Anderson's interpretation of English history in his essay 'The Peculiarities of the English' (1965). The central criticism that Thompson made of 'Origins of the Present Crisis' was of its normative structure: 'There is, indeed, throughout their analysis an undisclosed model of Other Countries, whose typological symmetry offers a reproach to British exceptionalism.' In contrast to this methodology, Thompson insisted that capitalist development 'happened in one way in France, in another way in England'.[262] Specifically, Thompson criticised Anderson's model of England's seventeenth-century revolution. While he agreed with Anderson that the revolution had been made by landowners, he insisted that they were in fact a 'superbly successful and self-confident capitalist class'.[263] Those landowners also had influenced the production of, in Adam Smith's political economy, a distinctive and cogent ideology.[264] Furthermore, Thompson argued that the English revolution had, as one of its main effects, the settlement of 1688, which facilitated capitalist development, and did so in a framework that was flexible enough to survive for a century-and-a-half. Then, in 1832, those small capitalists who had been excluded from the original agreement, but who had since grown in stature, were incorporated into a new settlement that restored the original's 'flexibility'.[265] Thompson insisted that England had experienced a bourgeois revolution in the seventeenth century, irrespective of its ability to match up to a normative model of the French revolution of 1789.

Anderson's account of English history was influenced by a range of 'Western Marxists' including Georg Lukács, whose *The Destruction of Reason* (1954) had examined Germany's national characteristics with a view to explaining the rise of the Nazis.[266] While he accepted the Stalinist claim that Nazism represented the interests of monopoly capital, Lukács attempted to overcome the crudities of this argument through an analysis of the growth of an irrationalist ideology in Germany from the nineteenth century onwards. While his model was undoubtedly more sophisticated than was the orthodox Stalinist interpretation of the rise of Hitler, *The Destruction of Reason* paralleled the traditional Stalinist interpretation of this process by explaining Hitler's victory as an inevitable consequence of the telos of German history after its failure to follow France or England's historical trajectory; a process against which the left was powerless to resist. Where Holland, England and France had experienced 'normal' bourgeois revolutions, Germany's unification under Bismarck was 'too late'.[267]

In contrast to Lukács's use of a normative concept of bourgeois revolution in his history of German irrationalism, David Blackburn and Geoff Eley have produced, in relation to German history, one of the most powerful re-statements of the classical Marxist interpretation of the bourgeois revolution as a process which liberates capital accumulation from pre-capitalist fetters. Blackburn and Eley, in *The Peculiarities of German History* (1984), extend Thompson's critique of normative models of the bourgeois revolution to Bismarck's unification of Germany. In so doing they incomprehensibly claim that their thesis supports Anderson's rather than Hill's interpretation of bourgeois revolutions.[268] Despite this eccentric suggestion, they convincingly argue that bourgeois revolutions should not be measured against a normal pattern, but should be understood as a 'complex of change . . . which cumulatively established the conditions of possibility for the development of industrial capitalism'.[269] According to this model, Bismarck's reforms should be understood as a bourgeois 'revolution from above' which facilitated Germany's industrial development.[270] Like Hill and Thompson, Blackburn and Eley insist that bourgeois revolutions should be judged by their success in unfettering capitalist development, rather than by the agency through which they are made.

Interestingly, the most prominent Marxist historian of the French revolution conceptualised this momentous process along lines that were broadly similar to those suggested of the English and German bourgeois revolutions by Hill, Thompson, Blackburn and Eley. Albert Soboul (1913–82)[271] argued that the bourgeois nature of the French revolution of 1789 was not a consequence of a uniform bourgeoisie overthrowing an equally homogeneous aristocracy. While the revolution 'destroyed the feudal regime of production . . . [and] the landed aristocracy . . . it also ruined the factions of the bourgeoisie who, on several accounts, were integrated into the society of the Ancien Régime'.[272] The bourgeois character of the revolution was, by contrast, determined, at least partially, by its consequences: 'the Revolution assured the economic expansion and the political preponderance of the bourgeoisie'.[273] This was true precisely because, alongside the aristocracy, the bourgeois revolution had removed those parts of the bourgeoisie who helped reproduce the old order: the 'bourgeoisie which profited from the Revolution was no longer the same as the bourgeoisie which triggered it'.[274]

In an attempt to generalise this argument, Callinicos has suggested that the notion of bourgeois revolution should be understood not, as it was sometimes entertained by Marx, as a process that necessarily involves the active participation of the bourgeoisie as a class, but rather as a series of interconnected developments whose 'effects' include unfettering the emerging dominance of the capitalist mode of production. This 'shift in focus', suggests Callinicos, would provide historical materialism with the necessary conceptual defences against revisionist criticisms of the Marxist interpretations of the English and French revolutions.[275]

Neil Davidson, following Callinicos's general model, has argued that Scotland experienced a bourgeois revolution in the eighteenth century. In

Discovering the Scottish Revolution (2003), Davidson develops the thesis that bourgeois revolutions should be understood primarily by their outcomes rather than by the agents that made them: 'bourgeois revolution is a sequence of social and political conflicts which remove institutional barriers to local capitalist development and allow the establishment of an independent centre of competitive accumulation within the framework of the nation state'.[276] This is not to suggest that Davidson ignores the question of agency; far from it. He argues that bourgeois revolutions can occur when three 'objective conditions' are fulfilled: the feudal order experiences an 'organic crisis'; a potential 'capitalist solution to the crisis' exists; and, some agency emerges which might realise the potential offered by the development of capitalist relations within the crisis ridden feudal mode.[277] Whether the bourgeoisie as a class plays this latter role is dependent on a variety of factors: the nature of the bourgeoisie itself; the nature of the proletariat; and the existence, or otherwise, of other possible agencies through which the revolutionary potential might be realised. Developing this argument, Davidson, following Hal Draper, differentiates the bourgeoisie into its 'hard core' and its 'outer penumbra', and insists that even in its most revolutionary moments, in the Dutch, English and French revolutions, it was the outer penumbra rather than the hard core that manned the barricades. Even this limited revolutionary role came to an end from the middle of the nineteenth century, from which point the emergence of a working class pushed the bourgeoisie in an increasingly conservative direction, while other agencies had emerged – such as Bismarck's State – which could act to make bourgeois revolutions 'from above'.[278]

The power of Davidson's argument, like those of Hobsbawm, Hill, Manning, Soboul and Thompson, is premissed on the assumption that the preceding social formation was non-capitalist. Unfortunately, as Brenner has pointed out, Dobb's interpretation of the transition from feudalism to capitalism, on which Hobsbawm, Hill and Manning base their analyses of the English revolution, implied that feudalism was dead in England two centuries before the revolution that was apparently needed to revolutionise it.[279] If feudalism was to be equated with serfdom, and serfdom had, to all intents and purposes, as Dobb argued, disintegrated by the fifteenth century, then it was hard to imagine how the English revolution of the seventeenth century can be described as a bourgeois revolution against feudalism. Brenner's response to this conundrum was to analyse the changing class relations of the fifteenth century, which he re-described as the process through which agrarian capitalism emerged out of the feudal class struggle. While this framework provided the basis from which Brenner explained the English revolution as a struggle, led by the new merchants, against a patrimonial state, this interpretation, as Manning and Anderson argued, was a far from adequate model of the scale of social upheaval involved in the revolution.

Fortunately, there is another way out of Dobb's conundrum. In his contribution to the 1950s' debate in *Science and Society*, Paul Sweezy suggested that if the growth of towns could be integrated into Dobb's analysis of the feudal dynamic, then the latter's endogenous account of the transition could be defended. In the absence of such a synthesis Sweezy's exogenous account of feudalism's demise was the best available alternative: the growth of trade had led to the disintegration of feudalism.[280] While Dobb had negatively refuted this argument in the sense that he showed that the expansion of trade per se could not have entailed the disintegration of feudalism, he failed to provide a coherent alternative account of the transition to capitalism. Nonetheless, Dobb made three crucial points which lend themselves to a fuller treatment of the problem: first, feudalism was a dynamic system; second, the transition to capitalism required an increase in the productivity of labour; and, third, the transitional petty mode of production was orientated towards the market. The way out of Dobb's problem lay in synthesising these elements of his analysis. If the feudal dynamic included a tendency to increase the productivity of labour, such that at a certain point in its development production for the market became a possibility, then the emergence of towns as centres of trade could be explained in terms intrinsic to feudalism. Such a model would also cohere with Marx's account of capitalism emerging from within the womb of feudalism.

One attempt to advance the Marxist interpretation of the transition in such terms is that of Rodney Hilton (1916–2002).[281] Hilton's analysis of the transition shares much ground with Brenner's thesis: both men stress the explanatory importance of the class struggle between peasants and lords as the prime mover in the transition. On the other hand, Hilton, unlike Brenner, integrates into his model an analysis of the development of the forces of production. While Hilton argued that 'the determining factor in the movement of feudal society was the conflict of classes', he was careful to point out that the level of the development of the forces of production 'set limits to – or on the contrary, opened possibilities to – developments in the nature of production relationships'.[282] This framework immunised Hilton against some of the more questionable conclusions of those Marxists who have afforded primacy to changing relations of production in explaining epochal transitions. Hilton could not have claimed, as did Wickham, that the outcome of the class struggle between lords and peasants could range, with no reference to the development of the forces of production, from the re-enslavement of the peasantry to the socialist reconstruction of society.[283] Despite this obvious strength, Hilton appeared to equate those Marxist models which stress the primacy of the development of the forces of production to the explanation of historical patterns with crude technological determinism, and distanced his ideas from them.[284] In so far has Hilton rejected the crude economic reductionism so often labelled 'Marxism', but which so few Marxists practise, this is an undoubted strength of his work.

Nevertheless, this standpoint is problematically actualised in Hilton's discussion of the position of urban centres in the feudal system. While he strongly argues that a consequence of the existence of petty commodity production was that urban development was an *inevitable* feature of feudalism; he does not integrate this process into his model of the transition. Despite this claim for the certainty of urban growth, he points out that the urban revival was a long time coming; it began in the eleventh and twelfth centuries – or some five or six centuries after the collapse of Rome. Given the importance of towns to the traditional Marxist model of revolution, this temporal development suggests a process of the first significance: for towns could act as political alternatives to the old order in a way that peasants alone could not. Hilton himself points out that 'for the feudal mode of production to be utterly undermined, it would be necessary for developments among the basic producers to reach such a level that there would be a viable alternative to replace the previous socio-economic relationships', and continues that this alternative must be actualised at the 'political level'.[285] But if the class conflict between lords and peasants was endemic to the feudal system, surely the emergence of towns provided that novel feature which could provide the peasants with a political alternative to lordly rule. This issue does not unduly trouble Hilton because, or so he argued, 'urban class struggles never threatened the feudal powers in the same fashion as peasant revolt'. This argument is compelling only if we assume, with Dobb *et al.*, that serfdom, and thus feudalism, ended in the fifteenth century. Hilton agreed with Brenner that the class struggles in England of the 'fourteenth and fifteenth centuries prepared the ground for the development of agrarian capitalism, itself the precursor of industrial capitalism'.[286] Whatever the merits of this argument, in assuming the early triumph of capitalism in England it undermines the social explanation of the seventeenth-century revolution as a bourgeois revolution and opens the door to revisionism.

In contrast to this perspective, Peter Kriedte, Hans Medick and Jurgan Schlumbohm have argued powerfully that Marx's 'two ways' of transition from feudalism to capitalism – either the producer becoming a merchant and a capitalist or the merchant taking 'direct control of production'[287] – should not be regarded as *alternative* routes to capitalism, but as 'two parts of the same historical process'.[288] As Kriedte argues, while early medieval merchant capital – all other things being equal – was solidly tied to feudal relations of production, because feudalism was itself a dynamic mode of production, merchants found themselves in a situation where they began to act in such a way as to help dissolve feudalism from within. According to Kriedte, the feudal economy experienced a series of 'long-term upswings' followed by crises. This process was not simply cyclical, but resulted in a secular tendency towards the expansion of towns, within which there grew an artisanal form of manufacture. Merchants then invested in this process, and acted as 'the decisive stimuli in the development of the non-agricultural economy until the onset of industrialisation'.[289] This process of proto-industrialisation was further strengthened as the dynamic of the feudal mode tended to generate a 'new stratum of agricultural producers with little or no land who were dependant on a subsidiary source of income. It was on these people that the merchants were able to rely, if they opted for building up production centres in the countryside.'[290] In this context, capitalism began to grow, as Marx argued, within the womb of feudalism. However, these two modes of production were not altogether congruent, and the new states 'developed a more ambiguous role' as they attempted to maintain 'feudal domination', while simultaneously stimulating the – increasingly capitalist – economy.[291]

Building on this argument, Chris Harman[292] has attempted to synthesise Dobb's insights into a more coherent analysis of the transition that is also able adequately to explain the English revolution. Harman argues that Brenner's dismissal of an, albeit slow, feudal dynamic flies in the face of a swathe of evidence to the contrary. A series of related studies of feudal Europe have cohered with Kriedte *et al.*'s claims, in pointing to a *systematic* increase in labour productivity during this period. Jacques Le Goff, for instance, argued that 'from the moment when the ruling class established itself in the countryside and became a class of great landowners, the landed aristocracy encouraged progress in agricultural production'. Le Goff went so far as to write of an 'agricultural revolution' around the year 1000;[293] while, more recently, he has argued that 'the Middle Ages constituted a period of creativity, innovations, and extraordinary progress'.[294] Similarly, Jean Gimpel argued that 'the Middle Ages was one of the great inventive eras of mankind', and that 'between the tenth and the thirteenth centuries, western Europe experienced a technological boom'.[295] Guy Bois has attempted to underpin Georges Duby's conception of a 'feudal revolution' at the year 1000 with the argument that it was around this point that the 'slave system taken in its entirety' ended, such that 'a new relation of exploitation in the form of seigneurie was substituted for the ancient slavery'. Bois then attempts to relate this revolution to the explosion in agricultural productivity that commenced slightly prior to the year 1000.[296]

Harman is critical of some of the analytical detail of, for instance, Bois's account, suggesting that he tends to confuse the legal and the Marxist categories of slavery; and Harman argues, in slight contrast to Bois, that the transformation at the year 1000 marked the point at which Europe's political superstructure finally adjusted to its relatively new basis.[297] Nevertheless, despite these caveats, Harman builds his analysis of the transition on those of Bois *et al.* He argues that the systematic increase in the productivity of labour under feudalism was a consequence of two interrelated factors: first, serfs were 'necessarily more attentive' to the land than slaves had been; while, second, the new lords, because they were a rural class with close links to their lands, were also more attentive to production than the city-based slave owners had been.[298] These two factors underpinned feudal society's dynamic tendency to increase labour productivity, which in turn created the economic basis for production for the market. This process had as one of its consequences the slow re-emergence and expansion of towns across Europe after the tenth century.[299] Commenting on the resistance of serfs to the introduction by lords of water-mills, mentioned above in relation to Wood's argument, Harman suggests that this example shows precisely that 'even the violence of the feudal lord could, on occasion, raise general productivity'.[300] Reiterating the classical Marxist interpretation of the pivotal role of towns in revolutionary upheavals, Harman argues that while peasant revolts were endemic to feudalism, such revolts could act as the basis for the creation of a systemic alternative to feudalism only once the towns had grown to such a size and social weight that they might lead the revolution against the old order.[301] Harman follows Le Goff in ascribing to towns an evolving role, such that, while in their earliest form they acted as a mere appendage of the feudal mode, as they expanded they slowly began to impose their own priorities on the system of production.[302] Harman does not suggest that, once they had expanded, the towns automatically acted as revolutionary alternatives of feudalism; nonetheless, he does point out that as European feudalism entered a period of 'demographic' crisis from the fourteenth century, those areas within which large towns existed, and could act as an alternative pole of attraction to the old order, could potentially exit crises in a very different, capitalist, direction, than was the case in those areas within which towns were weaker.[303] All the same, even at this point, nothing was inevitable about the triumph of capitalism: Harman points out that Polisensky's analysis of the Thirty Years' War showed that even the most economically and culturally advanced areas of Europe – Bohemia in the early seventeenth century – could be crushed by feudal reaction in the struggle between emergent capitalist and entrenched feudal interests.[304]

Harman analyses the period between the decline of serfdom and the epoch of the bourgeois revolutions as a transitional era characterised by a tendency towards absolutism. Whereas Berktay had argued that it was only if the feudal mode of production was defined in abstraction from its particular manifestation through states that absolutism could be regarded, as he suggests it must, as a feudal state form; Harman agrees that a narrow definition of feudalism would lead to the conclusion that absolutist France was no longer feudal.[305] He suggests that the economic changes in the two centuries prior to the seventeenth meant that it would be inadequate to describe the absolutist states simply as 're-organised' feudal structures; or 'redeployed and recharged apparatus of feudal exploitation'.[306] Rather, Harman preferred Engels's characterisation of absolutism as the form taken by the state in the period when capitalist and feudal interests were more or less balanced.[307] The re-organised feudal structures of absolutism could act to balance capitalist and feudal interests only because capitalism had emerged from within the womb of feudalism. In the early period, the umbilical cord between feudalism and capitalism was necessary if the embryo was to survive; but once capital had matured it could flourish only by breaking the bond with its parent.

A bourgeois revolution was needed in England, and elsewhere in Europe, if the State was to be remade so that it might coherently represent the interests of capital. However, because the absolutist states acted to represent both feudal and capitalist interests in a contradictory unity, then the revolution could not be manifested as a simple opposition between feudalism and capitalism. Rather, the absolutist states acted to foster a certain degree of capital accumulation, but because they remained tied to the old feudal interests they failed to fully realise the potential of such a strategy. This structure of accumulation had the contradictory consequences of creating an increasingly self-confident capitalist class, while simultaneously fettering the full realisation of the potential of this class. So, while absolutism would tend to tie some elements of the capitalist class to feudal structures, it did so by excluding other elements of the same class from effective power. This model of the contradictory structure of England's pre-revolutionary regime could easily make sense of the empirical findings deployed in Brenner's *Merchants and Revolution*. Moreover, Harman's framework allowed him to situate the English revolution, as Brenner's could not, as a response to Hobsbawm's general, feudal, crisis of the seventeenth century.

Harman argues, following Le Goff and Duby, that the feudal system was prone to deep crises every few centuries.[308] At each crisis point the ruling class would attempt to increase the rate of exploitation, while peasants fought back. This occurred, so Harman argues, until the crisis of the seventeenth century, when urban centres had evolved such power that they were able to offer a new way out of the crisis. This potential could be realised, or frustrated, only at the level of the class struggle. Like Hilton, Harman therefore understands the level of the development of society's forces of production as setting the parameters from which the outcome of the class struggle could emerge. However, unlike Hilton, Harman argues that under feudalism there was a systematic development of the productive forces, such that the feudal mode essentially created its own – potential – gravediggers in the urban bourgeoisie. As crises erupted, this class could, and did in London in the 1640s for instance, act as an alternative to the status quo.

Conclusion

Marx's emancipatory political project demanded a theory of human nature as a basis from which people of whatever epoch might be understood to resist oppression and to fight for freedom. Nevertheless, Marx distinguished between human nature and the nature of man; that is between species-being and social-being. While human nature included some transhistorical needs and capacities – among them the need to eat, sleep, find shelter, etc., and the capacity to think rationally – the nature of man was a much more historically specific concept relating to historically constituted needs and capacities.[309] Marx's concept of modes of production was designed to make sense of the realisation of this latter attribute by relating historical periods to the nature of production undertaken therein. Marxist historians have produced fascinating, and contradictory, interpretations of a whole series of these modes of production, both as distinct totalities and as dynamic systems that are related to each other across space and time. For obvious political reasons, this debate has focused on the emergence of capitalism with a view to informing Marxist analyses of the struggle for socialism. To that end, Marxists have tended, in one way or another, to engage with the debate on the uniqueness and the nature of European feudalism, and its relation to the emergence of capitalism. Given that the direct producers in feudal Europe were peasants working the land in circumstances similar to those under which others have worked the land in various places and various times throughout history, these historians have sought to provide the conceptual tools through which either the feudal mode or its European variant might be delimited from its near neighbours. On the one hand, many Marxists have argued that European feudalism was a distinct mode of production, and it was its unique characteristics that explained the rise of capitalism. On the other hand, some Marxists have universalised the concept of feudalism, and argued that Europe's specificity is to be located in the relative strength and coherence of the states that emerged within it. Whatever else may be said about this debate, it cannot be denied that Marx fostered a positive research programme which has contributed to our understanding of the past, and through that understanding a more complete sense of awareness of the present.

While the debate over the contested conceptualisations of modes of production may appear to be somewhat arcane, these theoretical debates do have some practical significance: they are designed to help make sense of the chaos of historical facts such that, first, historical processes may be explained and, second, those explanations may inform contemporary socialist practice. As Chris Wickham argues, 'we try to categorize world history in Marxist terms' so that 'we understand the world better by doing so, so that we can change it'.[310] While this goal may seem far removed from the day-to-day concerns of historians of antiquity, the very real need felt by all historians to adequately delineate between distinct periods in history can help inform, at the very least, the socialist critique of ahistorical and ideological attempts to naturalise patterns of behaviour that are in fact specific to capitalism.

Robert Brenner's analysis of the transition from feudalism to capitalism is framed in precisely those terms: he has attempted to uncover an explanation for the development of capitalist relations of production and, hence, the evolution of capitalist rationality, rather than assume the universality of this type of behaviour:

> it is only given the prevalence of certain quite specific, historically developed property relations . . . that the individual economic actors will find it rational and possible to follow the patterns of economic actions supportive of modern economic growth outlined by Adam Smith.[311]

While Brenner makes explicit the political consequences of the theory of historical periodisation, similar concerns have informed the work of all the Marxist historians whose ideas I have discussed.

Notes

1 I. Roxborough *Theories of Underdevelopment* (London, 1979), p. 1.
2 Marx Preface to *A Contribution to the Critique of Political Economy*, pp. 21–2.
3 C. Wickham 'The Uniqueness of the East' in C. Wickham *Land and Power* (London, 1994), p. 45; the essay was originally published in the *Journal of Peasant Studies* 12, 1985.
4 I have borrowed this subheading from the title of Bruce Trigger's excellent study of Childe's work: B. Trigger *Gordon Childe: Revolutions in Archaeology* (London, 1980).
5 Ibid., p. 95.
6 Childe was born in Sydney, Australia, where he completed his first degree. He then did graduate work at Oxford, before returning to left-wing activism in Australia – where he worked as the private secretary to the Labour premier of New South Wales. After becoming disenchanted with Australian politics, he returned to England in 1922. In 1925 he published his classic *The Dawn of European Civilisation*, and in 1927 he became the first holder of the Abercromby chair of archaeology at Edinburgh – making him 'one of the few professional archaeologists in Britain at that time'. In 1946 he became professor of European archaeology and director of the Institute of Archaeology at the University of London. He retired in 1946, and died a year later, after he had returned to Australia: Trigger *Gordon Childe*, pp. 9–10.
7 T. Patterson *Marx's Ghost: Conversations with Archaeologists* (Oxford, 2003), p. 33.
8 Trigger *Gordon Childe*, p. 95.
9 M. Rowlands 'Childe and the Archaeology of Freedom' in D. Harris ed. *The Archaeology of V. Gordon Childe: Contemporary Perspectives* (Melbourne, 1994), p. 38.
10 D. Harris 'Introduction' to *The Archaeology of V. Gordon Childe*, p. 4; C. Renfrew 'Concluding Remarks: Childe and the Study of the Culture Process', in ibid., p. 123.
11 In a recent survey of Childe's influence on late twentieth-century archaeology, David Harris claimed that Childe was 'the scholar who for the first time *made sense* of the prehistoric past' (Harris 'Introduction', p. 1), while Bruce Trigger labelled Childe 'the most renowned and widely read archaeologist of the 20th century': 'Childe's Relevance to the 1990s' in ibid., p. 9. In the same collection, Kent Flannery argued that 'Childe had a vision of evolution at a time when other archaeologists had only chronology charts': Flannery 'Childe the Evolutionist: A Perspective from Nuclear America' in ibid., p. 110; and Michael Rowlands

suggested that, while the detail of Childe's arguments was necessarily of transient interest, his method was important because 'he was asking all the right questions': Rowlands 'Childe and the Archaeology of Freedom', p. 35.

12 P. Gathercole 'Discussion' in ibid., p. 28.
13 V. Gordon Childe *History* (London, 1947), p. 77.
14 R. McGuire *A Marxist Archaeology* (San Diego, 1992), p. 58.
15 Patterson *Marx's Ghost*, p. 44.
16 V. Gordon Childe *Man Makes Himself* (London, 1965 [1936]), p. 6.
17 Trigger 'Childe's Relevance', p. 15.
18 Childe *Man Makes Himself*, p. 6.
19 Patterson *Marx's Ghost*, p. 57; Trigger *Gordon Childe*, p. 97.
20 Trigger *Gordon Childe*, p. 97.
21 Childe *History*, pp. 73–5.
22 Trigger *Gordon Childe*, p. 99.
23 Childe *Man Makes Himself*, p 98.
24 Ibid.
25 Patterson *Marx's Ghost*, p. 47.
26 Childe *Man Makes Himself*, p. 238.
27 Trigger *Gordon Childe*, p. 102.
28 Childe *Man Makes Himself*, p. 99.
29 Ibid., pp. 29, 75, 87.
30 Ibid., p. 71.
31 Ibid., pp. 1–14.
32 Ibid., p. 238.
33 Ibid., p. 105.
34 V. Gordon Childe *What Happened in History* (London, 1964 [1942]), pp. 73–6.
35 These were the areas around the Nile and the Indus, and that between the Tigris and the Euphrates. Childe seemed to argue that the breakthrough originally occurred in one area and was copied, but the general validity of his revolutionary model is unaffected if we accept that similar transformations occurred at a number of times in various places: ibid., pp. 168–70.
36 Childe *Man Makes Himself*, pp. 106, 154.
37 Ibid., pp. 179, 227.
38 Ibid., p. 228.
39 Ibid., pp. 229–36.
40 Marian Sawer *Marxism and the Question of the Asiatic Mode of Production* (The Hague, 1977), p. 191.
41 Trigger *Childe's Relevance*, pp. 31–2.
42 Childe *Man Makes Himself*, p. 231.
43 Ibid., p. 134.
44 Childe *What Happened in History*, p. 191.
45 Ibid., p. 196.
46 Ibid., pp. 233, 209, 268.
47 Ibid., p. 233.
48 Ibid., pp. 260–2.
49 Ibid., p. 277.
50 Ibid., p. 246.
51 Ibid., p. 283.

52 Ibid., p. 284.
53 Ibid., p. 286.
54 Ibid., p. 288.
55 Ibid., p. 289–90.
56 Ibid., p. 292.
57 Ellen Wood was, until her retirement, professor of political science at York University, Toronto.
58 On Political Marxism see my 'Political Marxism: Towards an Immanent Critique' *Studies in Marxism* 9, 2002–3.
59 R. Brenner, 'The Social Basis of Economic Development' in J. Roemer ed., *Analytical Marxism* (Cambridge, 1986), pp. 27ff.
60 E. M. Wood *Peasant–Citizen and Slave* (London, 1988), p. 157.
61 Ibid., p. 161.
62 Ibid., p. 159.
63 Ibid., pp. 157–8.
64 Ibid., pp. 5–42.
65 Ibid., p. 37.
66 Ibid., p. 38.
67 Geoffrey de. Ste Croix broke with his 'thoroughly right-wing upbringing' in the 1930s when he was radicalised by the growing threat of fascism. Before the war he trained as a solicitor, but after military service in the RAF he studied Greek and Roman history at the University of London from where he graduated at the age of 39. After a brief spell at the LSE, he became a fellow at New College, Oxford, from where he published his two magna opera, *The Origins of the Peloponnesian Wars* (1972), and *The Class Struggle in the Ancient Greek World* (1981; revised 1983) in his seventh and eighth decades respectively. He is probably unique among Marxist historians in having played tennis on the centre court at Wimbledon (1929), and definitely unique in having beaten the great Fred Perry there! For biographical details on Ste. Croix see G. E. M. de Ste. Croix 'Class in Marx's Conception of History, Ancient and Modern' *New Left Review* no. 146, July–August 1984; see also P. A. Cartledge and F. D. Harvey 'Editors' Preface' in 'Crux: Essays in Greek History Presented to G. E. M. de Ste. Croix', special issue of *History of Political Thought* 6:1–2, 1985.
68 P. Anderson 'Geoffrey de Ste. Croix and the Ancient Greek World' in P. Anderson *A Zone of Engagement* (London, 1992), pp. 2–4; essay originally published in *History Workshop Journal* 16, 1983.
69 Ste. Croix *The Class Struggle in the Ancient Greek World*, p. 52.
70 Ibid. p. 133.
71 Ibid., p. 173.
72 Ibid., pp. 159–60.
73 Wood *Peasant Citizen and Slave*, pp. 1, 64; Ste. Croix *The Class Struggle in the Ancient Greek World*, pp. 505–6.
74 A. Callinicos 'The Foundations of Athenian Democracy' *International Socialism* 2:40, 1988, p. 128.
75 Anderson 'Geoffrey de Ste. Croix', p. 8.
76 Ste. Croix *The Class Struggle in the Ancient Greek World*, p. 141.
77 Anderson 'Geoffrey de Ste. Croix', p. 10.
78 Ste. Croix *The Class Struggle in the Ancient Greek World*, p. 90.

79 Ibid., pp. 92–3.
80 Ibid., pp. 464–5.
81 Ibid., p. 287.
82 Ibid., p. 453.
83 Ibid.
84 Ibid., p. 463.
85 Ibid., pp. 502–3.
86 Ibid., p. 146.
87 Anderson 'Geoffrey de Ste. Croix', pp. 17–18. A brilliant exposition of the process through which common 'pidgin' languages evolved out of the myriad local languages encountered by eighteenth-century sailors in the Atlantic has been outlined by Linebaugh and Rediker. Moreover, as they argue, while this language developed to facilitate the international capitalist labour process, it was utilised by these sailors in their resistance to capitalist exploitation – it is not hard to imagine elements of a similar process evolving in the classical world: P. Linebaugh and M. Rediker *The Many Headed Hydra* (London, 2000), pp. 153–4.
88 Anderson 'Geoffrey de Ste. Croix', p. 16.
89 P. Anderson *Passages from Antiquity to Feudalism* (London, 1974), pp. 42–3.
90 Ibid., p. 24.
91 Ibid., p. 22.
92 Ibid., p. 141.
93 Ibid., p. 269.
94 Chris Wickham is professor of early medieval history at the University of Birmingham.
95 C. Wickham 'The Other Transition: From Ancient World to Feudalism' in C. Wickham *Land and Power*, p. 9; the essay was first published in the *Past and Present* 63, 1984.
96 Wickham 'The Other Transition', pp. 12–13.
97 Ibid., p. 16.
98 Ibid., p. 19.
99 Ibid., p. 20.
100 The title of this section is borrowed from H. Mukhia ed. *The Feudalism Debate* (New Delhi, 1999). Most of the essays in that collection were published in the *Journal of Peasant Studies* 12, 1985, which was itself produced as a response to Mukhia's 'Was There Feudalism in Indian Society?' *Journal of Peasant Studies* 8, 1981, which is also in the collection.
101 S. Dunn *The Fall and Rise of the Asiatic Mode of Production* (London, 1982), pp. 23, 41.
102 N. Harris *The Mandate of Heaven: Marx and Mao in Modern China* (London, 1978), pp. 3–15.
103 Ibid., pp. 11–13.
104 L. Krader *The Asiatic Mode of Production* (Assen, 1975), p. 315.
105 L. Trotsky *Leon Trotsky on China* (New York, 1976), pp. 403, 263.
106 Draper *Karl Marx's Theory of Revolution* Vol. 1, p. 629; Krader *The Asiatic Mode*, p. 315; T. Brook 'Introduction' in T. Brook ed. *The Asiatic Mode of Production in China* (London, 1989), p. 12ff. Compare these with A. Bailey and J. Llobera 'Editors' Introduction' in A. Bailey and J. Llobera eds *The Asiatic Mode of Production* (London, 1981), pp. 51–2.

107 N. Harris *Beliefs in Society* (London, 1968), p. 152.
108 For some classic Marxist studies of the French revolution see the selection of A. Soboul's essays on the subject: *Understanding the French Revolution* (London, 1988); A. Soboul *A Short History of the French Revolution* (London, 1977 [1965]); G. Lefebvre *The Coming of the French Revolution* (London,1967 [1947]); G. Lefebvre *The French Revolution* Vols 1 and 2 (London, 1962, 1964 [1951, 1957]); D. Guerin *Class Struggle in the First French Republic* (London, 1977 [1973]). As I point out in chapter 5, the English translation of Guerin's book is not, despite its title, of the 1946 edition of *La Lutte des classes sous la premiere republique*. Unfortunately, considerations of space preclude a discussion of this literature.
109 Draper *Karl Marx's Theory of Revolution* Vol. 1, pp. 515–71.
110 Ibid., p. 537; see also Krader *The Asiatic Mode of Production*, p. 310.
111 Draper *Karl Marx's Theory of Revolution* Vol. 1, p. 537.
112 K. Wittfogel *Oriental Despotism* (London, 1963 [1957]), p. 447.
113 P. Anderson *Lineages of the Absolutist State* (London, 1974), p. 487.
114 Maurice Godelier is an internationally renowned anthropologist, professor and director of studies at Ecole des Hautes Etudes en Sciences Sociales in Paris; Maurice Godelier is an officer in the French Legion of Honour, who has been awarded the French Academy Prize (1982), the International Alexander von Humbolt Prize for Social Sciences (1990) and in 2001 he was awarded the Gold Medal by the French National Centre for Scientific Research.
115 M. Godelier 'The Asiatic Mode of Production' in Bailey and Llobera eds *The Asiatic Mode of Production*, pp. 275, 264.
116 Ibid., 265.
117 Ibid., p. 266.
118 Ibid., p. 267.
119 Ibid., p. 268.
120 Ibid., p. 271.
121 Anderson *Lineages of the Absolutist State*, pp. 480, 483.
122 Ibid., p. 486.
123 Ibid., pp. 401–2.
124 Ibid., pp. 403–4.
125 Ibid., p. 414; Anderson *Passages from Antiquity to Feudalism*, pp. 147–8.
126 Anderson *Lineages of the Absolutist State*, p. 413.
127 Ibid., p. 416.
128 Ibid., p. 418.
129 Ibid., pp. 428–9.
130 P. Hirst *Marxism and Historical Writing* (London, 1985), p. 96.
131 Ibid., p. 106.
132 Ibid., p. 101.
133 Ibid., p. 110.
134 M. Fulbrook and T. Skocpol 'Destined Pathways' in T. Skocpol ed. *Vision and Method in Historical Sociology* (Cambridge, 1984), p. 183.
135 M. Sawer *Marxism and the Question of the Asiatic Mode of Production* (The Hague, 1977), p. 232. A. Bailey and J. Llobera 'The Asiatic Mode of Production: Sources and Formation of the Concept' in Bailey and Llobera eds *The Asiatic Mode of Production*, p. 14.

136 D. Parker *Class and State in Ancien Régime France* (London, 1996), p. 270.
137 Ibid., p. 21.
138 Ibid., p. 172.
139 S. Amin *Unequal Development* (New York, 1976 [1973]), pp. 51, 16.
140 Ibid., p. 15.
141 Ibid., pp. 53–4.
142 Ibid., pp. 53, 33–4.
143 *Capital* Vol. 3, p. 927.
144 Wickham 'The Uniqueness of the East', p. 69.
145 Ibid., p. 49; Wickham 'The Other Transition', p. 39.
146 Wickham 'The Uniqueness of the East', p. 56.
147 Ibid., p. 67; Wickham 'The Other Transition', p. 16.
148 Wickham 'The Uniqueness of the East', pp. 71–2.
149 Ibid., p. 71.
150 The bulk of the essays collected in this special issue were later published, alongside three other contributions to the debate, in a collection edited by Harbans Mukhia entitled *The Feudalism Debate* (New Delhi, 1999).
151 H. Berktay 'The Feudalism Debate: The Turkish End' in Mukhia ed. *The Feudalism Debate*, pp. 278, 287, 281; essay originally published in the *Journal of Peasant Studies* 14, 1987.
152 John Haldon is professor of Byzantine history and head of the School of Historical Studies at the Institute of Archaeology and Antiquity at the University of Birmingham.
153 J. Haldon *The State and the Tributary Mode of Production* (London, 1993), pp. 88, 75–8.
154 Ibid., pp. 10, 64.
155 Ibid., pp. 60, 25. Haldon's suggestion that Marx's concept of modes of production is an ideal type is surely mistaken. Weber's ideal types, because they are 'purely abstract and conventional', do not evolve over time, and therefore do 'not produce a line of development, but only a juxtaposition of ideal types selected and arranged casuistically': L. Colletti *From Rousseau to Lenin* (New York, 1972), p. 41; G. Lukács *The Destruction of Reason* (London, 1980), p. 612. As Adorno argued, ideal types are merely 'heuristic instruments, heuristic means, with which the historical material is to be compared': T. Adorno *Introduction to Sociology* (Cambridge, 2000), p. 119. Thus conceived, ideal types can be utilised to identify difference over time, but not continuity in change. Alternatively, in Marx's conception modes of production, as I noted in chapter 2, are defined as internally dynamic, and therefore transitory, totalities. Each mode of production has, at its heart, a distinct dynamic mode of surplus extraction, founded on a particular level of the development of the forces of production. This model allows Marxists to theorise change in a way that Weberians can not. In fact, there exists an insurmountable gap between Weber's ideal types and the real world, such that once Weberians move from theory to empirical investigations their method tends towards empiricism: W. Outhwaite *New Philosophies of Social Science* (London, 1987), p. 104. The empiricist implications of Weberianism, of course, converge with the practice of traditional historiography; and Weberians are wont to elaborate similar criticisms of Marxism's supposed reductionism to those developed within mainstream historiography.

156 Haldon *The State and the Tributary Mode of Production*, p. 65.
157 Ibid., p. 97.
158 Ibid., pp. 79–83, 103.
159 Indeed, Wickham, in a comment on his original essay, concedes that he has been persuaded that his original position was inadequate by the criticism articulated by Berktay, Haldon and others: Wickham 'The Uniqueness of the East', p. 75.
160 Wickham 'The Uniqueness of the East', p. 71.
161 Ibid., p. 45–6; Wickham 'The Other Transition', pp. 9–10; Haldon *The State and the Tributary Mode*, p. 89; Berktay 'The Feudalism Debate', p. 289.
162 Barry Hindess and Paul Hirst *Pre-Capitalist Modes of Production* (London, 1975), p. 310.
163 R. Brenner 'Dobb on the Transition from Feudalism to Capitalism' *Cambridge Journal of Economics* 2, 1978, p. 121.
164 E. M. Wood *The Origin of Capitalism* (London, 1999), p. 44; Harman *Marxism and History*, p. 65.
165 R. Brenner 'Dobb on the Transition from Feudalism to Capitalism', p. 121.
166 Dobb *Studies in the Development of Capitalism*, pp. 7–8.
167 Ibid., p. 11.
168 Ibid., p. 7.
169 Ibid., pp. 17, 41; M. Dobb 'A Reply' in R. Hilton ed. *The Transition from Feudalism to Capitalism* (London, 1976), p. 60.
170 Dobb *Studies in the Development of Capitalism*, p. 55.
171 Ibid., pp. 70–1.
172 Ibid., pp. 72–5.
173 Ibid., pp. 89, 121.
174 Ibid., pp. 123–4.
175 Paul Sweezy, like so many of his generation, was radicalised in the early 1930s by the depression and the threat of fascism. He became a Marxist in 1932. In 1942 he published *A Theory of Capitalist Development*, and after a period of war service, he returned to the USA to launch the magazine *Monthly Review* in 1949. In 1954 he was indicted by the McCarthyites, but fought them all the way to the Supreme Court, where, in 1957, he had a conviction for contempt of court overturned. In 1966 he co-authored the classic *Monopoly Capitalism* with Paul Baran.
176 P. Sweezy 'A Critique' in Hilton ed. *The Transition from Feudalism to Capitalism*, pp. 33, 35.
177 Ibid., p. 41.
178 Ibid., pp. 42–3.
179 G. Procacci 'A Survey of the Debate' in Hilton ed. *The Transition from Feudalism to Capitalism*, p. 130.
180 Dobb *Studies in the Development of Capitalism*, p. 170.
181 Ibid., p. 172.
182 Ibid., pp. 174–6.
183 R. Brenner 'Dobb on the Transition from Feudalism to Capitalism', p. 132.
184 Dobb *Studies in the Development of Capitalism*, p. 181.
185 Ibid., pp. 71–2.
186 Robert Brenner is a professor of history and director of the Centre for Social Theory and Comparative History at the University of California, Los Angeles.

He is a prominent revolutionary socialist and member of the editorial board of *New Left Review*.

187 R. Brenner, 'Agrarian Class Structures and Economic Development in Pre-Industrial Europe' in T. H. Aston and C. H. E. Philpin eds *The Brenner Debate* (Cambridge, 1985), p. 30.
188 G. Bois, 'Against Neo-Malthusian Orthodoxy' in ibid., p. 115.
189 R. Brenner, 'Bourgeois Revolution and the Transition to Capitalism' in Beier, Cannadine and Rosenheim eds *The First Modern Society*, p. 272.
190 Ibid., p. 279.
191 Ibid., p. 296.
192 Ibid., pp. 303, 295.
193 R. Brenner 'Economic Backwardness in Eastern Europe in Light of Developments in the West' in D. Chirot ed *The Origins of Backwardness in Eastern Europe* (Berkeley, CA 1985), p. 18.
194 Ibid., p. 50.
195 R. Brenner, 'Agrarian Class Structures and Economic Development in Pre-Industrial Europe', p. 34.
196 Ibid., p. 38.
197 R. Brenner 'The Low Countries in the Transition to Capitalism' in P. Hoppenbrouwers ed. *Peasants into Farmers* (Turnhout, 2002), pp. 276, 289.
198 R. Brenner 'Feudalism' in J. Eatwell, M. Milgate and P. Newman eds *The New Palgrave Marxian Economics* (London, 1990), p. 182; R. Brenner 'Property Relations and the Growth of Agricultural Productivity in Late Medieval and Early Modern Europe' in A. Bhaduri and R. Skarstein eds *Economic Development and Agricultural Productivity* (Cheltenham, 1997), pp. 14–15.
199 R. Brenner *Merchants and Revolution* (Cambridge, 1993), p. 638.
200 Ibid., p. 641.
201 Ibid., p. 648.
202 Ibid., p. 653.
203 Ibid., p. 643.
204 Ibid., p. 652.
205 Ibid., p. 653.
206 Ibid., p. 648.
207 Ibid., p. 651.
208 Ibid., p. 657.
209 Ibid., p. 665.
210 J. Morrill 'Conflict Probable or Inevitable?' *New Left Review* no. 207, p. 121.
211 Brenner *Merchants and Revolution*, p. 83.
212 Ibid., pp. 225, 91.
213 Ibid., p. 160.
214 Ibid., pp. 160, 54.
215 Ibid., p. 317.
216 J. Morrill 'Conflict Probable or Inevitable?', p. 121.
217 P. Anderson 'Maurice Thompson's War' *London Review of Books*, 4 November 1993, p. 16.
218 Ibid., pp. 16–17.
219 B. Manning *The English People and the English Revolution* (London, 1992 [1976]), pp. 319–20.

220 Ibid., p. 326.
221 B. Manning *1649: The Crisis of the English Revolution* (London, 1992), pp. 49–78; C. Hill (1956) 'Recent Interpretations of the Civil War' in C. Hill *Puritanism and Revolution* (London, 1958), pp. 17–18.
222 Manning *1649*, p. 51.
223 B. Manning 'The English Revolution and the Transition from Feudalism to Capitalism' *International Socialism* 2:63, 1994, p. 84; 'The English Revolution: The Decline and Fall of Revisionism' *Socialist History* 14, 1999, p. 50. More generally for an empirical criticism of Brenner's assessment of capitalist agriculture see M. Overton *Agricultural Revolution in England* (Cambridge, 1996), p. 205; and R. Albritton 'Did Agrarian Capitalism Exist?' *Journal of Peasant Studies* 20:3, April 1993, pp. 419–41.
224 B. Manning 'The English Revolution and the Transition from Feudalism to Capitalism', pp. 84–6; 'The English Revolution: The Decline and Fall of Revisionism', p. 50; 'The Nobles, The People, and the Constitution' in T. Aston ed. *Crisis in Europe* (New York, 1965), pp. 261–8.
225 Manning 'The English Revolution: The Decline and Fall of Revisionism', pp. 45, 51.
226 Brenner *Merchants and Revolution*, p. 638.
227 Ibid., p. 639.
228 On the distinction between Hill's earlier and more mature works see R. C. Richardson *The Debates on the English Revolution* (Manchester, 1998), p. 125; for his earlier opinion see C. Hill (1948) 'The English Civil War Interpreted by Marx and Engels' in B. Jessop and C. Malcolm-Brown eds *Karl Marx's Social and Political Thought: Critical Assessments* Vol. 3 (London, 1990), p. 644.
229 C. Hill *Change and Continuity in Seventeenth Century England* (London, 1974), p. 280.
230 In this sense, Hill's argument coheres with Manning's reassertion of the Marxist commonplace that class interpretations of social movements by no means imply that the classes involved in those struggles are in any sense homogeneous: 'The English Revolution: The Decline and Fall of Revisionism', p. 44.
231 C. Hill *Economic Problems of the Church* (London, 1971 [1956]), pp. 10–13, 35.
232 Ibid., pp. 347–8.
233 Ibid., p. 80.
234 Ibid., p. 120.
235 Ibid., p. 108.
236 Ibid., p. 162.
237 Ibid., p. 121.
238 Ibid., p. 241.
239 Ibid., pp. 341, 346.
240 Ibid., pp. 344, 45.
241 Ibid., p. 350.
242 C. Hill 'A Bourgeois Revolution?' in J. G. A. Pocock ed. *Three British Revolutions: 1641, 1688, 1776* (Princeton, NJ, 1980), p. 110.
243 C. Hill *Reformation to Industrial Revolution* (London, 1969), pp. 146ff., 169ff.
244 C. Hill *Intellectual Origins of the English Revolution Revisited* (Oxford, 1997), p. 321.

245 Albritton 'Did Agrarian Capitalism Exist?', p. 436.
246 Manning 'The English Revolution: The Decline and Fall of Revisionism', p. 44.
247 B. Manning 'The Outbreak of the English Civil War' in R. H. Parry ed. *The English Civil War and After 1642–1658* (Berkeley, CA, 1970), p. 3; B. Manning 'The Aristocracy and the Downfall of Charles I' in B. Manning ed. *Politics, Religion and the English Civil War* (London, 1973), pp. 68, 79. Laud was also executed, but in 1645.
248 Manning *The English People and the English Revolution*, pp. 71, 101; 'The Aristocracy and the Downfall of Charles I', p. 80.
249 Manning *The English People and the English Revolution*, p. 130.
250 Manning 'Religion and Politics: The Godly People' in Manning ed. *Politics, Religion and the English Civil War*, p. 105; *The English People and the English Revolution*, p. 230.
251 Manning 'Religion and Politics: The Godly People', p. 123; *The English People and the English Revolution*, p. 241.
252 Manning *Aristocrats, Plebeians and Revolution in England: 1640–1660* (London, 1996), p. 8.
253 Manning *The English People and the English Revolution*, p. 230; *1649*, p. 60.
254 Manning 'The Nobles, The People, and the Constitution', pp. 261–2.
255 Hill 'A Bourgeois Revolution?', p. 112.
256 C. Hill 'Introduction' in Aston ed. *Crisis in Europe*, p. 3.
257 E. Hobsbawm 'The Crisis of the Seventeenth Century' in Aston ed. *Crisis in Europe*, pp. 15, 5; for a more recent general survey of this concept see G. Parker and L. Smith eds *The General Crisis of the Seventeenth Century* (London, 1997).
258 Hobsbawm 'The Crisis of the Seventeenth Century', pp. 13, 57.
259 R. Blackburn *The Making of New World Slavery* (London, 1997), pp. 515, 572.
260 R. Johnson, 'Barrington Moore, Perry Anderson and English Social Development' in S. Hall, D. Hobson, A. Lowe and P. Willis eds *Culture, Media, Language* (London, 1980), pp. 59, 61.
261 P. Anderson 'Origins of the Present Crisis' in P. Anderson *A Zone of Engagement* (London, 1992), pp. 17–19; essay first published in *New Left Review* 24, 1964.
262 E. P. Thompson 'The Peculiarities of the English' in E. P. Thompson *The Poverty of Theory and Other Essays* (London, 1978), pp. 247, 257; essay originally published in R. Miliband and J. Saville eds *The Socialist Register* 1965 (London, 1965).
263 Ibid., p. 252.
264 Ibid., p. 254.
265 Ibid., p. 260.
266 P. Blackledge *Perry Anderson, Marxism and the New Left* (London, 2004), p. 16.
267 Lukács *The Destruction of Reason*, pp. 76–7, 57, 37.
268 D. Blackburn and G. Eley *The Peculiarities of German History* (Oxford, 1984), pp. 59, 52, 170, 136, 82.
269 Ibid., p. 144.
270 Ibid., p. 84.
271 Albert Soboul, a professor of history at the Sorbonne, was after the death of

Georges Lefebvre, the most prominent defender of the Marxist interpretation of the French revolution.
272 A. Soboul *Understanding the French Revolution* (London, Merlin, 1988), p. 36.
273 Ibid., p. 18.
274 Ibid., p. 41.
275 Callinicos 'Bourgeois Revolution and Historical Materialism', p. 124.
276 N. Davidson *Discovering the Scottish Revolution* (London, 2003), p. 8.
277 Ibid., p. 9.
278 Ibid., pp. 10–15.
279 E. Hobsbawm ''The Historians' Group of the Communist Party' in M. Cornforth ed. *Rebels and Their Causes* (London, 1978), p. 23; Hill 'A Bourgeois Revolution?', p. 130.
280 Sweezy 'A Critique', p. 40.
281 Rodney Hilton was a member of the Communist Party Historians' Group before becoming an activist in the New Left in 1956; he was professor of medieval social history at the University of Birmingham.
282 R. Hilton *Class Struggle and the Crisis of Feudalism* (London, 1990), p. 5; see also his 'A Crisis of Feudalism' in Aston and Philpin eds *The Brenner Debate*, p. 119.
283 Wickham 'The Uniqueness of the East', p. 71.
284 Hilton *Class Struggle and the Crisis of Feudalism*, p. 4.
285 Hilton 'A Crisis of Feudalism', p. 133.
286 Hilton *Class Struggle and the Crisis of Feudalism*, pp. 7, 212, 9.
287 *Capital* Vol. 3, p. 452.
288 P. Kriedte, H. Medick and J. Schlumbohm *Industrialisation Before Industrialisation: Rural Industry and the Genesis of Capitalism* (Cambridge, 1981), pp. 9–10.
289 P. Kriedte *Peasants, Landlords and Merchant Capitalists: Europe and the World Economy 1500–1800* (Leamington Spa, 1983), pp. 7–9.
290 Ibid., p. 14.
291 Ibid., p. 16.
292 Chris Harman is the editor of *International Socialism*, a leading member of the British Socialist Workers' Party and the author of the popular *A People's History of the World* (London, 1999).
293 J. Le Goff *Medieval Civilization* (Oxford, 1988 [1964]), p. 57.
294 J. Le Goff *The Birth of Europe* (London, 2005), p. 198.
295 J. Gimpel *The Medieval Machine* (London, 1988 [1976]), p. viii.
296 G. Bois *The Transformation of the Year One Thousand* (Manchester, 1992), pp. 25, 32, 135, 128.
297 C. Harman 'Change at the First Millennium' *International Socialism* 2:64, 1994, pp. 94–5.
298 Harman *Marxism and History*, p. 76.
299 Ibid., p. 81.
300 Ibid., p. 78.
301 Ibid., p. 101; see also W. Kula *An Economic Theory of the Feudal System* (London, 1976 [1962]), p. 143.
302 Harman *Marxism and History*, p. 84.
303 Ibid., pp. 94, 96.

304 Ibid., pp. 103–5; J. V. Polisensky *The Thirty Years' War* (London, 1971 [1970]).
305 Berktay 'The Feudalism Debate', p. 287; C. Harman 'The Rise of Capitalism' *International Socialism* 2:102, 2004, p. 85.
306 V. Kienan 'Foreign Mercenaries and Absolute Monarchy' in Aston ed. *Crisis in Europe*, p. 124; Anderson *Lineages of the Absolutist State*, p. 18.
307 Harman *Marxism and History*, p. 98.
308 Ibid., pp. 93–6.
309 S. Creaven *Critical Realism and Marxism* (London, 2000), p. 75.
310 Wickham 'The Uniqueness of the East', p. 44.
311 Brenner 'Economic Backwardness in Eastern Europe', p. 19.

5

Structure, agency and the struggle for freedom

In 'The Eighteenth Brumaire' Marx famously wrote that 'men make history, but not of their own free will; not under circumstances they themselves have chosen but under given and inherited circumstances with which they are directly confronted'.[1] While, through this aphorism, he made a formal solution to the problem of synthesising structure and agency within his theory of history, it did not provide Marxists with a clear guide as to the relative weight which may be ascribed to each of these elements of the historical process at any given moment. It is difficult to imagine how Marx could have offered such a formulation, for some historical processes – for instance the concentration and centralisation of capital – seem to progress by a much more structurally given logic than do other processes: revolutions, for instance. Nevertheless, despite the appeal of the suggestion that structural and agential moments of the historical process have more or less importance in different circumstances, the post-war Marxist debates on structure and agency have tended to polarise around attempts to reduce either agency to structure or vice versa.

Jean-Paul Sartre (1905–80) made one of the earliest contributions to this discussion, in which he placed the free individual at the centre of his reconstruction of historical materialism; and while his project must ultimately be regarded as a failure, his critique of the schematic historiography of Stalinism undoubtedly marked a positive contribution to the renewal of historical materialism in the post-war decades.

While Sartre's was the towering voice of the post-war French and international left, his star began to wane at the turn of the 1960s, when the cutting edge of Parisian thought moved away from existentialism and towards structuralism. The Marxian variant of this general intellectual shift was developed most systematically by Louis Althusser (1918–90). Althusser emerged as a significant thinker in the context of, first, a communist reaction against the emergence of an anti-communist left after 1956; second, the Sino-Soviet split of the early 1960s; and, third, the shift towards structuralism within the French academy. He simultaneously rejected the stress on human agency in Sartre's interpretation of historical materialism, and attempted to replace it with a form of Marxist structuralism, according to which history was understood to be a process without a subject.

Meanwhile, a parallel process was unfolding across the Channel. In the decade after the war, a regime of benign neglect within the British Communist Party helped facilitate the emergence of a libertarian strand of Marxism within the Communist Party Historians' Group. In the context of the events of 1956 – Khrushchev's 'secret speech', the Soviet invasion of Hungary and the Anglo-French invasion of Egypt – this theoretical framework informed the break with the CPGB made by many within the Historians' Group, which in fact provided the British New Left with a number of its key leaders; including, most prominently, Edward Thompson.

Alongside his political role, Thompson was to become, after the publication of his classic *The Making of the English Working Class* (1963), the most outstanding representative of the new movement for history from below. In respect of the power of Thompson's contribution to Marxist historiography specifically, and radical historiography more generally, this chapter focuses on the debate occasioned by, on the one hand, the publication of his book and, on the other hand, his seminal contributions to two debates in the 1960s and 1970s: first, his passionate critique, in *The Peculiarities of the English* (1965), of Perry Anderson's schematic history of England; and, second, his onslaught, in *The Poverty of Theory* (1978), against the influence of Althusser on radical historiography.

Finally, I move to discuss Gerry Cohen's evolutionary Marxist response to the debate opened by Althusser and Thompson, Alasdair MacIntyre's early contribution to a debate on Thompson's work, and later attempts by Perry Anderson and Alex Callinicos to synthesise the more powerful contributions to this debate into a defensible interpretation of historical materialism.

Sartre: the existentialist revolt against mechanical materialism

The Communist Party of France (PCF) was, in the immediate post-war years, perhaps the most Stalinist of all the communist parties in Western Europe. As such it demanded that intellectuals within its ranks play two particularly unappealing roles: first, to 'twist Marxism' in any way necessary to defend the actions of the Soviet State; and second, to give a revolutionary spin to the Party's Soviet-dictated conservative practice. Party members were also expected to realise these roles within the rhetoric of Stalin's crude distortion of Marxism.[2] To many intellectuals the combination of these roles made life within the party an unappealing prospect. However, the party did maintain an appeal to intellectuals on the basis of, first, the fresh memories of its central role within the *résistance*; second, the crucial part played by Russia in the defeat of Hitler; and, third, the PCF's considerable presence within the French working class. Together, these factors meant that many radical intellectuals continued to gravitate towards the PCF in the post-war years.

Among those who felt simultaneously repulsed and attracted to the PCF in the 1940s and 1950s was Jean-Paul Sartre.[3] Sartre was first pulled into the orbit of the PCF during the period of resistance, when, as Ian Birchall argues, the party supplied the organisation demanded by the struggle against Germany. However, even at that juncture Sartre was aware that the PCF's monolithic structure was a barrier to emancipatory politics.[4] Nevertheless, he recognised, and continued to recognise after the war, that if he was to have any influence on socialist politics in France he must learn to work, if not *in*, then *with*, the PCF.[5] This relationship became strained in the immediate post-war years when the PCF played, in Sartre's words, a 'hesitant' role vis-à-vis domestic politics, while its government ministers voted for war credits to pursue the imperialist conflict in Indo-China.[6] It was this context that spurred Sartre's attempt to form an independent socialist organisation in the late 1940s. However, at a global level, the outbreak of the Cold War mediated against the success of this organisation, and many of its leading members swung quickly from positions that were independent of the communists to become rabidly anti-communist.[7] Sartre responded to this, and parallel pressures, in the early 1950s by moving to occupy a position of intellectual fellow-traveller to the PCF.[8] However, the news of Khrushchev's invasion of Hungary, and the PCF's support for that policy, forced Sartre to rethink this stance. The most important consequence of this rethink was that Sartre broke with the PCF in 1956, which he described as 'monstrous' for its defence of Russia's intervention. Sartre described the Soviet attack on Hungary as a moment when 'the concrete struggle of the masses [was] drowned in blood in the name of a pure abstraction'.[9]

This criticism is especially interesting, for it demonstrates that Sartre was not, as he is often represented to have been by his right-wing critics, a simple apologist for Stalinism,[10] while also illuminating a recurrent theme of his critique of mechanical interpretations of historical materialism. Sartre argued that crude Marxists, from whose number he generally excluded Marx himself, tended to impose on reality abstract Platonic ideals rather than base their strategic pronouncements on detailed studies of concrete historical processes. This is the thrust of one of Sartre's earliest engagements with Marxism, 'Materialism and Revolution' (1946), in which he drew a distinction between Marx and his epigones: 'Marx had a much deeper and richer conception of objectivity' than did the Stalinists. He claimed that his criticisms of Marxism in the essay were 'not directed against' Marx, but against 'Neo-Stalinist Marxism'.[11]

According to Sartre, the materialist pretensions of Stalinist Marxism acted to negate its revolutionary intent; for materialism tended towards 'the elimination of human subjectivity' from history. This was important for more than moral reasons; for if the revolutionary is defined by her 'going beyond the situation' in which she finds herself, then revolutionary politics demands that the revolutionary evolve a total comprehension of her 'situation' within society.

Consequently, for Sartre, 'revolutionary thinking is thinking within a situation; it is the thinking of the oppressed in so far as they rebel together against oppression; it cannot be reconstructed from the outside'. Revolutionary thought is therefore, first and foremost, the thinking of revolutionary activists, and cannot be equated with Stalin's contemplative materialism.[12]

Sartre repeated this theme a decade later in a prefatory essay to his *Critique of Dialectical Reason* (1960), the much less formidable *Search for a Method* (1957), in which he argued that while Marxism was 'the one philosophy of our time which we cannot go beyond', the malign influence of Stalinism meant that Marxism itself had 'stopped'. With the aim of restarting Marxism, Sartre took it on himself to 'reconquer man within Marxism' by reminding contemporary Marxists that 'men themselves make their history', despite the fact that they do so 'in a given environment which conditions them'.[13] To the extent that this project had concrete Marxist adversaries, Sartre argued that the Trotskyists, just as much as the Stalinists, were guilty of the methodological sin of dissolving real history in a bath of generalising 'sulphuric acid'.[14] Specifically, Sartre argued, in response to the Soviet invasion of Hungary, that both Trotskyists and Stalinists analysed real events through a series of *a priori* assumptions – the former assumed that the mass movement in Hungary was a socialist movement, the latter that it was fascist: 'I have not heard it said', he wrote, 'that even one Marxist changed his opinion' on hearing the news from Hungary.[15]

Against both these tendencies, Sartre reiterated his claim that revolutionary thought could advance only if it aimed at the scientific analysis of the 'projects' of free individuals to move from one concrete situation to another.[16] Sartre labelled the scientific approach to understanding this process the 'progressive–regressive method' and suggested that it involved assessing both the concrete situation in which actors found themselves, and the actions through which they aimed to move beyond that situation.[17] Interestingly, while Sartre insisted that this method involved the affirmation of the 'specificity of the historical event', he immediately introduced two transhistorical concepts into the heart of his theory of history: *scarcity* – the 'principal characteristic' of all historical struggles of exploited against exploiter[18] – and *the practico-inert*.

While Sartre had suggested, in *Search for a Method*, that scarcity is a historical concept which could be overcome in some far distant future by 'technical progress',[19] in his *Critique of Dialectical Reason* the weight of his arguments tended towards a much more pessimistic conclusion: scarcity, he argued, is the 'fundamental relation of our history': Jameson described scarcity as the 'unanalyzable starting point' of Sartre's system.[20] This starting point had dramatic consequences for Sartre's Marxism. He argued that because scarcity 'produces everyone in a multiplicity as a mortal danger for the Other', its existence implied that reciprocal relations of solidarity between individuals must, of necessity, be transient.[21] So, Sartre argued, while social atomisation may be challenged through revolutionary struggles, the 'fused groups' thus created could hope only to reproduce themselves for short periods of time before they became 'institutionalised'. Once institutionalised those groups would break down and antagonistic relations between individuals would re-emerge. Sartre labelled this type of relationship 'seriality', and suggested that this condition was the basis for the formation of states. Accordingly, he dismissed as 'absurd' the Marxist concept of dictatorship by the proletariat: for the proletariat could not possibly rule collectively.[22]

The pessimistic implications of Sartre's conception of scarcity are reinforced by his concept of the practico-inert. By this concept, Sartre means to explain the 'equivalence between alienated praxis and worked inertia'.[23] The practico-inert is, in Poster's words, 'matter which has absorbed the past actions and meanings of human beings'.[24] The practico-inert is therefore much more than the human created world around us: it is an alienated context, the product of our praxis, the 'unintended consequences' of which constantly 'thwart' and 'confound' our intentions. Sartre elaborates this concept through the example of the tree-clearing practice of Chinese peasants, one consequence of which was massive flooding. Through this example, Sartre aimed to show that while man attempted to control his environment, in fact he becomes controlled by it: he becomes 'a product of his product'.[25]

Nevertheless, as Aronson points out, Sartre fails to convince the reader that his concept of the practico-inert is of universal significance, because the production relations of the Chinese peasantry – individuals working independently but in a shared context – is 'clearly too general and timeless': 'Sartre scarcely entertains the possibility that other social groupings might organise their relations to the material field differently, and so achieve different relations to their product.'[26] This failure to delineate distinct historical moments leads Sartre to conclude, in stark contrast to the Marxist attempts at historical periodisation discussed in chapter 4, that 'in a sense there is only one pre-socialist order and that is capitalism'.[27] Indeed, his unversalisation of the concept of scarcity implied that even socialism offers no escape from seriality.[28]

Following the logic of this claim, Sartre analysed the rise of Stalinism, as Aronson points out, as an 'inevitable' consequence of the Bolshevik revolution.[29] In an attempt to justify this suggestion Sartre notes that as both Stalin and Trotsky realised, in the mid-1920s, that 'it was necessary to embark on the difficult stage of pre-socialist accumulation', it was generally accepted that something like Stalin's project of forced industrialisation was inevitable.[30] However, in opposition to mechanical economic reductionism Sartre insisted that the concrete form taken by Stalinism could be 'reduced simply' neither 'to the isolation of the first socialist country within an ensemble of capitalist powers' nor to its 'underdeveloped' nature.[31] Rather, the specific characteristics of Stalinism grew out of the struggle between Stalin and Trotsky in the 1920s. The ideology of 'socialism in one country', for instance, could best be understood as emerging concretely from Stalin's critique of Trotsky's theory of permanent revolution; other actors would have struggled using different ideological tools, and would have produced a distinct legitimising ideology for the Soviet Union.[32] In this way, Sartre hoped to explain both the necessity of Stalinism, and, contra Plekhanov's crude interpretation of the role of individuals in history, its specific features.[33]

To give a flavour of what he meant by his method of analysis, in 1956 he pointed Pierre Naville towards the discussion of the roles of Lenin and Trotsky in the October revolution as richly described in the first volume of Isaac Deutscher's biography of Trotsky (1954): 'Deutscher shows us simultaneously the objective movement of history through the historical individual and the mark made by the individual on the historical movement.'[34] To reinforce this point, and to give French readers the opportunity of reading the truth of Trotsky's role in the revolution – long censored by the Stalinists – Sartre republished the relevant chapter of Deutscher's biography in *Les Tempes Modernes* in 1957.[35] Unfortunately, despite Sartre's praise for Deutscher's detailed and scholarly method, his own forays into historical writing were much less successful.

Sartre's first work to include a deep historical dimension, *The Communists and Peace* published in *Les Tempes Modernes* between 1952 and 1954, was his attempted justification of his policy of fellow-travelling with the PCF. This perspective obviously clashed with his previous criticisms of the PCF's political 'hesitancy' in the immediate post-war context. In *The Communists and Peace* he attempted to invert his earlier appreciation of the evidence for this hesitancy: it was the working class, not the Communist Party, which had hesitated. Sartre elaborated this argument in a polemic against Ernest Mandel – a leading member of the European Trotskyist movement, then writing under the name Germain.[36] Whereas Mandel had argued that the PCF had, on a number of occasions since the Second World War, done 'violence to the instincts and the revolutionary dynamism of millions of militants', Sartre countered that it was not the PCF that was at fault, but rather Mandel's methods, which were inadequate to the task because he counterposed an 'ideal' class struggle to the 'real' struggles of the French masses.[37]

In contrast to Mandel's supposed 'idealism', Sartre maintained: 'I don't concern myself with what would be desirable nor with the ideal relationship which the party-in-itself sustains with the Eternal Proletariat; I seek to understand what is happening in France today before our very eyes.'[38] Additionally, Sartre deepened his case against Mandel by arguing that Mandel had misunderstood the relationship between party and class.

To be bourgeois, asserted Sartre, was easy; one simply had to choose the right parents and then to exist. To be proletarian, by contrast, a worker must fight against her existence: there must be a praxis, which must have an organisational form.[39] Trade unions were incapable of playing this role because they reflected the sectional interests of the workers and fought only against effects rather than with causes.[40] Sartre therefore insisted that the proletariat needed a party through which it could be constituted as a class; and furthermore that such a party must necessarily be conceived as 'authority'.[41] In fact, the party was required if political unity was to be imposed on the class: 'it is the party which demands of the masses that they come together into a class under its direction'.[42] Sartre went so far as to suggest that 'without the CP the French proletariat would not have an empirical history'.[43]

To criticise the bureaucratisation of the CP, as did Mandel, was therefore anachronistic: 'Will you speak after that of "communist betrayal"? Come off it! This "bureaucratisation" is a necessity in the period of scientific management.'[44] The politics of the PCF merely reflected the real needs and aspirations of the French workers, rather than the needs and aspirations that Mandel ascribed to them. In an attempt to defend this claim, Sartre provided a schematic overview of French history through which he aimed to make sense of the peculiarities of France's class struggle:

> I maintain that the development of capital, taken in its generality, accounts for the aspects common to all workers' movements. But these, in-principle, considerations will never of themselves explain the particular traits of the class struggle in France or England. A concrete fact . . . can be explained in its singularity only by singular reasons . . . The French proletariat is a historical reality whose singularity was made manifest in recent years by a certain attitude: I do not go looking for this attitude in the universal movement of societies, but in the movement of French society; that is to say in the history of France.[45]

While Sartre's suggestion that historical research must be empirically grounded was eminently laudable, his refusal to distinguish between the concepts of party and class meant that, in effect, he reduced his history of France to a justificatory narrative for the contemporary politics of the PCF. This form of political fatalism, as Mandel argued, seemed to sit uneasily with the stress on human freedom that characterised all of Sartre's work. Merleau-Ponty charged that it was precisely because Sartre's analysis of the relationship between party and class did not probe below the level of free action that it was innocent of a sense of how workers may move towards a socialist consciousness of their collective experience of class.[46]

Although this theoretical weakness was to reappear in Sartre's later work through the transhistorical concepts of scarcity and the practico-inert, in the immediate context of the fallout from the events of 1956 Sartre's attempts to write history were hindered by a much more mundane failings. This is evident in his *Search for a Method*, within which his own historical analysis of the various Marxist responses to the events of 1956 appeared to suffer from just the sort of dissolving, sulphuric, bath of which he was so critical in others. Specifically, his claim that no 'Marxist changed his opinion' of the Soviet regime in 1956 is simply untrue. One needs look no further than Sartre's own texts for evidence of Marxists who did change their opinions in 1956. For instance, while in *Search for a Method* he refers positively to Henri Lefebvre's 'simple and faultless method for integrating sociology and history in the perspective of a materialist dialectic', he fails to mention that Lefebvre, alongside a number of other leading communist intellectuals, either left or were expelled from the PCF as a consequence of their opposition to the Soviet invasion of Hungary.[47] In his most considered response to the events in Hungary, *The Spectre of Stalin* (1956–57), he actually referred to the journalism of Pete Fryer without mentioning that this correspondent for the British *Daily Worker* went to Hungary a Stalinist and came back a Trotskyist.[48]

More generally, as Birchall argues, because Sartre concentrated on the supposed methodological failings of all the competing Marxist interpretations of the Hungarian events, he 'evaded the real question, namely, which was the most important of the class conflicts [in Hungary]?' Sartre was thus content to conclude his analysis of the Soviet invasion with the rather trite suggestion that the truth about this act lay somewhere between the Trotskyist and Stalinist interpretations.[49] This position, as C. L. R. James argued, led Sartre, despite his own revolutionary credentials, to ignore that which was most politically important to a revolutionary analysis of Hungary: the re-emergence of workers' councils for the first time since the war.[50]

Rather than address this contemporary process, Sartre discussed the emergence of a collective revolutionary agency during the French revolution. This project, like the bulk of his historical essays, was executed through a critique of the work of other historians. The target of his criticism this time was the Trotskyist Daniel Guerin, who had produced in *La Lutte des classes sous la Premiere Republique* (1946)[51] what Sartre described as a 'fascinating' account that was 'rich in new insights'. Despite labelling Guerin 'one of the best Marxist writers' of his time, Sartre suggested that Guerin's history of the revolution 'totalizes too quickly', reducing 'the political to the social'.[52] Sartre's suggestion that crude Marxism tended to dissolve real men in a generalising bath of sulphuric acid was used directly against Guerin. However, Birchall points out, it was Sartre who jumped to conclusions a little early in this matter. Guerin had argued that in 1793 there had emerged in Paris an 'embryo of an anti-bourgeois or pre-proletarian revolution'.[53] As Norah Carlin argues, while Guerin believed that this movement was doomed to failure because of France's relative economic backwardness, his arguments were systematically distorted by communist historians who caricatured his thesis, suggesting that he believed that a successful workers' revolution was possible in France in the 1790s.[54] Birchall points to the political basis of this distortion: Guerin was a critic of, on the one hand, the Jacobins and, on the other hand, the Communists' popular front strategy of socialist unity with liberal bourgeois parties, while the Jacobins, who the Communist historians tended to eulogise, played a central part in the myth of the popular front.[55] For his part, Sartre never challenged the popular front strategy,[56] and simply repeated the standard Communist criticisms of Guerin's critique of the policies of the French middle class of the 1790s, with no suggestion of the political subtext to their arguments.[57]

Sartre accepted the Stalinist myth that Communist parties, East and West, continued to be revolutionary organisations, and that the 'stoppage' of Marxism was a consequence of the conflict between the 'revolutionary action' of the Communist movement 'and the Scholastic justification of this action'.[58] Specifically, in the second volume of the *Critique of Dialectical Reason*, which remained unfinished and unpublished in his lifetime, Sartre argued that Stalin's ideology of '"socialism in one country" was the product of revolutionary practice', because it grew out of the October revolution, and that had Trotsky led the Comintern in the early 1920s 'its policy towards the European and Asiatic Communist Parties would doubtless not have been perceptively different'. In fact, Sartre went so far as to argue that 'Stalin himself, despite innumerable acts of treachery, did still help the Chinese, Spanish etc. to the extent he believed possible'.[59]

Whatever the veracity of these claims, in making them Sartre rode roughshod over three decades of debate and analysis of Stalin's foreign policy. Sartre was able to maintain this approach only by ignoring the Marxist criticisms of the popular front strategy. Rather than analyse the subjective intentions of the actors involved in the European revolutionary upheavals of the 1920s and 1930s, he explained the failures of these movements as an inevitable consequence of the October revolution: because that revolution led to the split of the European labour movement between Communists and social democrats, the workers' movement was irretrievably damaged, such that it was incapable of threatening the power of capital.[60]

This conclusion was all too typical of the apparently fatalistic nature of many of Sartre's historiographic arguments:[61] a historical and political fatalism that appeared to leave little room for the kind of committed intellectual practice that he aimed to underpin. More intellectually damaging, however, was the failure, in Sartre's eyes at least, of his attempt to construct an intelligible total history from the chaotic interaction of individual 'projects'. As Aronson argues, Sartre construed 'individual praxis' in such a way as to negate the possibility that he would uncover any 'intrinsic links' within larger totalities. In fact, he was so opposed to 'lazy Marxist' generalisations about collective concepts, such as class, that he inverted their error and 'hypostatised' an individualist negation of class analysis.[62] A consequence of this approach was that his discussion of the degeneration of the Russian revolution collapsed under the inadequacies of his method: the discussion of the conflict between Stalin and Trotsky, as Anderson points out, 'abruptly breaks off', leaving Sartre unable to 'demonstrate how the ravaging struggles of the time generated an ultimate structural unity'.[63] So Sartre's reworking of Marx's theory of history from the point of view of the free agent eventually collapsed in the unpublished second volume of the *Critique*.

The structuralist reaction

The first volume of Sartre's *Critique* was published in 1960, two years before Claude Lévi-Strauss[64] published, in *The Savage Mind* (1962), his devastating critique of Sartre's methodology. While Sartre, in his *Critique*, had praised Lévi-Strauss's earlier work, Lévi-Strauss, as Poster argues, 'felt compelled to challenge Sartre' if he was to 'insure the victory' of his brand of structuralism over Sartre's existentialism.[65] In the event, such was the power of Lévi-Strauss's critique of existentialism, that the publication of his book marked the point of an 'abrupt shift in the French intellectual mood toward structuralism'.[66]

In *The Savage Mind* Lévi-Strauss criticised Sartre for becoming 'the prisoner of his Cogito'.[67] By this he meant that because Sartre's analysis, like Descartes's, began with 'the allegedly self-evident truths of introspection' but, unlike Descartes's, could not appeal to God to furnish him with knowledge of the universe beyond his cogito, his method, far from ensuring knowledge of the world, actually became trapped within introspection. Substantively, Lévi-Strauss argued that Sartre's concept of the practico-inert was an inadequate model of the structures within which humans live.[68] This criticism did not amount to a complete rejection of Sartre's approach, for Lévi-Strauss borrowed 'a certain amount of Sartre's vocabulary' and granted that Sartre's analysis of the French revolution was 'the richest' to date. However, he insisted that 'it does not follow that his meaning just because it is the richest should be the truest'.[69] Lévi-Strauss argued that this was the case because history, truly represented, would appear simply as 'chaos', and in their efforts to make sense of this chaos, all historians write not the truth but contemporary history. So, while he maintained that the 'anthropologist respects history', he insisted that they do 'not accord it a special value'.[70] In contrast to historiography's necessarily subjective and partial accounts of human systems, Lévi-Strauss argued that a true science could only be one which dissolved this subjectivity, decentring human intention from its study and analysing 'men as if they were ants'.[71] This method led Lévi-Strauss, according to Callinicos, to privilege 'the study of synchrony, of the universal structures underlying concrete sets of beliefs and social institutions, over the diachrony, of historical transformations', such that the subject of history is assigned 'a secondary and constituted place rather than a primary and constitutive place'.[72]

As Poster argues, Sartre's unconstructive response to Lévi-Strauss's arguments suggested something of the severe limitations with his interpretation of Marxism. For rather than confront Lévi-Strauss's rejection of the claim that history could be studied scientifically, Sartre's replies were 'often more defensive and harsh than pertinent'.[73] Some French Marxists did make more positive responses to Lévi-Strauss's challenge to historical materialism, and the dominant voice among them was that of Louis Althusser.[74] However, as Anderson argues, Althusser, 'rather than engaging with Levi-Strauss's attack on history or his interpretation of humanism, endorsed and incorporated them into Marxism'.[75]

The context in which Althusser made his contribution to Marxism was very different from that experienced by Sartre in the 1940s and 1950s. For where Sartre wrote at the height of the Cold War, Althusser wrote during a period of thaw in the relations between the superpowers. This geopolitical context was translated into French when the PCF shifted towards a much more conciliatory rhetoric in its relations with the French Government. In contrast to the period after 1947, when the Party had reacted to its exclusion from government by fostering political strikes and demonstrations, in the late 1950s and early 1960s the PCF moved to the right in an attempt to foster a working relationship with the Gaullist regime. This new perspective was given a degree of ideological respectability through the party's embrace of the ideology of socialist humanism. This increasingly moderate stance vis-à-vis the State obviously created a degree of resentment among the more militant sections of the organisation. And, in 1962, when news came of the Sino-Soviet split, it was only natural that some of the more militant members of the Party should look to the Chinese regime for leadership, especially as the critique made of the Soviet regime by the Maoists was couched in the rhetoric of a left-wing critique of the Soviet's increasingly rightward deviation from Marxism. In 1964, in one of his more extreme condemnations of the Soviet regime, Mao claimed: 'the Soviet Union today is the dictatorship of the bourgeoisie, a dictatorship of the grand bourgeoisie, and a Hitlerite dictatorship. They are a bunch of rascals.' Commenting on the intellectual merits of this passage, Harris wrote that 'Mao's "analysis" was no more than an expression of extreme irritation after the Sino-Soviet break, not the theoretical justification for the break itself'.[76] Nevertheless, whatever the provenance of Mao's critique of Khrushchev's regime, the fact of its existence created a split in the previously monolithic world of international communism, and it was in this space that Althusser wrote.

Following the Maoist critique of the 'rightward' trajectory of the Soviet regime, generally, and the Soviet's embrace of the ideology of socialist humanism, more specifically, Althusser sought to counter the Communist movement's 'over-reaction' to Stalinism through a critique of theoretical humanism.[77] Althusser rejected the humanist contention that men made history, and argued conversely that history was 'a process without a subject'.[78] According to Althusser the 'true "subjects" [of history] are . . . the relations of production'.[79] Developing this point, his collaborator, Balibar, located a series of 'invariant' elements within history – the labourer, the means of production and the non-labourer – which could be combined and recombined in various ways through two relations: the *production* process and the *exploitation* process. Balibar believed that the various combinations of the three elements and the two relations gave rise to various modes of production, and explained the transition from one mode of production to another through the changing combinations of those elements.[80] Whereas Marx had argued that history's prime mover was the force of production, Althusser and Balibar rejected any such evolutionary schema and argued that history proceeded as a series of distinct relations of production.[81]

Althusser's model of a mode of production was such that it seemed uncertain how it might give rise to change. Althusser and Balibar attempted to solve this problem by stressing Marx's distinction between a mode of production and a social formation. They argued that while the first of these was a theoretical construct, the latter referred to actual societies that existed as unique combinations of modes. Change occurred as a consequence of already existing modes, defined by their relations of production, attaining and losing dominance in a specific social formation. While this model of historical periodisation inverted Marx's theory of history, it powerfully restated the distinction between real societies and abstract modes; a distinction that is obviously suggestive of both the need for historical research into the concrete combination of modes of production within specific social formations and, conversely, of the inadequacy of any attempt to deduce Marxist strategic conclusions from *a priori* claims on the dynamic structure of any single mode of production. The elaboration of Marx's distinction between modes of production and social formations is perhaps Althusser's most positive contribution to historical materialism.[82] However, Althusser's insistence that it is changes in the relations, rather than the forces, of production that is the prime mover in history also allowed that Maoist China be characterised by socialist relations of production, irrespective of the low level of development of the forces of production. So, where scarcity, for Sartre, had acted as a universal limitation to the realisation of socialism, Althusser's approach lent support to those who wished to bypass this problem altogether.[83]

Althusser argued that whereas the Marxist humanists believed that they had overthrown crude economic reductionism, the fundamental weakness of their approach paralleled that of (Stalinist) economism: for both shared the 'leftist' error of denying the autonomy of society's various levels – the political, ideological, economic, theoretical, etc.[84] Althusser insisted that each of these levels experienced a relative autonomy, and explained the defects of Stalinism as a consequence of Stalin's failure to realise that while he had instituted socialist production at the economic level, this did not entail that the Soviet superstructure would passively follow the base to become socialist. Rather, 'the new society produced by the Revolution may itself *ensure the survival, that is, the reactivation, of older elements*'.[85]

Althusser explained the relative autonomy of each social formation's levels by means of the concept of 'overdetermination'. As I have noted, Althusser argued that both Stalin and his humanist critics shared a similarly weak model of the historical totality: Stalin, economistically, reduced the totality to the economy, while the humanists reduced it to human practice. Althusser claimed both of failings to be variants of one more generally inadequate approach to the study of history– *historicism* – and suggested that the historicist weakness of contemporary Marxism could be traced back to the influence on Marxism of Hegel's expressive conception of the social totality. Hegel's totality was expressive, Althusser argued, because each aspect of the whole expressed a central contradiction: Stalin and the humanists were historicists because they reduced the complexity of the social whole to one historical process; either economic progress or human practice. Marx's conception of the social whole was very different from this: 'it is no longer the Hegelian dialectic but a quite different dialectic'.[86] Following suggestions in Mao's *On Contradiction*, Althusser insisted that each totality is made up of a plurality of contradictions, each of which exhibits a relative autonomy from the others.[87] In contrast to the simple model of the social totality as a determined product of the economy, Althusser insisted that each relatively autonomous level 'overdetermines' all other levels. He therefore argued that 'all historical societies [are] constituted of an infinity of concrete determinations', none of which is the final determination.[88] Or, rather, the economic does determine in the last instance, but, famously, 'the lonely hour of the "last instance" never comes'.[89]

If the totality is defined as a series of independent levels, none of which determine the others, it is difficult to see how society can be conceived as a totality rather than simply as a chaotic collection of practices. Althusser attempted to answer this criticism through his concept of conjuncture, or 'ruptural unity'. He described such a unity as a point at which 'an accumulation of "circumstances" and "currents"' allows one of society's contradictions to 'become "active" in the strongest sense' such that the various levels 'fuse' into a 'single national crisis'.[90] Althusser thus explained the Russian revolution, not as an extreme manifestation of a general contradiction, but as an 'exceptional situation', that was explicable only as a unique fusion of a multiplicity of contradictions.[91]

Whatever the strengths of this model, and it is clear that it opens the door to a detailed study of concrete historical moments,[92] it is also apparent that it includes one fundamental failing, a failing that was to have dire consequences for Althusserianism after 1968. The main strength of Althusser's model lay in his powerful stress on the role of 'structural causality' in history. By this he meant to explain historical processes by analysing the changing interrelationship among 'structural relations'. In contrast to both the traditional mechanical model of causality and the Hegelian essentialist model of causality, he argued that historical transitions occurred as a consequence of shifts within the social formation's structures which were simultaneously the cause and the effect of change.[93] While this model obviously lent itself to the explanation of certain historical processes – for instance Guy Bois's analysis of the dynamic of feudal society is informed by it,[94] Althusser's rejection of any form of humanism meant that his model of history was of little use as a guide to political action: Poster has labelled it a form of 'cosmic fatalism'.[95]

Despite his stated aim of improving on Stalin's fatalist interpretation of Marx's theory of history, Althusser's alternative tends to a similar error.

In the context of the low level of class struggle in France in the early to mid-1960s, the implications of this error were somewhat hidden. However, with the explosion of human agency in the mass movement of 1968, the inadequacies of Althusser's system were revealed. As one of Althusser's students explained:

> In this conjuncture, the political significance of Althusserianism was shown to be quite different from what we had thought. Not only did the Althusserian theoretical presuppositions prevent us from understanding the political meaning of the student revolt. But further, within a year we saw Althusserianim serving the hacks of revisionism in a theoretical justification for the 'anti-leftist' offensive and the defence of academic knowledge.[96]

Additionally, while the events of 1968 exposed Althusser's inability to theorise human agency, it became increasingly apparent that his conception of 'ruptural unity' was inadequate to the attempt to theorise society as a totality. This was the conclusion reached by one of the few historians to engage theoretically with Althusser's oeuvre. Pierre Vilar argued that one of the great strengths of Marx's insistence that capitalism be analysed as a totality, was that it informed radical historiography's critique of the empiricism and pluralism that emerged spontaneously from the specialised structure of the academy. Althusser's model of overdetermination, he suggested, necessarily implied the return 'to a division of history into so many "histories"'.[97] Hence Vilar located himself in the idiosyncratic position of a historian who criticised a philosopher of history for the empiricist and pluralist implications of his theory.[98]

Developing a similar critique, Peter Osborne argued that because each level within Althusser's system operates along a differential temporality, there was 'no common time' through which those levels may be united. Consequentially, Althusser's system makes it impossible to imagine 'the transition from one mode of production to another', because he rules out 'any conception of the development of the whole as a whole'.[99] Althusser therefore had not only followed the structuralists in decentring man from history, he now seemed to prefigure the post-structuralist denial of totality and meta-narrative. As Perry Anderson has argued, when Althusser 'radicalised' Lévi-Strauss's anti-humanism it was almost certain that someone would come along, as Foucault did, to announce the 'full-throated "end of man"'.[100] French Marxism appeared to have run out of steam at just the moment, in 1968, when a mass strike of French workers appeared to suggest that Marxism was more relevant than it had been for a generation. From that moment, as Paris moved from structuralism to post-structuralism, it was in the Anglophone world that the most powerful contributions to the Marxist theory of history were made.

Edward Thompson: the reassertion of agency

In the 1950s the political bipolarity of the Cold War was refracted within organised working-class politics in Britain through the Communist and Labour Parties, with the latter, then as now, maintaining a position of hegemony on the British left. However, this position did not go unchallenged; in particular the CPGB, while much smaller than the PCF, positioned itself as the left opposition to Labour. Unsurprisingly, the CP had long since proved its willingness to perform any number of elaborate political contortions at the behest of its mentors in Moscow, while, more counter-intuitively, the Labour Party leadership had developed a parallel relationship with Washington. This situation was, of course, unconducive to the development of an independent left capable of articulating a political programme that went beyond Cold War dualism.

The Asia–Africa Conference at Bandung in 1955 provided the first sign of an alternative to this bipolar worldview. At that conference what later became known as the 'Third World' declared itself for the first time as a major independent player in world affairs. If that event opened a crack in the world order, the events of 1956 – Khrushchev's secret speech, his invasion of Hungary and the Anglo-French invasion of Egypt – together created a space for widespread criticism of the world order as a whole. In striking deep at the heart of the international system these events opened a space from which independent political forces could emerge in Britain. As a response a 'New Left' was born which sought to map a third way between the West and the East, and their left-wing political allies: social democracy and Stalinism. Two journals, the *New Reasoner* and the *Universities and Left Review*, which were to merge in 1959 to form *New Left Review* (*NLR*), represented the most visible signs of the new space created on the English political scene. However, while the events of 1956 marked the point at which an independent left first emerged in post-war Britain, it was a further eighteen months or so before a movement erupted that offered this milieu the opportunity to test its politics against those of the Labour and Communist Parties. The force that brought a new generation of activists onto the streets, and then into the New Left's meeting rooms, was CND, whose marches from early 1958 saw thousands of the dissatisfied youth come into conflict, not only with the Government but with the leaderships of the Labour and Communist Parties.[101]

Unfortunately, despite its early promise, by 1962 the New Left was – in Britain at any rate – a spent force.[102] At that point the editorial board of *NLR* broke up, and a new generation led by Perry Anderson took the helm. One of Anderson's short-term goals was to explain the demise of the New Left, so as to help overcome its limitations. The vehicle through which he executed this project was a *schematic* history of England. Anderson's hope was that through this history, which was informed by the work of Sartre, Lukács and

Gramsci, he might make sense of the weaknesses of the English left relative to its European counterparts. However, Anderson's history, *Origins of the Present Crisis* (1964), provoked the anger of Edward Thompson and sparked the first instalment of a two-part contest between Thompson and Anderson that was to dominate the Anglophone debate on historical materialism for the next two decades.[103]

As I pointed out in chapter 4, Anderson argued that England had 'had the first, most mediated, and least pure bourgeois revolution of any major European country', the 'ideological legacy' of which was 'almost nil'.[104] In the wake of that revolution, England industrialised in a period when the threat of Napoleon, coupled with that of a rising working class, pushed the leadership of the bourgeoisie towards a rapprochement with the capitalist aristocracy; and those two classes thereafter fused to form a new ruling class.[105] A malign consequence of that fusion was that the bourgeoisie ended its crusade against aristocratic privilege and sold its birthright for title and land. It was able to do so because, while the aristocracy was not a bourgeoisie, it was a capitalist class: 'no fundamental antagonistic contradiction between the old aristocracy and the new bourgeoisie' existed.[106] In this, Anderson suggested, lay 'the most important single key to modern English history'.

The corollary of England's early industrialisation was the growth of the world's first proletariat. Unfortunately, this proletariat was 'premature', for it had developed before an indigenous socialism had time to mature. Too early for Marx, the English workers were intellectually ill-equipped to take on the British State in the great battles of Chartism. Tragically, therefore, Chartism ended in defeat. After 1848 there was a 'caesura' in British working-class life, so that when proletarian militancy did again spring up at the end of the century the key beneficiary was Labourism, not Marxism.[107] Next, imperialism swept all classes and parties along in its train, ideologically incorporating them into the aristocratic worldview.[108]

Anderson stressed that, alone of the European states, England had suffered no defeat or revolution between 1914 and 1945. Ironically, the defeats suffered by the other European powers, coupled with their experience of revolutionary upheaval, led to the modernisation of those states. While all around were modernised, England was never forced to break with the past. The resultant continuation of the hegemony of the aristocracy, Anderson suggested, was reflected in the choice of the Conservatives rather than the Liberals as the natural party of government in the twentieth century. While England's economic base had been transformed over the previous few centuries, its superstructure remained intact. The economy was a bastion of industrial capitalism, but the aristocracy had managed through a cumulative series of conjunctures to maintain its hegemony over the whole of society. Workers, meanwhile, had been industrially militant, but had never challenged for leadership of the State: they were 'separate but subordinate'.[109]

As I noted in the chapter 4, Edward Thompson (1924–1993)[110] made a powerful critique of the normative structure of this thesis in his essay 'The Peculiarities of the English' (1965).[111] Substantively, Thompson criticised Anderson's model of England's seventeenth-century revolution. While he agreed with Anderson that the revolution had been made by landowners, he insisted that those aristocrats were in fact a 'superbly successful and self-confident capitalist class',[112] who had influenced the production of, in Adam Smith's political economy, a distinctive and cogent ideology.[113] Thompson argued that the English revolution had, as one of its main consequences, the settlement of 1688, which both facilitated capitalist development, and did so in a framework that was flexible enough to survive for a century-and-a-half. Then, in 1832, those small capitalists who had been excluded from the original agreement, but who had since grown in stature, were incorporated into a new settlement that restored the original's 'flexibility'.[114] As to the issue of the supposed dominance of an aristocratic ideology, Thompson directed Anderson's attention to Bagehot's description of the royal family as a 'retired widow and an unemployed youth'. This 'cynicism' and 'self confidence', he argued, exemplified 'emasculated bourgeois republicanism in England'.[115]

However, it was Anderson's conceptualisation of class that more than any other element of his thesis outraged Thompson: Anderson, he wrote, tended to clothe classes 'throughout in anthropomorphic imagery'.[116] He flattened the struggles for hegemony that had occurred within the proletariat into an overarching unity, within which Labourism was never seriously challenged. Class, perceived as a unified *it*, had two immediate consequences for Anderson's work: first, it enabled him to ignore the real struggles for hegemony that had taken place between reformists and revolutionaries within the British labour movement over the preceding century; second, it permitted him to read-off the attitudes of the mass of workers from the ideologies of their leaders in the Labour Party and trade-union movement.[117] As a consequence of this method, 'history is flattened, stretched, condensed; awkward facts are not mentioned; awkward decades are simply elided', in the pursuit of an untenable argument. So, while Thompson did not deny that Labourism was hegemonic within the English working class, he did deny that this hegemony was written in stone. In particular, he took offence at Anderson's dismissal of the existence of minority socialist traditions within the English proletariat.[118] In contrast to Anderson's schematic history, which had the effect of misrepresenting crucial periods of struggle, Thompson maintained that 'we can only describe the social process . . . by writing history'.[119] From that standpoint, Anderson's schema was particularly debilitating because he was reluctant to seriously investigate any of the periods of working-class resistance that he briefly mentioned. For Thompson, the schematic structure of Anderson's history, by focusing on overarching themes, tended to act as an objectivist apologia for the status quo. The schematic structure of his thesis was therefore not a forgivable vice, given the overall nature of his work; rather it masked a further shift towards an idealism in which the past was not simply viewed through the lens of the present, but was constructed from the ideologies of the present with scant regard for accuracy. Anderson's schematic method therefore led to 'reductionism' whereby there occurred a 'lapse in historical logic by which political or cultural events are "explained" in terms of the class affiliation of the actors'.[120]

Anderson's reply to Thompson, *Socialism and Pseudo-Empiricism*, was ostensibly an aggressive defence of his own model of English social development against Thompson's criticisms. However, in the text he both acknowledged the implicit idealism to be found in *Origins of the Present Crisis*, and noted that there were signs of 'a counter idealistic trend within European Marxism of a potentially comparable strength and sophistication' to the earlier tradition on which he had drawn: 'Althusser's work has this promise'. While it is doubtful that Anderson ever wholly adopted Althusserianism – he followed the remarks just quoted with the caveat that Althusser's system could be criticised on account of its borrowings from idealist systems[121] – Elliott is right to suggest that Anderson's *NLR* could be characterised, between 1968 and 1970, 'as politically quasi-Maoist and theoretically neo-Althusserian'.[122] Nevertheless, by 1972 at the latest, Anderson had been convinced of Althusser's idealism by, among others, Norman Geras and Andre Glucksmann.[123] In an anonymous introduction to the latter's essay, originally published in 1972, Anderson argued that Glucksmann's analysis of Balibar's conceptualisation of mode of production 'reveals insurmountable gaps and contradictions within it'.[124] Glucksmann had shown that Althusser's method was an 'amphibology: a terminological round trip that never leaves its conceptual starting point except in its own imagination'.[125]

Whatever the merit of this argument, it is apparent that by the 1970s *NLR* was no longer an Althusserian journal. Irrespective of this development, Thompson's growing anger at the influence of Althusser on the British left, generally, and within Anglophone historiography, more specifically, led him to extend his earlier polemic against Anderson's schematic historiography to a general critique of Althusserian Marxism, within which category he subsumed Anderson and the *NLR*. The result was Thompson's passionate defence of the historian's craft against any reductionist methodology: *The Poverty of Theory* (1978).

Thompson argued in *The Poverty of Theory* that Althusser came 'not to offer to modify [Marxism] but to displace it'.[126] Althusser's epistemology, he argued, 'consists of an idealist mode of theoretical construction' that created a 'self-generating conceptual universe which imposes its own ideality upon the phenomena of material and social existence, rather than engaging in a continual dialogue with these'.[127] Althusser confused 'empirical procedures, empirical controls, with something he calls empiricism'.[128] By contrast, historical materialism, Thompson observed, 'differs from other interpretive orderings of historical evidence not (or not necessarily) in any epistemological premises, but in its categories, its characteristic hypotheses and attendant procedures'.[129]

Thompson contended that Althusserianism was built on the weaker elements of Marx's thought: in *Capital* Marx deployed historical concepts to explain capitalism, while in the *Grundrisse* his thought remained trapped within the static structure of political economy.[130] It was from within this second tradition that Althusser arose: 'Althusser and his colleagues seek to thrust historical materialism back into the prison of the categories of Political Economy'.[131] Thompson saw an ancestor of Althusser's structuralism in Stalin's *Marxism and Linguistics*, and Althusserianism was, like Stalin's Marxism, a static system which could not begin to understand history as a process: it was, he argued with characteristic directness, 'unhistorical shit'.[132] Against this form of structuralism, Thompson remarked, 'I feel myself revert to the poetry of voluntarism'.[133] Thompson argued that Marxists should move from the scientific and static analysis of capital to the historical analysis of capitalism.[134] To make this leap, the historical materialist method ought to have at its heart the aim of analysing the intentions of actors in real historical time. And as individuals understand their experiences through culture – the middle term between capitalism and the individual – Marxists were asked to prioritise the analysis of this sphere in their theoretical work.[135]

Thompson's reinsertion of human agency into the centre of Marxist theory was nowhere clearer than in *The Making of the English Working Class* (1963). In the Preface to this masterpiece, he defended his book's 'clumsy title' with the claim that through it he was seeking to convey the sense of class formation as 'an active process, which owes as much to agency as to conditioning'. He noted that his title referred to the working class rather than to the more 'descriptive term' working *classes*, because the former term's analytical power would allow him to explain history as a process. However, in contrast to Stalinist Marxism, he defined class 'not as a "structure", nor even as a "category", but as something which in fact happens (and can be shown to have happened) in human relationships'. While 'class experience is largely determined by the productive relations into which men are born . . . [c]lass consciousness is the way in which these experiences are handled in cultural terms'. So, where class experience is 'determined', class consciousness is not. This humanist framework allowed Thompson, first, to reject crude Stalinist deductions of class consciousness from class location; and, second, to examine human action in its own terms, with the hope that the participants even in failed struggles will help teach us something of the 'social evils which we have yet to cure'. This latter point is used to justify the memorable passage in which he notes his aim of rescuing 'the poor stockinger, the Luddite cropper, the "obsolete" handloom weaver, the "utopian" artisan, and even the deluded follower of Joanna Southcott, from the enormous condescension of posterity'.[136] In contrast to many of the 'historians from below' who have followed his lead, Thompson's democratic methodology had nothing in common with academic specialisation.[137] Rather, he aimed to unearth the stories of human struggles for freedom with the goal of informing contemporary socialist practice. In that sense, his work has more in common with C. L. R. James's *The Black Jacobins* (1938) than it does with much modern history from below. For its execution recalls James's aim, in his magnificent book, not of writing of African slaves as mere victims, but of recording their actions as conscious fighters for freedom in even the worst conditions.[138]

Thompson's characterisation of Althusserianism cannot be divorced from this project generally and his own break with Stalinism more specifically. So, when he asked which group had been the target of Althusser's attack, and found that it was the socialist humanists, he concluded his critique of Althusserianism with the claim that it had emerged 'as a manifestation of a general police action within ideology, as the attempt to reconstruct Stalinism at the level of theory'.[139] While Thompson confused his own form of socialist humanism with the much less progressive form espoused by the leadership of the PCF in the 1960s, the power of his defence of the role of agency in history, and the need for historians to engage with that agency cannot be underestimated. Interestingly, despite his call for the accurate portrayal of the intensions of agents in history, his mistaken conflation of Althusser's critique of PCF humanism with his own was matched by an equally inept insistence that the *NLR* and Anderson were guilty of the same crimes against historiography as was Althusser. Whatever the veracity of this claim, Thompson once again threw down the gauntlet to Anderson and his collaborators.

Anderson: a flawed synthesis

Perry Anderson's[140] response to this challenge, *Arguments within English Marxism* (1980), was a much less polemical work than had been his rejoinder to Thompson's earlier critique of his work *Socialism and Pseudo-Empiricism* (1966). It was through this medium that he attempted to synthesise the insights suggested by both Althusser's structuralist Marxism and Thompson's voluntarist alternative. Further, while *Arguments* was written as a theoretical and political response to Thompson's critique of Althusserianism, Anderson wrote it at a moment when his own understanding of Marxism was evolving. For, by the late 1970s, he had moved from his earlier flirtations with Althusserianism to embrace the more orthodox interpretation of historical materialism associated with the work of G. A. Cohen.

Cohen's interpretation of Marxism is characterised by its analytically rigorous defence, in his *Karl Marx's Theory of History: A Defence* (1978), of two key propositions: first, 'the forces of production tend to develop throughout history (the developmental thesis)'; and, second, 'the nature of the production relations of a society is explained by the level of development of its productive forces (the primacy thesis)'.[141] This version of Marxism has something in common with Darwinian evolutionism, in that they both offer functionalist accounts of historical transformations.[142] Beyond criticisms of the application of evolutionary models to cultural history,[143] two problems with Cohen's method are to be noted. First, in defending the proposition that the forces of production develop over time Cohen is committed to elaborating some reason for this. In this respect he assumes that human agents will find it rational to develop those forces of production over time: 'Men are . . . somewhat rational. The historical situation of men is one of scarcity. Men possess intelligence of a kind and degree which enables them to improve their situation.'[144] Thus Cohen commits himself to accepting what Wright *et al.* call a 'transhistorical' model of human rationality.[145] Cohen is also compelled to address a conjunctural political problem for his Marxism that did not exist for his nineteenth-century predecessors: his hypothesis appears to have been refuted by history even before it was written. The Russian and Chinese revolutions, among others, occurred on the basis of relatively low levels of the development of the forces of production, while Western Europe and America have, thus far at least, survived the socialist threat, despite having much higher levels of technological advancement. Unfortunately, Cohen never adequately deals with this problem for his Marxism.[146] This lacuna led Callinicos to argue that as the 'inevitability of revolution is almost a *reductio*' of Cohen's reinterpretation of historical materialism, the very fact that history is much more complex than this model allows suggests that his 'recasting of Marxism is untenable'.[147] Nevertheless, despite the power of their criticisms of Cohen's reinterpretation of Marxism, both Callinicos and Wright *et al.* accept that his book is 'the most sustained defence' of what the latter call 'classical' Marxism, and Callinicos labels 'orthodox historical materialism' – but is perhaps more properly understood as an updated version of the Marxism of Kautsky's *The Materialist Conception of History*.[148] It was the very power of this reinterpretation of historical materialism that so attracted Anderson in the late 1970s.[149]

Anderson engaged in his role as mediator between Thompson and Althusser from a position greatly influenced by Cohen. *Arguments* opens with the ironic comment that while Thompson was perhaps the greatest historian of his generation and Althusser's work was marked by a paucity of historical insight, Althusser had formulated the problem of the nature of history far more clearly than had Thompson. Whereas Thompson equated history with the past *per se*, Althusser, more clearly, argued that a historical fact was one that caused change within existing structural relations.[150] It was towards a comprehension of such social change that Anderson then turned.

Anderson developed his account of social change through a critique of Thompson's magnum opus *The Making of the English Working Class*. He criticised the book at three levels. First, he argued that it was marred by the idealistic thesis of 'co-determination', by which Thompson argued that the working class 'made itself as much as it was made'; second, Thompson mistakenly had equated class 'in and through' class consciousness; and, third, Thompson had implied that the process of working-class formation had, essentially, been 'completed by the early 1830s'.[151]

Anderson's critique of Thompson's theory of co-determination is perhaps the most persuasive of the three points. For despite Thompson's claim that class formation was an equal product of both objective and subjective circumstances, in practice he left largely unexamined the structural side of the structure–agency couplet and hence proposed a thesis that could not be 'adjudicated' on, given the evidence cited in his book. Anderson noted several contextual elements that Thompson had left largely unexplored, including the impact of the French and American revolutions, the commercial nature of London and the 'spearhead sectors of the industrial revolution'.

Anderson's criticism of Thompson's equation of class with class consciousness, centred on the claim that Thompson had made abusive generalisation from a peculiar history that could lead to voluntarist and subjectivist deviations from materialism. Against Thompson's model of class, Anderson cited Cohen's 'fundamental work', of 'exemplary clarity and subtlety', which was 'unlikely to need further restatement'.[152] Third, in contrast to Thompson's implied claim that the making of the English working class had been closed in 1832 Anderson called for an analysis of the re-making of that class.[153] The thrust of Anderson's critique of Thompson's theorisation of class was against the idealistic and voluntarist drift that he detected in Thompson's work, and towards a restatement of the materialist insights of Marx which, he believed, Althusser had stressed and Cohen had formulated best. Practically, this meant that Anderson took issue with Thompson's approach to the problem of intentionality.

Thompson's model of class, Anderson argued, implied a 'rehearsal' of Sartre's attempt to construct a model of ordered social relations based on the interaction of a multiplicity of individual intentional praxes. However, as Sartre's *Critique of Dialectical Reason* had unsuccessfully attempted to theorise society thus, in presuming such a framework, Thompson was assuming an untenable account of the structure of social order. By contrast, Anderson argued, 'the problem of social order is irresolvable so long as the answer is sought at the level of intention . . . it is and must be the dominant mode of production that confers a fundamental unity on a social formation'.[154] Anderson insisted that Cohen had produced an interpretation of historical materialism 'whose intellectual force supersedes virtually all previous discussion . . . a fundamental work'.[155]

Cohen argued that the transition from one mode of production to another was always a consequence of the realisation of the structural conflict between forces and relations of production. As the forces of production developed, the relations of production, which once had facilitated their expansion, slowly began to impede further development. From then onwards people acted rationally to transform the social relations through revolution.[156] Anderson agreed that the 'most fundamental of all mechanisms of social change, according to historical materialism, are the systemic contradictions between forces and relations of production, not just social conflicts between classes generated by antagonistic relations of production alone'.[157] He claimed that this stress on structure was characteristic of Althusser's rather than Thompson's Marxism:

> Althusser's unilateral and remorseless stress on the overpowering weight of structural necessity in history corresponds more faithfully to the central tenets of historical materialism, and to the actual scientific study of the past – but at the price of obscuring the novelty of the modern labour movement and attenuating the vocation of revolutionary socialism. Thompson's passionate sense of the potential of human agency to shape the collective conditions of life, on the other hand, is much closer to the political temper of Marx and Engels themselves in their own time – but tends to be projected backwards as a uniform weft of the past, in defiance of the millennial negations of self determination in the kingdom of necessity.[158]

The problem that Marxism needed to face, as Anderson saw it, was of how to synthesise these two elements, the voluntaristic and the structural, into a viable interpretation of historical materialism.

Anderson attempted a solution to this puzzle through an analysis of the Marxist concept of agency. While Thompson's *oeuvre* centred on the 'key organising theme' of agency, he had, unfortunately, left this concept unelaborated, and as a consequence his model of active agency elided over three distinct connotations, understood in terms of the goals aimed at by active agents. These three types of goal included agents acting to realise private goals, for example marriage, or public goals that did not seek to remodel social relations, for example wars and diplomacy. However, it was with the third type of agency that Anderson was most concerned – the 'collective project' of the 'conscious creating or remodelling of all social structures'. By contrast with Thompson's elision, Anderson argued, the concept of a collective and transformative agency could be retained 'even on rigorously determinist premises' as 'conscious, goal directed activity'. However, this was possible only if the nature of the goals aimed at, and around which 'everything turns', were themselves analysed.[159] Hence, Anderson sought to elaborate on the distinctive nature of the goal of socialism, so that he could better conceptualise the novelty of socialist agency.

Anderson argued that the new type of agency, inaugurated by the Russian revolution, had 'premonitions' in the agencies involved in 'political colonisation, religious heterodoxy or literary utopia in earlier centuries'. More specifically, the French and American revolutions were 'the first historical figurations of agency in this, decisive sense'. The specificity of the Bolshevik revolution lay in the way in which it was led by individuals who believed themselves to be possessed of a scientific understanding of the social world that enabled them to *predict* the revolution: in contrast, the American and

French revolutions began as 'largely spontaneous explosions'.[160] Lenin and Trotsky could be differentiated from Robespierre and Washington in that, among other attributes, the former, by contrast with the latter, were aware, in advance, that they aimed to transform social relations. The specificity of the socialist project could best be understood as the scientifically predicted transformation of social structures. This formulation of the concept of socialist agency allowed Anderson formally to agree with Marx, that socialism was predicated on a novel type of agency, while simultaneously redefining this novel model of socialist agency so that it could encompass both the Eastern European and Chinese experiences. Anderson's mentor, Isaac Deutscher, had explicitly noted that while Marx had insisted that socialism could only be built upon a new form of agency, his equation of socialism with proletarian self-emancipation could not be maintained if it were accepted that the Eastern bloc and China were in some sense socialist: 'The old Bolsheviks . . . believed in revolution from below . . . The revolution now carried into eastern Europe was primarily a revolution from above.'[161] Following a similar line of argument, Anderson replaced Marx's claim, that socialism could be the product only of self-conscious proletarian agency, with the suggestion that it was the consciousness of the goal that was of prime importance to the socialist project, not the proletarian character of the agency itself.

Following Timpanaro, Anderson's alternative to Thompson's 'voluntaristic' model of agency was intended not to collapse into fatalism, but rather to insist that a cognitive element should be added to the aspirational element in Thompson's account: 'the attainment of communism [is] not only a product of will, but equally and indivisibly of knowledge'.[162] The knowledge to which Anderson refers includes both that of the goal of socialism itself, and the parameters within which material conditions – the development of the forces of production – allow agents to realistically actualise their aspirations.

Whatever the power of this assessment of Thompson's model of agency, Anderson was unable to outline a coherent materialist alternative to it that was free of both fatalism and voluntarism. He introduced his discussion of agency by noting that the concept had 'two opposite connotations. It signifies at once active initiator and passive instrument.'[163] His discussion of agency, as we have seen, then followed Thompson in stressing the former of these associations. Unfortunately, where Thompson had elided over the differing goals of human agency, Anderson makes his own elision between two connotations of active agency as, first, goal-directed activity, and, second, the concrete embodiment of such activity. While Thompson may have made some confused comments regarding the nature of the goals aimed at by agents, his discussion was aimed at uncovering the real processes whereby working people had in faltering, mediated and never complete ways attempted to 'become' a collective agent of change through historical processes of struggle.[164] Whatever the undoubted merits of Anderson's critique of Thompson's voluntarism, he nowhere addresses this, the most salient feature of his work. This is the key elision in Anderson's discussion of the concept of agency. For in the 1980s, he essentially accepted an anthropomorphic conceptualisation of class that rendered it unnecessary that he discuss the contested processes through which activists inside the workers' movement, operating in circumstances that were more or less conducive to their success, fought with varying degrees of success to make class agencies: his model, as Kaye points out, 'fail[s] to pose the . . . issue of class formation'.[165]

This failing became apparent in Anderson's re-engagement with his analysis, first developed in *Origins of the Present Crisis*, of the British working class. In 'The Figures of Descent' (1987), as in *Origins*, Anderson maintained that the British working class had experienced a 'deep caesura' between Chartism and the emergence of the Labour Party. He explained the shift from the two types of politics as a reflection of the changing structure of the English working class. Artisans and hand-workers dominated an economy up to 1848 in which 'the machine driven factory was the most advanced rather than the most typical unit': It was only in the second half of the nineteenth century that there emerged the modern labour movement forged in factory production.[166] This new movement was characterised by a profound schizophrenia, one which had not afflicted its predecessor: politics and economics were tightly separated.

The specificity of the new English working class lay in the contrast between its high degree of 'industrial organisation' compared with its exceptionally weak 'political project'. Politically, 'British labour as an organised force was a captive client of the Liberal party down to the end of the century after which the Labour Party grew as part of the liberal revival.'[167] Subsequently, Labour's path to power was no road of its own making: the First World War destroyed the Liberal Party, while the Second World War created the conditions for massive state intervention. The smooth transfer of power to the Conservatives in 1951 showed just how little the Labour Party had affected the 'structures of Britain's imperial economy'.[168]

As Looker argues, 'read as an account of the Labour Party there is little new or original here – Miliband's *Parliamentary Socialism* mapped this terrain decades ago'. However, Anderson went beyond Miliband, in assuming that Labourism set the 'structural limits to working-class consciousness and activity'.[169] Whereas previous Marxist analyses of the English working class had shown the impossibility of the Labour Party seriously challenging the status quo, Anderson deepened this thesis, to dismiss the potential of English working-class anti-capitalism. This dismissal is premised on the claim that 'the English 1848 closed a history'.[170] By this he meant to suggest that the political and organisational legacy of Chartism was almost nil: the new factory proletariat had no use for the old ideology. What is striking, therefore, about Anderson's analysis of Labourism is the way that it is, first, founded on a mechanical model of the relationship of consciousness to industrial structure, while, second, it is equated, anthropomorphically, with the politics of the working class itself. The two are, of course, intimately related: for if Labourism is the natural politics of a certain industrial structure, then to describe the history of the Labour Party is to describe the history of the working class.

This conceptualisation of the nature of the English working class as an essentially passive reflection of England's social structures is built on his reading of Cohen's critique of Thompson's conceptualisation of social class. In the second of his general criticisms of *The Making of the English Working Class* Anderson, as I noted above, rejected what he perceived to be Thompson's conflation of the concepts of class and class consciousness, and supported that rejection with the claim that Cohen's 'concept of class as an objective relation to the means of production, independent of will or attitude, is unlikely to need further reinstatement'.[171] Anderson's argument in 'The Figures of Descent' appears to be that his outline of the objective coordinates of England's social structure is sufficient to explain the nature of the consciousness of England's proletariat: 'The British Labour movement never exhibited one unchanging essence; but nor did it display indefinite variation. Through every transformation and vicissitude, its history developed within a set of structural limits that placed strict bounds on its identity. The modern form of that binding has been Labourism.'[172] Interestingly, this mechanical reading of the relationship between social structure, class and class consciousness goes beyond even Cohen's, for whom the phrase 'making of the English working class' was acceptable, despite his criticisms of Thompson, so long as it was meant to connote the process whereby the English working class moved from being a class in itself to acting as a class for itself, rather than connoting the process whereby the class itself was made.[173] Anderson, in as much as he neither traced the processes of the ebb and flow of socialist class consciousness within the English proletariat nor discussed the possibility of such a development, appeared to have moved beyond even the objectivism of Cohen to accept a crudely mechanical explanation of the relationship of social structure to political consciousness: in effect, inverting Thompson's voluntarism rather than correcting it. As Bob Looker argued, 'Anderson . . . has failed to grasp what Thompson's analysis of the English working class clearly demonstrated; the issue isn't a matter of conceptual distinctions but of real movements rising through class practice'.[174]

MacIntyre and Callinicos: towards a synthesis of structure and agency[175]

Unfortunately, despite the power of *The Poverty of Theory*, there was a somewhat quixotic character to Thompson's polemic: for, not only did he erroneously tax Althusser with adhering to theoretical positions against which he had been among the sternest critics, but he denounced others as Althusserians who had previously developed critiques of Althusserianism similar to his own.[176] Moreover, as is evident in Thompson's deployment in his mature work of the concept of 'desire', this lax attitude to theoretical concerns had a malign consequence for his strategic thought.[177] Anderson has pointed out that as it was used by Thompson in the second edition of *William Morris* (1977), the meaning of 'desire' had a genealogy that could be traced back to the post-Althusserian, post-structuralist, Parisian left, against which, a year later, he was to tangentially polemicise in *The Poverty of Theory*.[178] Anderson was quick to spot this incoherence, responding to Thompson's claim that Morris's moral theory could never be fully 'assimilated to Marxism' as 'one may not assimilate desire to knowledge', with the argument that for Marx '"knowledge" was itself a fundamental and illimitable human "desire"'.[179] Against Thompson's confused borrowing of this concept from the post-structuralists, Anderson insisted that neither socialism generally nor Marxism specifically has 'anything to gain from traffic' with any concept that posited the origin of the state in 'the masochistic "desire" to be dominated'.[180] Quite so; however, the irony with this argument is that Anderson was to an extent tilting at his own windmills. For while Thompson slipped into 'Parisian irrationalism' with his deployment of the concept of 'desire' in the Postscript to *William Morris*, elsewhere he had attempted to build on a much more historically rooted reading of this concept. In his 1973 essay 'An Open Letter to Leszek Kolakowski', he had endeavoured to underpin his strategic thought with theoretical foundations borrowed from Alasdair MacIntyre's deployment of 'desire' in his early essay 'Notes from the Moral Wilderness'.[181]

In that essay MacIntyre had attempted to outline a preliminary Marxist critique of both Stalinist defenders and liberal critics of the Soviet Union by developing a specifically Marxist approach to morality. He had sought to imbue the concept of 'desire' with precisely the 'clear and observable meaning' that Anderson later demanded of Thompson.[182] Unfortunately, Anderson, in his critique of Thompson's Marxism, chose to ignore this aspect of the genealogy of Thompson's use of the concept. Among the unwritten reasons for this dismissal can perhaps be counted MacIntyre's move away from Marxism in the late 1960s, which Anderson took as a clear sign of the dangers of 'rightism' in the moral critique of the generation of 1956.[183] This dismissive stance was only reinforced by the publication of the first edition of MacIntyre's magnum opus *After Virtue* (1981), which, despite its great strengths, could easily be disregarded by the left because of its concluding despair at the possibility of building a moral community in the modern world. However, the Marxist left's dismissal of MacIntyre's early Marxist works is unfortunate, for MacIntyre's engagement with Thompson's analysis of Stalinism points to a method through which structure and agency can be synthesised in a defensible reinterpretation of historical materialism.

Thompson made his first, and most developed, critique of Stalinism in his essay 'Socialist Humanism: An Epistle to the Philistines' (1957).[184] This was his attempt to theorise his break, a year earlier, with the CPGB. In effect it acted as a locus for debate within the New Left on the nature of Stalinism. The essay opened with the claim that 'a quarter of the earth's surface is a new society, with a new economic structure, new social relations, and new political institutions'.[185] However, despite the novelty of these social relations, oppression in many varied forms continued as a reality of life in those states: the persistence of oppression, despite the suppression of private property, convinced Thompson of the falsity of the traditional Marxist view that all forms of oppression were rooted in economic exploitation.[186] Against such 'economistic' models of historical materialism Thompson sought to re-emphasise human agency at the heart of his Marxism, and in particular to reaffirm the importance of ideas as the basis for action. This reinterpretation of Marxism allowed him to conceptualise both the rise of Stalinism and the revolt against it in 1956. He explained the anti-Stalinist revolt as the rebellion of the human spirit against the deadening grip of authoritarianism,[187] while Stalinism itself had arisen out of, in part, malign ideas within the Marxist canon: 'Stalinism did not develop just because certain economic and social conditions existed, but because these conditions provided a fertile climate within which false ideas took root, and these false ideas became in their turn part of the social conditions.' Those false ideas had, in turn, a basis in the classical Marxist tradition. As an inheritor of that tradition Trotskyism shared with Stalinism a key theoretical weakness in that it attempted 'to derive all analysis of political manifestations directly and in an over-simplified manner from economic causations'.[188] This mistake linked Stalinism to crude Marxism, as, in their cruder moments, Marx and Engels had a tendency to dissolve agency into abstraction: revolution was seen sometimes to occur simply as and when forces and relations of production clashed, rather than through the actions of real men and women. This weakness in their oeuvre was most apparent when Marx and Engels used the metaphor of base and superstructure to aid their conceptualisation of reality. Thompson insisted that this was a 'bad and dangerous model, since Stalin used it not as an image of men changing in society but as a mechanical model, operating semi-automatically and independently of human agency'.[189] This 'denial of the creative agency of human labour', when combined with working-class 'anti-intellectualism' and 'moral nihilism', acted to rob Marxism of its human element and to freeze it into the dogma of Stalinism, which was itself 'embodied in institutional form in the rigid forms of democratic centralism'.[190] Tragically, as the tiny Trotskyist groups were organised along democratic centralist lines and shared with Stalinism a crude and vulgarly materialist interpretation of historical materialism, Thompson's analysis implied that they manifested all of the evils of Stalinism with none of its advantages. So, while both the CPGB and the British Trotskyists regurgitated similar dogma, the latter had not the former's large base of committed socialists: Trotskyism was therefore a type of anti-

Stalinism in the sense that there once existed 'anti-Popes', but without the benefit of a mass congregation.[191]

So, according to Thompson, the Stalinist distortions of Marxism, as embodied in the authoritarian, elitist and 'rigid' organisational form of democratic centralism, could be explained as the consequences of the application of the more mechanical side of Marx's legacy. However, while they were distorted, the Stalinist states remained, in an important sense, socialist structures: 'the fact that British socialists do not like all the features of this society has no bearing upon the fact of its existence. It was obviously only short-sightedness which ever led socialists to conceive of the new society stepping, pure and enlightened, out of the fires of the old.'[192] To help explain this contradictory phenomenon, Thompson wanted to reclaim Marx's dialectical interpretation of progress – 'that hideous pagan idol, who would not drink the nectar but from the skulls of the slain' – and apply it to the interpretation of Stalinism, such that he explained it as a system that was simultaneously economically progressive and morally reactionary.[193] The central characteristic of Stalinism was that it fashioned a rigid and reactionary ideology from ambiguities that exist in Marx's legacy and which had become fallacies under Lenin.[194] For Thompson, it was through the ideology of *economism*, or mechanical Marxism, as embodied in the organisational structure of democratic centralism, that Marxism became ossified and socialism was distorted. Anderson has argued that this is a far from satisfactory analysis of Stalinism because it downplays the explanatory importance of material scarcity, which is the key common characteristic of all the Stalinist states.[195]

Anderson's comment suggests a deeper failure of Thompson's method. For, at its heart, Thompson's essay embraced a fatal contradiction, which even his grand rhetorical flourishes were unable to fully conceal. Thompson opened his essay with the claim that one-quarter of the earth's surface was controlled by a new society, which, despite its many abhorrent features, represented a qualitative break with capitalism: 'The instruments of production in the Soviet Union are socialised. The bureaucracy is not a class, but is parasitic upon that society. Despite its parasitism, the wave of human energy unleashed by the first socialist revolution has multiplied the wealth of society, and vastly enlarged the cultural horizons of the people.'[196] However, in contrast to this characterisation of the Soviet system as being at once socialist while yet morally unpalatable, elsewhere he insisted that 'the "end" of Communism is not a "political" end, but a human end'.[197] This formulation suggested a tremendous gap between the human ends of the Soviet experiment and the inhuman means through which those ends were, at least partially, being realised. So while Thompson implied that a plurality of means could be utilised to achieve the end of communism, he was aware that those means were not morally equivalent. Concretely, in the Soviet case, he argued that the flaws of the Stalinist system could best be understood as a consequence of the inadequate model of Marxism that had guided the

Bolsheviks. They, or so he claimed, had embraced a mechanical interpretation of the Marxist base–superstructure metaphor such that agency, in the form of the conscious activity of the masses, was lost, only to find expression through the monolithic party which became the guardian of true socialist consciousness. Then the 'immorality' of replacing the actions of real individuals with those of cardboard abstractions became 'embodied in institutional form in the rigid forms of "democratic centralism"'.[198] Thompson's moral critique of Stalinism involved a call both for a more flexible interpretation of Marx's theory of history and a rejection of the Leninist form of political organisation.

For all its undoubted power, Thompson's thesis was susceptible to two distinct, but related, criticisms. First, could a mechanical version of Marxism as embodied in a democratic centralist organisation bear the weight of his explanation of the rise of Stalinism? Second, what, if any, are the relations between socialism and Communism in his model, and if the latter is a human 'end', then what could be said of the abhorrent means through which the Stalinists had gone some, at least, of the way to realising that end? Thompson's implicit answers to these questions suggest that he had not broken with as much of the common sense of his age as he imagined. First, traditional consequentialist ethics, which included, for the little they were worth, the ethical justifications of their actions deployed by the Stalinists, suggest that good ends can come from bad means; while, second, the dominant liberal and Stalinist histories of the Soviet system were agreed on one point at least: Leninism led to Stalinism. In tacitly accepting both of these positions, Thompson opened his moral critique of Stalinism to an immanent critique from those who saw a contradiction between his humanist claim that socialism represented the realisation of historically (self-)created human potentialities,[199] and any suggestion that the Stalinist system might represent, in however distorted a form, a progressive break with capitalism. This is more or less the form of the critique that was formulated by Harry Hanson in the autumn 1957 issue of the *New Reasoner*.

Hanson argued that modern 'Communism is not the creed of the proletariat. Rather, it is, first and foremost, a technique, operated by a revolutionary elite, of pushing forward the economic development of an underdeveloped country at the fastest possible rate . . . [which] is a very painful process.'[200] Hanson insisted that, for all Thompson's rhetoric and his indisputable honesty, his was an untenable critique of Stalinism, as it shared with the Stalinists, and Marxism more generally, a consequentialist moral framework which, despite fine talk of the interdependence of means and ends, tended to subordinate the former to the latter, offering an unsatisfactory basis from which to criticise Stalinist immorality. In place of such a moral framework, Hanson suggested that the left should look to Kant as a guide to action.[201] This was a compelling critique of Thompson's rather weak analysis of Stalinism, and, as Thompson had largely rejected Marx's revolutionary political theory for a form of militant left reformism,[202] it was unclear how he might reply to the substance of Hanson's claims. In fact it was MacIntyre who came to the defence of a sophisticated version of socialist humanism, which, while building on Thompson's insights, began to outline a project capable of offering a powerful alternative to both Hanson's Kantianism and to Stalinist consequentialism. In developing this perspective, MacIntyre also began to outline one of the more sophisticated defences of the revolutionary politics of his day.

MacIntyre's critique of Hanson's reply to Thompson's moral critique of Stalinism, 'Notes From the Moral Wilderness' (1958–59), while written as a defence of Thompson's general perspective, was simultaneously an implicit critique of the weaknesses of Thompson's own exposition of the doctrine of socialist humanism. MacIntyre opened this essay with a classically Marxist critique of the implied Kantianism of Hanson's morality: 'The ex-Communist turned moral critic of Communism is often a figure of genuine pathos . . . They repudiate Stalinist crimes in the name of moral principle; but the fragility of their appeal to moral principles lies in the apparently arbitrary nature of that appeal.'[203] However, MacIntyre was just as critical of those apologists for Stalinism for whom socialism's moral core was lost amid a mechanical theory of historical progress. As to their theory of history, while MacIntyre acknowledged that it was accepted both by Stalin and Karl Popper as being authentically Marxist, he insisted that it could not be truthfully read into either Marx's early or more mature writings. Rather, he suggested, Engels had played a negative role in the history of Marxism, when, through his likening of Marx to Darwin, he had helped foster a mechanical interpretation of historical materialism which reduced human history to a special case of natural history.[204] In place of the orthodox interpretation of historical materialism, MacIntyre insisted that if the moral core of Marxist political theory was to be retrieved and reconstructed from the fragments that Marx had written on the subject then it must be carried out alongside a similar reconstruction of Marx's theory of history.

MacIntyre suggested that it was the Stalinists, through the medium of a teleological vision of historical progress, who identified 'what is morally right with what is actually going to be the outcome of historical development', such that the '"ought" of principle is swallowed up in the "is" of history'.[205] It was not enough to add something like Kant's ethics to this existing Stalinist theory of historical development if one wished to reassert moral principle into Marxism, for that theory of history negated moral choice. However, neither was it right to reject, as immoral, any historical event from some supposed higher standpoint, as 'there is no set of common, public standards to which [one] can appeal'. Any such manoeuvre would tend to gravitate to an existing tradition of morality which, because it had generally evolved to serve some particular dominant class interests, would 'play into the hands of the defenders of the status quo'.[206] So, MacIntyre suggested, apologists for both the East and the West in the Cold War based their arguments on inadequate theoretical frameworks; but, if this was true, what would be the structure of an alternative 'third moral position'? MacIntyre's answer was that such a position could be built only by 'replacing a misconceived but prevalent view of what Marxism is by a more correct view'.[207]

The Stalinist insistence that history's general course was predictable rested, or so MacIntyre maintained, on a misconception of the role of the base–superstructure metaphor in Marxist theory. What Marx was suggesting when he deployed this metaphor was neither a mechanical nor a causal relationship. Rather, he was utilising Hegelian concepts to denote the process through which the economic base of a society provides 'a framework within which superstructures arise, a set of relations around which the human relations can entwine themselves, a kernel of human relationships from which all else grows'. MacIntyre wrote that in 'creating the basis, you create the superstructure. These are not two activities but one.' The Stalinist model of historical progress, in which political developments were understood to follow automatically from economic causes, could not be further from Marx's model: in Marx's view 'the crucial character of the transition to socialism is not that it is a change in the economic base but that it is a revolutionary change in the relation of base to superstructure'.[208] As the essence of the human condition is historically conditioned freedom, while general predictions can reasonably be made as to the tendency of people to revolt against capital and other oppressive systems; Marxists would be mistaken to predict mechanically either revolts or successful revolutions as the automatic consequence of any particular economic process. So, where both Stalin's teleology of historical progress and Kant's ahistorical categorical imperative were found to be wanting, MacIntyre suggested that we look for a 'theory which treats what emerges in history as providing us with a basis for our standards, without making the historical process morally sovereign or its progress automatic'. In his search for a basis from which to reconstruct a Marxist ethics, MacIntyre insisted, contrary to 'the liberal belief in the autonomy of morality', that it was the purposive character of human action that could both distinguish human history from natural history and provide a historical–materialist basis for moral judgements.[209]

MacIntyre suggested that Marxists should follow Aristotle specifically and the Greeks more generally in insisting that a link be maintained between ethics and human desires: 'we make both individual deeds and social practices intelligible as human actions by showing how they connect with characteristically human desires, needs and the like'.[210] He proposed to relate morality to desire in a way that is radically at odds with Kant, for where, in Kant, 'the "ought" of morality is utterly divorced from the "is" of desire', MacIntyre insisted that to divorce ethics from activities which aim to satisfy needs and desires in this way 'is to make it unintelligible as a form of human action'. So, in contrast to the Kantian categorical imperative, MacIntyre argued that we need a morality which relates to our desires. However, while these desires are related to human needs, MacIntyre refused to reify his concept of human nature. Instead, he followed Marx in radically historicising human nature, without losing sight of its biological basis: 'it is only with Hegel that Man begins to possess and with Marx that Man achieves a real history', for in Marx history 'becomes one with the history of men'.[211] It is in thus historicising 'Man' that Marx's greatness lies, for he refuses to follow either Hobbes into a melancholic model of human needs and desires or Diderot into a utopian counterposition of the state of nature against contemporary social structures. Instead, Marx comprehends the limited historical truth of Hobbes's insight, but counterposes to it, not a utopia, but the real movement of workers in struggle through which they realise that solidarity is a fundamental human desire.

MacIntyre sought to ground this suggestion of Marx's through a peculiar rewriting of the history of ethics. He suggested that such a history could be written as a synthesis of three strands: first, a 'history of moral codes'; second, 'a history of human attitudes to desire'; and, third, a history of 'human nature'. Moral codes, he argued, relate initially to human desires; however, with the Protestant Reformation the connection between desire and morality is broken. For the Protestants, as Man is by nature corrupt, then human desires cannot act as the basis for moral codes. What is more, as men are finite beings, they cannot hope to understand the mind of God and cannot hope to fathom God's moral code. Consequently, 'the moral law becomes a connection of divine fiats', which are 'so far as we are concerned totally arbitrary'. In such a world, 'desire becomes something anarchic and amoral', and once moral codes lose their religious colouration and take on a secular form they are seen to act, for instance in Hobbes, as 'at best an uneasy truce or peace between warring desires'. To counterpose desires, in their natural state, to these moral codes, as Diderot did, was an inadequate response to the post-Reformation view because this strategy fails to acknowledge that 'in class society desire itself is remoulded, not simply repressed'.[212] Two questions necessarily arise from this claim. Can this remoulding be absolute? And, if this process of remoulding is not absolute, is it possible that it may be transcended? To understand these issues historically we must ask if a form of human nature could emerge such that the needs and desires of individuals are not felt to be in simple atomised opposition one to the other? Marx's greatness, according to MacIntyre, was to comprehend both the deep historical and sociological content to this question when he suggested that 'the emergence of human nature is something to be comprehended only in terms of the history of class-struggle. Each age reveals a development of human potentiality which is specific to that form of social life and which is specifically limited by the class-structure of that society.' Specifically, under advanced capitalism, according to MacIntyre, 'the growth of production makes it possible [for man] to reappropriate his own nature'. This is true in two ways: first, the increasing productivity of labour produces the potential for us all to lead much richer lives, both morally and materially; and, second, capitalism also creates an agency – the proletariat – which, through its struggles for freedom, embodies a new collectivist spirit, through which individuals come to understand both that their needs and desires can best be satisfied through collective channels, and that they do in fact need and desire solidarity. For, according to MacIntyre, the proletariat in its struggles against capital is beginning to create the conditions for the solution of the contemporary problems of morality: it is beginning to embody the practice which could overcome the 'rift between our conception of morality and our conception of desire'.[213] In acting thus the proletariat comes to realise that solidarity is not simply a useful means through which its individual members struggle to meet their needs, but it is in fact what they naturally desire.[214]

MacIntyre therefore understood the history of morality as 'the history of men ceasing to see moral rules as the repression of desire and as something that men have made and accepted for themselves', and which concretely culminates in the socialist struggles of the proletariat against its alienation and against reified ways of perceiving the world. Conversely, 'both the autonomy of ethics and utilitarianism are aspects of the consciousness of capitalism; both are forms of alienation rather than moral guides'.[215] So, once the political left has rid itself both of the myth of the inevitable triumph of socialism and of the reification of socialism as some indefinite end which justifies any action taken in its name, socialists will truly comprehend the interpenetration of means and ends through the history of class struggle, and they will understand Marxist morality to be, as against the Stalinists, 'an assertion of moral absolutes', while 'as against the liberal critic of Stalinism it is an assertion of desire and history'.[216]

Elsewhere MacIntyre extended this analysis of the relationship between structure and agency to make more general claims for historical materialism. For instance, in his 1960 essay 'Breaking the Chains of Reason' – his contribution to a New Left collection edited by Thompson, *Out of Apathy* (1960), he confronted Popper's critique of Marxism. Popper had argued that it was Marx's attachment to methodological collectivism that led to his embrace of mechanical materialism. In opposition to this approach, Popper insisted that social interaction could be adequately understood through the methodological individualist approach.

Against Popper, MacIntyre insisted that 'the characterisation of individuals and classes has to go together. Essentially these are not two separate tasks.' So, while Popper 'is right to stress that there is no history and no society which is not the history or society of concrete individuals', it is equally true that 'there are no individuals who exist apart from their history or apart from their society'.[217] In opposition to both methodological individualism and methodological collectivism, MacIntyre claimed that both mechanical, rule-governed, models of behaviour and lawless individual models of action broke the link between 'understanding and action'. The problem with both of these approaches to social action is that they entail political fatalism:

> Either men can discern the laws which govern social development or they cannot. If they can, then they must avow that their own behaviour is subject to these laws and consequently they must admit that they have discovered themselves to be not agents, but victims, part of a social process which occurs independently of human mind, feeling and will. If they cannot discern such laws, then they are necessarily helpless, for they have no instruments of change at their hands. So in any case human agency is bound to be ineffective.[218]

While my discussions of Sartre's and Althusser's interpretations of historical materialism seem to confirm this argument, as I pointed out in my discussion of Trotsky's *History of the Russian Revolution*, MacIntyre made a similar criticism of Deutscher's Marxism. In the third volume of his biography of Trotsky, Deutscher suggested, on the basis of a reworked version of Plekhanov's analysis of the role of the individual in history, that Trotsky's 'grappling with the classical problem of personality in history' is the 'least successful' aspect of his *History of the Russian Revolution*.[219] Criticising this proposition, MacIntyre argued that Trotsky's Marxism cannot be reduced to Deutscher's analysis, because Trotsky recognised that 'from time to time history presents us with real alternatives', so that our actions cannot be understood at such junctures as 'just part of an inevitable historical progress'.[220] MacIntyre insisted that 'Trotsky himself evades all the categories of Plekhanovite Marxism'.[221]

Alex Callinicos, in *Making History* (1987), aims to outline a similar model of historical materialism that escapes Plekhanovite fatalism, without succumbing to methodological individualism. To realise this project he has sought to meet Anderson's challenge to articulate structural and agential 'types of causality' into a defensible 'theory of historical materialism'.[222] Regarding Marx's attempt to solve the relationship between structure and agency in 'The Eighteenth Brumaire', Callinicos argues that Marx's famous 'formula suffers from a fundamental flaw, namely that it conceives the role of structure as essentially negative'. Moreover, he notes, following Anderson, that Marx also fails to distinguish between the various kinds of goals of human action.[223]

To overcome these lacunae, Callinicos has attempted to integrate an historically constituted version of the 'orthodox conception of agents' – the proposition that it is individuals, themselves products of history, who make history by choosing between unactualised potentials – with an interpretation of social structure as capacity as well as constraint.[224] According to Callinicos, while human agents continue to make history in circumstances not of their own choosing, those circumstances can aid, as well as hinder, the attempts made by agents to realise their goals. Thus conceived, the level of the development of the forces of production sets the parameters of that which is possible in a positive as well as a negative sense.[225] This is, of course, a relatively orthodox statement. However, Callinicos combined with it a critique, borrowed from Eric Olin Wright *et al.*, of Cohen's interpretation of historical materialism.

Through a discussion of Cohen's *Karl Marx's Theory of History: A Defence*, Wright *et al.* attempt to defend what they called a 'weak restricted historical materialism'.[226] They argue that while both Darwinism and Marxism are evolutionary theories, they are historical theories in quite different ways. For where Darwinian evolution is 'historical in the same way that thermodynamics is', Marxism is a developmental theory in the Lamarckian sense.[227] However, they argue that this claim does not imply that Marxism is a crude theory of social development *à la* Cohen. Rather, while Cohen provides an account of 'the necessary (material) conditions for change; the direction of change; the means through which change is achieved', his defence of the argument that history will automatically provide 'the sufficient conditions for change' is less convincing.[228] Declaring a broad agreement with the first three of these conditions, Wright *et al.* merely reject the fourth condition in their 'reconstruction' of historical materialism. In effect this amounts to their rejection of Second International notions of inevitability and irresistibility. This model implies an open-ended and flexible approach to history. It is this flexibility, alongside Wright *et al.*'s defence of the proposition that there existed a 'weak impulse' for the productive forces to develop over time, rather than Cohen's suggestion of a 'strong impulse', which appealed to Callinicos.[229]

In his Introduction to the 2004 edition of the book, Callinicos extends his defence of the proposition that there exists a weak impulse for the forces of production to develop through history via a discussion of Carling and Nolan's pseudo-Darwinian explanation of the tendency for the forces of production to develop through history. Carling and Nolan argue that in a social system consisting of a plurality of social subsystems – for instance the European feudal system – there does not need to exist a capitalist drive for accumulation for intensive development of the forces of production to occur. Rather, the unintended consequence of the intensive growth of any particular subsystem would tend to include military victory over more static subsystems. Accordingly, they conceive of a tendency for the forces of production to develop as generalised through military (and non-military) competition between groups. This mechanism, Callinicos suggests, is a more defensible account of the development of the forces of production in precapitalist societies than is Cohen's transhistorical model of rationality.[230] In explaining the long-term tendency for the forces of production to develop – Cohen's developmental thesis – Carling and Nolan's model helps sustain something like Cohen's primacy thesis – that it is the level of the development of the forces of production that is the prime *explanandum* in history.

While he broadly accepts this thesis, by insisting on the orthodox conception of agency Callinicos ensures that his interpretation of historical materialism is immunised against the appeal of crude productive force determinism. Consequently as long as individual humans are considered to be the agents of history, then there can be no tendency to reduce historical materialism to a form of crude economic determinism. However, in opposition to methodological individualism, Callinicos – because he insists that 'an adequate theory of agency must be a theory of the causal *powers* persons have' and that 'the productive forces are . . . best understood as the productive *powers* of humanity' – resists the temptation, most fully embraced by Sartre, of perceiving individual agents as transhistorical subjects of history.[231]

This attempt to marry structure and agency without subsuming either term by the other is built on foundations suggested by Bhaskar, who defines structure as 'both the ever present condition (material cause) and the continually reproduced outcome of human agency'.[232] In the new Introduction to his book, Callinicos extends this argument to insist, contra Wright *et al.*, that structures cannot be reduced to individual agency even if they are reproduced by that agency. So while the subjects of history are always individuals, because individuals can move into and out of various structural locations – for instance a position as a manager – these locations are best understood as so many 'empty spaces', the properties of which determine the roles executed within them.[233] In making this argument, Callincos follows Margaret Archer's 'morphogenetic' approach to the conceptualisation of the structure–agency debate.[234]

In her seminal study of the issue, Archer argues for a dualist approach to the structure–agency problem such that agency and structure are understood to emerge each from the other, but to be irreducible one to the other.[235] More recently, Sean Creaven has argued that while this approach liberates the social scientist from the antinomies of traditional structuralist and agential models of the social, Archer's own model is susceptible to the criticism that it opens the door to idealism and pluralism, and suggests that her method would be strengthened if she embraced Marxism.[236]

This model obviously indicates an objective account of class, as a location within the relations of production. Similarly, Callinicos defends Ste. Croix's 'analytical' conceptualisation of class as an objective relationship against Stedman Jones's conception of class as structured through discourse.[237] This procedure has profound consequences, because Ste. Croix's model implies a particular historical dynamic where Stedman Jones' model does not. Ste. Croix insists that Marx's relational model of class is analytical because it implies class struggle and social change.[238] Such an objective model of class does not, however, imply that the determination of class interests can be reduced to 'a merely technical exercise', for, Callinicos argues, it is only through class struggle that class interests (and desires) become potentially apparent.[239] However, if this potential is to be realised,

Callinicos argues (following Gramsci), then political struggles must be engaged, within the ideological superstructure, between old and new ways of conceiving the world.[240]

Callinicos suggests that these ideological struggles involve contestation between competing identities. To illuminate the point he cites the British miners' strike of 1984–85. In this strike, or so he argues, debates between miners

> typically involved a choice between two kinds of identity. The strikers were encouraged to see themselves as acting for their communities, their union, their industry, their class. The scabs, especially in Nottinghamshire, were invited to regard themselves as trade unionists of a different kind, committed to a high wage, high-productivity, strike free industry and taking their decisions through procedures such as the use of the secret ballots which mirror the serial structures of bourgeois democracy.[241]

So, while the class struggle was objectively grounded in conflictual relations of production, it was articulated through an ideological struggle. The ability of workers to realise their potential class powers was therefore limited because they remained politically fragmented, and this fragmentation was contested ideologically.[242] The point is of central importance to Callinicos because he believes that the class struggle is the central mediating 'bridge' between long-term historical tendencies and short-term revolutionary upsurges.[243]

However, if Marx was wrong when, occasionally, he suggested that class struggles would inevitably generate revolutionary socialist consciousness within the proletariat as a whole,[244] then the class struggle between workers and capitalists could conceivably continue indefinitely. The importance of winning the ideological struggle could therefore not be overstated. In this context Callinicos discussed and rejected Walter Benjamin's conception of the socialist revolution as 'a tiger's leap into the past'.[245] In contrast to Benjamin, Callinicos argues (following Marx), that where bourgeois revolutions clothed themselves in the mythological imagery of the past so as to construct the coalition of disparate forces needed to overthrow the old order, socialist revolutions 'do not need to conceal their real character'.[246]

At this point, Callinicos's argument converges to a degree with Sartre's discussion of the need for the revolutionary to attain a scientific understanding of her concrete situation if she is to help realise the potential of that situation: 'To constitute itself fully as a collectivity, that is, to achieve revolutionary class-consciousness', the working class 'requires a lucid understanding of its position within capitalist society and the power and interest which this position gives it to build communism'. Proletarian self-awareness is essential if workers are to realise their political potential. This self-awareness obviously involves the disavowal of any myths through which bourgeois society is legitimised. Moreover, as one of the key myths through which bourgeois legitimation is realised is that of nationalism, Callinicos argues that for the working class to imagine itself as part of the nation is politically 'disabling'.[247] Where communist historians of the 1930s and 1940s were asked to write national histories of progress culminating in the contemporary national workers' movement, Callinicos argues that Marxist historians should aim to keep alive traditions of struggle with which to inform contemporary political practice.[248] There is evidently some continuity between these two goals, but real self-awareness cannot be content to cut the struggles of the oppressed to fit a procrustean nationalist bed.

Conclusion

Callinicos closed the Introduction to the 2004 edition of his book with the suggestion that his argument was not intended as a 'definitive "answer"' to the problematic conceptualisation of the relationship between structure and agency in social and historiographic thought, but was 'a contribution to debates that have ceased to be merely theoretical'.[249] The sentence alludes, of course, to the changed political context between the publication of the book's first edition in 1987, when the defeat of the British miners' strike appeared to silence those who spoke of the continuing salience of class-based politics, and the post-Seattle contemporary context, when the concept of anti-capitalism has been forcefully reinstated within mainstream political debate.

The emergence of the modern anti-capitalist movement suggests that Marx was right to argue that however many defeats it experiences, the struggle for freedom can never be entirely extinguished because it is written into our very nature. Nevertheless, Marx held to a historical view of human nature, in which human needs and capacities evolved in a complex interplay between the development of the forces of production and the struggle between classes. In this chapter I have traced the ways in which a number of key Marxist theoreticians have attempted to marry the structural and agential aspects of Marx's theory of history. I have argued that neither the extremes of Althusser's structuralism nor Sartre's individualism were able to provide a defensible reinterpretation of historical materialism. Further, I have argued that while Thompson scored many direct hits against the schematism of structural history, his own positive alternative was ultimately unpersuasive. Finally, I have argued that the attempt to synthesise structure and subject into a Marxist theory of agency, suggested by Anderson and present in the early work of MacIntyre, and developed by Callinicos, is the most powerful reinterpretation of historical materialism to date. Nevertheless, despite the theoretical weaknesses that I have identified in each of the preceding frameworks, all have informed the work of Marxist historians of the highest rank. Thompson's own work clearly heads the list, but it should not be forgotten that Althusser inspired historians of the calibre of Pierre-Phillippe Rey, Guy Bois, Perry Anderson and Peter Kriedte,[250] while Sartre has inspired Jim Holstun's recent history of the English revolution.[251]

Notes

1 Marx 'The Eighteenth Brumaire', p. 146.
2 M. Poster *Existential Marxism in Postwar France* (Princeton, NJ, 1975), p. 38; A. Hirsh *The French Left* (Montreal, 1982), pp. 10–11; A. Callinicos *Is There a Future for Marxism?* (London, 1982), p. 55.
3 Sartre was one of the more important figures of the post-war French left. In 1964 he was awarded the Nobel Prize for literature – and refused it. Althusser likened him to Rousseau – 'he was our Jean Jacques'.
4 I. Birchall *Sartre Against Stalinism* (Oxford, 2004), p. 36.
5 R. Aronson *Jean Paul Sartre: Philosophy in the World* (London, 1980), p. 161.
6 Birchall *Sartre Against Stalinism*, p. 53.
7 Ibid., pp. 93–105.
8 J. P. Sartre *The Communists and Peace* (New York, 1968 [1952–54]).
9 J. P. Sartre *The Spectre of Stalin* (London, 1969 [1956–57]), pp. 104, 87.
10 Birchall *Sartre Against Stalinism*, p. 2.
11 J. P. Sartre 'Materialism and Revolution' in J.P. Sartre *Literary and Philosophical Essays* (London, 1955 [1946]), pp. 188, 185.
12 Ibid., pp. 188, 210–12.
13 J. P. Sartre *Search for a Method* (New York, 1963 [1957]), pp. xxxiv, 21, 83, 85.
14 Ibid., p. 44.
15 Ibid., p. 23.
16 Ibid., p. 91; see Sartre 'Materialism and Revolution', p. 220. In the first volume of his *Critique of Dialectical Reason* (London, 1976 [1960]), p. 36, he wrote that 'if we do not wish the dialectic to become a divine law, a metaphysical fate, it must proceed from individuals and not from some kind of supra-historical ensemble'.
17 Sartre *Search for a Method*, pp. 133, 145, 159.
18 Ibid., pp. 124, 127.
19 Ibid., p. 34.
20 Sartre *Critique* Vol. 1, p. 125. F. Jameson *Marxism and Form* (Princeton, 1971), p. 233.
21 Sartre *Critique* Vol. 1, p. 735.
22 Ibid., p. 662.
23 Ibid., p. 67.
24 M. Poster *Sartre's Marxism* (London, 1979), p. 60.
25 Aronson *Jean Paul Sartre*, pp. 258–9.
26 Ibid., pp. 260–1.
27 J. P. Sartre *Critique of Dialectical Reason* Vol. 2 (London, 1991), p. 115.
28 Sartre *Critique* Vol. 1, p. 85.
29 Aronson *Jean Paul Sartre*, p. 280.
30 Sartre *Critique* Vol. 2, p. 99.
31 Ibid., p. 107.
32 Ibid., p. 98.
33 Aronson *Jean Paul Sartre*, p. 283; R. Aronson *Sartre's Second Critique* (Chicago, IL, 1987), p. 161.
34 Birchall *Sartre Against Stalinism*, p. 180.

35 Ibid.
36 Sartre *The Communists and Peace*, p. 105.
37 Ibid., pp. 105–6.
38 Ibid., p. 120.
39 Ibid., p. 128.
40 Ibid., p. 181.
41 Ibid., p. 128.
42 Ibid., p. 129.
43 Ibid., p. 134.
44 Ibid., p. 213.
45 Ibid., p. 134–5.
46 Aronson *Jean Paul Sartre*, p. 224; M. Merleau-Ponty *Adventures of the Dialectic* (Evanston, IL, 1973), pp. 107–8.
47 Sartre *Search for a Method*, p. 51; Poster *Existential Marxism*, p. 212; Hirsh *The French Left*, p. 5.
48 Sartre *The Spectre of Stalin*, p. 27.
49 Birchall *Sartre Against Stalinism*, p. 164.
50 C. L. R. James 'Letter 10th February 1957' in A. Grimshaw ed. *The C.L.R. James Reader* (Oxford, 1992), p. 2265.
51 A dramatically cut version of this book was published in France in 1973 as *Bourgeois and Bras Nus*, and it was this book that was translated and published in English in 1977 with, confusingly, the English rendition of the 1946 French title: *Class Struggle in the First French Republic* (London: Pluto).
52 Sartre *Search for a Method*, pp. 37, 39, 45.
53 N. Carlin 'Daniel Guerin and the Working Class in the French Revolution' *International Socialism* 2:47, 1990, p. 199.
54 Ibid., pp. 201, 203.
55 Birchall *Sartre Against Stalinism*, p. 176.
56 Ibid., p. 179.
57 Sartre *Search for a Method*, p. 44.
58 Ibid., p. 29.
59 Sartre *Critique* Vol. 2, p. 106.
60 Ibid., p. 105.
61 Aronson *Jean Paul Sartre*, pp. 218, 231, 280.
62 Aronson *Sartre's Second Critique*, pp. 234–7.
63 Aronson *Jean Paul Sartre*, pp. 52–3.
64 Claude Lévi-Strauss became a professor of social anthropology at the College de France in 1958.
65 Sartre *Critique* Vol. 1, p. 480; Poster *Existential Marxism*, p. 307.
66 Poster *Existential Marxism*, p. 306.
67 C. Lévi-Strauss *The Savage Mind* (London, 1972 [1962]), p. 249.
68 Poster *Existential Marxism*, p. 312.
69 Lévi-Strauss *The Savage Mind*, pp. 245, 254.
70 Ibid., pp. 256–7.
71 Ibid., p. 246.
72 A. Callinicos *Social Theory* (London, 1999), p. 269.
73 Poster *Existential Marxism*, pp. 331–2.
74 Louis Althusser was a professor of philosophy at the Ecole Normale Superior.

75 P. Anderson *In the Tracks of Historical Materialism* (London, 1983), p. 37.
76 Harris *The Mandate of Heaven*, p. 222.
77 Poster *Existential Marxism*, pp. 340–1.
78 L. Althusser 'Marx's Relation to Hegel' in L. Althusser *Montesquieu, Rousseau, Marx* (London, 1970), p. 183.
79 L. Althusser and E. Balibar *Reading Capital* (London, 1970 [1968]), p. 170.
80 Ibid., p. 215.
81 Ibid., p. 225.
82 G. Elliott *Althusser: The Detour of Theory* (London, 1987), p. 169; Anderson *Arguments within English Marxism*, p. 68.
83 Cf. C. Bettleheim *Class Struggle in the USSR* Vols 1 and 2 (London, 1976, 1978).
84 Callinicos *Is there a Future for Marxism?*, p. 61.
85 L. Althusser *For Marx* (London, 1969 [1965]), p. 116.
86 Althusser 'Marx's Relation to Hegel', p. 173.
87 Althusser *For Marx*, p. 94.
88 Ibid., pp. 101–2.
89 Ibid., p. 113.
90 Ibid., p. 99.
91 Ibid., p. 104.
92 Elliott *Althusser*, p. 156; Robert Paul Resch *Althusser and the Renewal of Marxist Social Theory* (Berkeley, CA, 1992), pp. 83–157.
93 Elliott *Althusser*, pp. 158–9; A. Callinicos *Althusser's Marxism* (London, 1976), p. 51.
94 G. Bois *The Crisis of Feudalism* (Cambridge, 1984 [1976]).
95 Poster *Existential Marxism*, p. 357.
96 J. Ranciere 'On the Theory of Ideology: Althusser's Politics' in R. Edgley and P. Osborne eds *Radical Philosophy Reader* (London, 1985 [1969]), p. 102.
97 Vilar 'Marxist History, A History in the Making: Towards a Dialogue with Althusser', p. 78.
98 For an Althusserian critique of Vilar see Resch *Althusser and the Renewal of Marxist Social Theory*, p. 371.
99 P. Osborne *The Politics of Time* (London, 1995), pp. 24–5.
100 Anderson *In the Tracks of Historical Materialism*, p. 38.
101 Both the Labour Party and the CPGB initially opposed CND's demand for unilateral nuclear disarmament: W. Thompson *The Good Old Cause* (London, 1992), p. 116; and *The Long Death of British Labourism* (London, 1993), p. 64.
102 P. Blackledge 'Reform, Revolution and the Question of Organisation in the First New Left' *Contemporary Politics* 10:1, March 2004.
103 P. Blackledge *Perry Anderson, Marxism and the New Left* (London, 2004), pp. 12–34.
104 P. Anderson 'Origins of the Present Crisis' in P. Anderson *English Questions* (London, 1992), pp. 17–19; essay originally published in *New Left Review* no. 24, 1964.
105 Ibid., p. 22.
106 Ibid., p. 20.
107 ibid., pp. 23–4.

108 Ibid., p. 27.
109 Ibid., p. 29.
110 Edward Thompson was perhaps the most gifted historian of his generation, a key figure in the British New Left of 1956, he became in the 1970s and 1980s a leading figure within CND, and European Nuclear Disarmament (END). *The Making of the English Working Class* (1963) is among the most influential history books of the twentieth century.
111 E. P. Thompson 'The Peculiarities of the English' in E. P. Thompson *The Poverty of Theory and Other Essays* (London, 1978), pp. 247, 257; essay originally published in R. Miliband and J. Saville eds *The Socialist Register* (London, 1965).
112 Ibid., p. 252.
113 Ibid., p. 254.
114 Ibid., p. 260.
115 Ibid., p. 263.
116 Ibid., p. 279.
117 'What our authors have done is to pick up a casual impression of the trade union conservatism and the intellectual inertia of the past fifteen years, and offer it as an interpretation of a hundred years of history' (ibid., p. 176).
118 Ibid., pp. 275–6.
119 Ibid., p. 289.
120 Ibid., pp. 275, 290.
121 P. Anderson 'Socialism and Pseudo-Empiricism' *New Left Review* no. 35, 1966, pp. 30–2.
122 G. Elliott *Perry Anderson: The Merciless Laboratory of History* (Minnesota, MN, 1998), p. 56.
123 A. Glucksmann (1972) 'A Ventriloquist Structuralism' in *NLR* ed. *Western Marxism: A Critical Reader* (London, 1977); see also N. Geras (1972) 'Althusser's Marxism: An Assessment' in ibid.
124 P. Anderson 'Introduction to Glucksmann' in ibid., p. 275; this essay was originally published anonymously in *New Left Review* no. 72, 1972.
125 Ibid., p. 279.
126 E. P. Thompson 'The Poverty of Theory' in *The Poverty of Theory*, p. 4.
127 Ibid., p. 13.
128 Ibid., p. 32.
129 Ibid., pp. 44, 57.
130 Ibid., p. 61.
131 Ibid., p. 68.
132 Ibid., p. 108.
133 Ibid., p. 72.
134 Ibid., p. 154.
135 Ibid., p. 171.
136 E. P. Thompson *The Making of the English Working Class* (London, 1980 [1963]), pp. 8–13.
137 B. D. Palmer *Descent into Discourse* (Philadelphia, 1990); W. Thompson *What Happened to History?* (London, 2000); for Marxist criticisms of some of the malign consequences of 'history from below' see J. Saville 'The Radical Left Expects the Past to Do its Duty' *Labour History* 18:2, spring 1977; J. Saville

Memoirs from the Left (London, 2003), p. 180; B. Kelly *Race, Class, and Power in the Alabama Coalfields, 1908–21* (Chicago, 2001), pp. 3–15; A Callinicos 'Marxism and the Crisis in Social History' in J. Rees ed. *Essays on Historical Materialism* (London, 1998), pp. 37–9.
138 Thompson *The Making of the English Working Class*, pp. 11–12; C. L. R. James *The Black Jacobins* (London, 2001 [1938]), p. xv.
139 E. P. Thompson 'The Poverty of Theory', p. 131.
140 Perry Anderson was the editor of *New Left Review* from 1962 to 1983, and again in 2000–4; he is a professor of history at the University of California.
141 Cohen *Karl Marx's Theory of History*, p. 134.
142 Ibid., pp. 285–9.
143 J. Elster 'Cohen on Marx's Theory of History' *Political Studies* 28:1, March 1980, pp. 124–5.
144 Cohen *Karl Marx's Theory of History*, p. 152.
145 E. O. Wright, A. Levine and E. Sober *Reconstructing Marxism* (London, 1992), p. 24.
146 Cohen *Karl Marx's Theory of History*, pp. 206, 389–95.
147 A. Callinicos *Making History* (Leiden, 2004), p. 69.
148 Wright *et al. Reconstructing Marxism*, p. 12; Callinicos *Making History*, p. 40.
149 Anderson *Arguments within English Marxism*, pp. 40, 72.
150 Ibid., p. 14.
151 Ibid., pp. 31–2.
152 Ibid., pp. 38–40.
153 Ibid., p. 45.
154 Ibid., pp. 53–5.
155 Ibid., pp. 72, 40.
156 Cohen *Karl Marx's Theory of History*, pp. 150–66.
157 Anderson *Arguments within English Marxism*, p. 55.
158 Ibid., p. 58.
159 Ibid., pp. 19–21.
160 Ibid., p. 20.
161 I. Deutscher *Stalin* (London, 1966 [1949]), p. 539; and *The Prophet Outcast: Trotsky 1929–1940* (Oxford, 1987 [1963]), p. 514; cf. P. Anderson *Considerations on Western Marxism* (London, 1976), p. 120.
162 Anderson *Arguments within English Marxism*, p. 24; S. Timpanaro *On Materialism* (London, 1975), p. 105.
163 Anderson *Arguments within English Marxism*, p. 18.
164 Thompson *Making of the English Working Class*, p. 8.
165 H. Kaye *The British Marxist Historians* (London, 1995), p. 240.
166 P. Anderson 'The Figures of Descent' in P. Anderson *English Questions* (London, 1992), p. 157; essay originally published in *New Left Review* no. 161, 1987.
167 Ibid., pp. 157–60
168 Ibid., p. 164.
169 R. Looker 'Shifting Trajectories' in C. Barker and D. Nicholls eds *The Development of British Capitalist Society: A Marxist Debate* (Manchester, 1988), p. 17.
170 Anderson 'The Figures of Descent', p. 157.
171 Anderson *Arguments within English Marxism*, p. 40.

172 Anderson 'The Figures of Descent', p. 168.
173 Cohen *Karl Marx's Theory of History*, p. 77.
174 Looker *'Shifting Trajectories'*, p. 27.
175 Alasdair MacIntyre is senior research professor of philosophy at the University of Notre Dame. In the early 1950s he was a member of the CPGB. He became a leading member of the British New Left in 1956, and shortly afterwards joined the Trotskyist movement. In the early 1960s he was a member of the *International Socialism* group. He drifted away from Marxism from the mid-1960s. Alex Callinicos is a professor of politics at the University of York, and a leading member of the Socialist Workers Party.
176 Anderson *Arguments within English Marxism*, pp. 67, 6.
177 E. P. Thompson *William Morris* (London, 1977 [1955]), p. 807.
178 Anderson *Arguments within English Marxism*, p. 161.
179 Ibid., p. 167; Thompson *William Morris*, p. 807.
180 Anderson *Arguments within English Marxism*, pp. 161–2.
181 Indeed, Thompson wrote that 'to the historian', MacIntyre's essays 'remain of the first importance': E. P. Thompson 'An Open Letter to Leszek Kolakowski' in *The Poverty of Theory*, pp. 359, 401; essay originally published in R. Miliband and J. Saville eds *The Socialist Register* (London, 1973).
182 Anderson *Arguments within English Marxism*, p. 162.
183 Ibid., p. 108.
184 In 1978, Thompson described the arguments deployed in this essay as 'immature, but not, I think, radically mistaken': 'The Poverty of Theory', p. 129.
185 E. P. Thompson 'Socialist Humanism' *New Reasoner* 1, summer 1957, p. 105.
186 Ibid., p. 106.
187 Ibid., p. 109.
188 Ibid., p. 108.
189 Ibid., p. 113
190 Ibid., pp. 132, 121.
191 Ibid., p. 139.
192 Ibid., p. 106.
193 E. P. Thompson 'Agency and Choice' *New Reasoner* 5, summer 1958, pp. 98–100.
194 Ibid.
195 Anderson *Arguments within English Marxism*, p. 121.
196 Thompson 'Socialist Humanism', pp. 105, 138.
197 Ibid., p. 125.
198 Ibid., p. 121.
199 Ibid., p. 124.
200 H. Hanson 'An Open Letter to Edward Thompson' *New Reasoner* 2, autumn 1957, p. 88.
201 Ibid., p. 79.
202 E. P. Thompson 'Revolution' in E. P. Thompson ed. *Out of Apathy* (London, 1960), p. 302.
203 A. MacIntyre 'Notes from the Moral Wilderness' in K. Knight ed. *The MacIntyre Reader*, pp. 31–2; essay originally published in two parts in *New Reasoner* 7, winter 1958–59, pp. 90–100, and *New Reasoner* 8, spring 1959, pp. 89–98.

204 Ibid., p. 38.
205 Ibid., p. 32.
206 Ibid., pp. 34–5.
207 Ibid., p. 37.
208 Ibid., p. 39.
209 Ibid., pp. 40–1.
210 Ibid., pp. 43, 41.
211 Ibid., p. 46.
212 Ibid., pp. 43–4.
213 Ibid., pp. 45–6.
214 Ibid., p. 48.
215 Ibid., pp. 42, 49.
216 Ibid., p. 47.
217 A. MacIntyre 'Breaking the Chains of Reason' in E. P. Thompson ed. *Out of Apathy* (London, 1960), p. 220; see also Thompson 'The Poverty of Theory', p. 30.
218 MacIntyre 'Breaking the Chains of Reason', p. 225.
219 Deutscher *The Prophet Outcast*, p. 241.
220 A. MacIntyre 'Trotsky in Exile' in A. MacIntyre *Against the Self-Images of the Age* (London, 1971), p. 59.
221 Ibid.
222 Callinicos *Making History*, p. xlviii.
223 Ibid., pp. 1–4.
224 Ibid., pp. 16, 94.
225 In the first edition of *Making History* Callinicos suggested a less orthodox reading of Marx, but his interpretation of historical materialism had become more orthodox by the time of the publication of the second edition in 2004: see p. xxxiii.
226 Wright *et al. Reconstructing Marxism*, p. 97.
227 Ibid., pp. 50, 58.
228 Ibid., pp. 89–90.
229 Ibid., pp. 102–6.
230 Callinicos *Making History*, pp. xxxiv–ix; for Nolan's essays see: P. Nolan 'A Darwinian Historical Materialism' in P. Blackledge and G. Kirkpatrick eds *Historical Materialism and Social Evolution* (London, 2002); A. Carling and P. Nolan 'Historical Materialism, Natural Selection and World History' *Historical Materialism* 6, summer 2000, pp. 215–64; see also the exchange between Nolan and Andrew Levine and Elliott Sober in *Historical Materialism* 10:2, 2002 and 11:3, 2003.
231 Callinicos *Making History*, pp. 274–5.
232 Ibid., p. 100.
233 Ibid., p. xxv.
234 Ibid., pp. xxvii–ix.
235 M. Archer *Realist Social Theory: The Morphogenetic Approach* (Cambridge, 1995), p. 14.
236 S. Creaven *Marxism and Realism* (London, 2000), pp. 8–9; see also A. Sayer *Method in Social Science* (London, 1992), pp. 96–8; C. Hay *Political Analysis* (London, 2002), pp. 122–34.

237 Callinicos *Making History*, pp. 53, 143.
238 Ibid., p. 54.
239 Ibid., pp. 147–50.
240 Ibid., pp. 174–9.
241 Ibid., p. 232.
242 Ibid., p. 214.
243 Ibid., p. 217.
244 Ibid., p. 260.
245 Ibid., p. 239.
246 Ibid., p. 244.
247 Ibid., p. 251.
248 Ibid., pp. 259, 264.
249 Ibid., p. xliii. Indeed, the journal *Historical Materialism* is presently organising a symposium on Callinicos's book which will be published shortly.
250 Resch *Althusser and the Renewal of Marxist Social Theory*, pp. 83–157.
251 J. Holstun *Ehud's Dagger: Class Struggle and the English Revolution* (London, 2000). Brian Manning once said to me that he thought that this was the most powerful study of the revolution.

6

The present as history:[1] Marxism and post-modernity

> Among intellectuals it has gradually become fashionable to greet any profession of faith in Marxism with ironical disdain.[2]

A theme revisited by almost all of the authors discussed in this book is that the study of history should inform contemporary emancipatory practice. This is not to suggest that areas of research such as medieval history, to take an example suggested by Charles Clarke when he was Tony Blair's philistine secretary of state for education and skills, are politically irrelevant; far from it. For while Marxist studies of pre-modern societies might appear to have a somewhat tenuous relation to modern socialist politics, the mere fact that historians of the pre-modern world have shown that people have lived in a number of very different societies with very different structures, priorities and rationalities supports the general critique of neo-liberal attempts to naturalise capitalist rationality. Nevertheless, if socialists are to distance themselves from the suggestion that such alternative social structures have been universally superseded by capitalism – that we have, in one way or another, joined Francis Fukuyama at the 'end of history' – then we must uncover the contradictions and dynamics of modern capitalism to show that it, like the older modes of production which preceded it, is a historically transitory phenomenon.

The exact form of socialist strategy suggested by the various historians and theorists discussed above varies widely; and debates continue as to the strategic significance of the various historical studies produced by Marxists. Part of the reason for this contestation is the existence of what Anderson has described as an 'inherent scissiparity' between Marxist historiography and Marxist politics.[3] Nevertheless, a number of Marxists, including Anderson, have attempted to follow Fredric Jameson's demand to 'always historicise',[4] by deploying Marx's concepts to periodise the present with a view to informing socialist strategic thought.

By contrast with the political imperative behind this project, Steve Rigby concludes his *Marxism and History* with the suggestion that the fates of historical materialism and Marx's revolutionary politics have no necessary connection, such that one might flourish while the other withers and dies. He goes so far as to claim that

> acceptance of Marx's historical claims entails no commitment to his revolutionary politics, nor are his revolutionary politics guaranteed by his historical method. It would thus be quite possible to accept Marxist accounts of the transition to capitalism or of the social appeal of Puritanism and yet vote Conservative tomorrow.[5]

Despite its apparent implausibility, this dualistic interpretation of Marxism has a pedigree that goes back to the period of the Second International, when, for instance, Rudolph Hilferding famously wrote that Marxism 'is only a theory of the laws of motion of society', and 'acceptance of the validity of Marxism . . . is one thing', it is 'quite another to work for that necessity'. Further, he suggested that 'it is quite possible for someone who is convinced that socialism will triumph in the end to join the fight against it'.[6]

Whereas few commentators would today claim that 'socialism will triumph in the end', it is not uncommon for historians who reject Marx's revolutionary politics to borrow insights from his theory of history. However, despite the implied compliment in this act, Marx understood his theory of history to be much more than a detachable complement to his revolutionary politics. Moreover, if, as I argued in the chapter 1, we accept that historical materialism is the interpretation of history from the standpoint of the revolutionary working class, this obviously poses a problem of perspective: can there be a Marxist interpretation of history in the absence of a revolutionary proletarian movement?

This question actually conflates two superficially related but in fact very different issues. What are Marxists to do when the real movement of workers is on the ebb? And what happens if the proletariat ceases to be a revolutionary class? The first poses few theoretical problems for Marxists, for no Marxist has ever denied that the real class struggle and the degree of class consciousness among workers will ebb and flow through history.[7] The second question, however, poses a much more serious problem, for if the proletariat ceases to be a revolutionary class, then, by its own logic, Marxism should be consigned to the dustbin of history. Unfortunately, while there is little difficulty in distinguishing the two issues theoretically, in practice it is very easy to confuse the evidence for one with the proof of the other. Indeed, a good deal of the debate within Marxist circles on the nature of post-modernity centres on the contested interpretation of the undoubted defeats inflicted on the left and the workers' movement since the 1970s.

Contesting post-modernity

Fredric Jameson[8] is perhaps the most prominent and influential Marxist to have joined the legion of theorists who have engaged in the debate over the nature of post-modernism. According to Jameson, the power of the argument that we inhabit a new post-modern era 'depends on the hypothesis of some radical break or *coupure*, generally traced back to the end of the 1950s or the early 1960s'.[9] While he predicates his own analysis of the transition from modernism to post-modernism, and previously the transition from realism to modernism, on Ernest Mandel's periodisation of capitalism, through its market, monopoly and multinational phases,[10] many of Jameson's critics have pointed out that his attempt to recruit Mandel to his project is somewhat 'precarious'. For Mandel understood the break between what he argued were the monopoly and the multinational phases of capitalism as occurring around 1945, whereas for Jameson the transformation to post-modernism is dated to the 1960s.[11] While Jameson has recently attempted to reinforce the economic foundations of his cultural theory by borrowing from Giovanni Arrighi's *The Long Twentieth Century*, it is perhaps fair to say that despite the power of his suggestion that post-modernism is predicated on an economic break, his own conceptualisation of this break is far from adequate.[12]

Among those who have followed Jameson's lead, none has stressed and developed his suggestion that post-modernism is build on a deep historical break in the history of capitalism more than Perry Anderson.[13] In 1992 Anderson, in a remarkably sympathetic response to Fukuyama's 'end of history' thesis, wrote that with the collapse of communism, and with welfare reformism undermined by globalisation, 'the central political fact today is that there are no programmes claiming to overcome capitalism left . . . history does appear to have come to its term'.[14] Specifically, he came to agree with Jameson that the late 1960s marked a real historical watershed, which he characterised by the transition of the economic itself, as

> life itself becomes so pervaded by the symbolic systems of information and persuasion that the notion of an independent sphere of more or less a-cultural production increasingly lost meaning. Henceforward, any major theory of culture was bound to encompass more of the civilization of capital than ever before. The traditional object of Western Marxism was enormously magnified.[15]

Developing Jameson's predication of the category of post-modernism on a qualitative transformation in the nature of the world economy, Anderson argued that a radical break in the nature of the system could be located, but that the transition was a long time coming. Whereas Anderson had previously held that the end of the Second World War marked the closure of the modernist epoch, he became convinced that

> the quarter century after the end of hostilities . . . seems in retrospect an interregnum, in which modernist energies were not subject to sudden cancellation, but still glowed intermittently here and there, where conditions allowed in an inhospitable environment. It was not until the turn of the seventies that the ground for an altogether new configuration was prepared.[16]

Anderson argued that modernism had been triangulated by

> an economy and society still only semi-industrial, in which the ruling order remained to a significant extent agrarian or aristocratic; a technology of dramatic inventions, whose impact was still fresh or incipient; and an open political horizon, in which revolutionary upheavals of one kind or another against the prevailing order were widely expected or feared.[17]

Post-modernism, by contrast, was triangulated by a 'the constellation of a *déclassé* ruling order, a mediatized technology and a monochrome politics'.[18] So, while modernism 'virtually defined itself as "anti-bourgeois", postmodernism is what occurs when, without any victory, that adversary is gone'; second, where once new technology was exciting, now it was commonplace; finally, the left had experienced a profound political defeat, which had begun in the 1970s and deepened through the 1980s. In particular, he stressed the significance of the collapse of Communism and the abandoning of the reformist impulse by Western social-democratic parties. Together, Anderson concluded, these changes suggested that 'capitalism as a whole [had] entered a new historical phase'.[19]

So while modernism was a world of 'sharp demarcations', in the post-modern era 'what moves is only the market'.[20] Not that Anderson believed that the post-modern world was without conflict. Rather, 'new poles of oppositional identification have emerged in the postmodern period: gender, race, ecology, sexual orientation, regional or continental diversity'. However, these 'have today constituted a weaker set of antagonisms' than that offered by Marx's proletariat to the traditional bourgeoisie.[21] The problem was thus posed of how to confront this new 'common nonsense of the age'?[22] Post-modernism, he argued, is like modernism, 'a field of tensions' and the arena of culture is a 'battlefield'.[23] However, while Anderson argued that the left must 'fight for a real alternative' to the right,[24] he insisted that the parameters within which such politics might operate had become much more narrowly defined than traditional Marxism had supposed.

Anderson developed this argument in his manifesto for the re-launched *NLR* in 2000. In this essay he claimed that the principal characteristic of the past decade is 'the virtually uncontested consolidation, and universal diffusion, of neo-liberalism'.[25] Comparing the context of the launch of the first *NLR* in 1960 with that of the present day, Anderson wrote that then a third of the planet had broken with capitalism; the discrediting of Stalinism in 1956 had unleashed a vital process of the rediscovery of authentic Marxism; while, culturally, there had been a qualitative break with the conformism of the 1950s.[26] Today, by contrast, American capitalism has reasserted its international primacy: European social-democratic governments are implementing policies designed to follow the American model, while the Japanese economy is experiencing a slump, the Russian catastrophe has produced no popular backlash and the Western powers have asserted themselves successfully in the

Balkans.[27] So, despite upsurges against neo-liberalism in the 1990s, 'no collective agency able to match the power of capital is yet on the horizon'.[28]

Anderson suggests three possible positions that socialists could take in such an unpromising conjuncture: accommodation, consolation or resignation. Commenting on each, he writes that while 'clamorous renegacy is quite rare . . . the depth of actual accommodation can be seen from episodes like the Balkan War, where the role of NATO was simply taken for granted . . . by a wide band of opinion that would not have dreamt of doing so ten or twenty years back'. Consolation, on the other hand, could be explained as an understandable, if misguided, 'propensity to over-estimate the significance of contrary processes . . . to nourish illusions in imaginary forces'. The third alternative, resignation, is, he argues, rarely articulated, but involves a 'lucid recognition of the nature and triumph of the system . . . without any belief in the chance of an alternative to it'. In contrast to these positions, Anderson believes that the left should combine 'uncompromising realism' with a refusal to accommodate 'to the ruling system': it should 'support any local movements or limited reforms, without pretending that they alter the nature of the system'.[29]

While Anderson overtly situated his defence of Jameson's general interpretation of the post-modern moment as a critique of the alternatives offered by Alex Callinicos, Terry Eagleton and David Harvey,[30] the interpretations of post-modernism articulated by those three theorists are far from uniform. Of the three, Harvey's reading of the post-modern conjuncture comes closest in execution to the analyses outlined by Jameson and Anderson.[31] In the introduction to his discussion, in *The Condition of Postmodernity*, of the 'transformation in the political economy of late twentieth-century capitalism', Harvey reminded his readers that 'we still live, in the West, in a society where production for profit remains the basic organising principle of economic life'.[32] Nevertheless, he insisted that 'the *regime of accumulation* and its associated *mode of social and political regulation*' had experienced important changes from around 1973, when the 'Fordist–Keynesian' mode began to 'break up'; even if it was 'by no means clear' that a new regime of accumulation had replaced it.[33] One aspect of the economic situation that was undeniably novel was the 'extraordinary efflorescence and transformation in financial markets' since the early 1970s.[34] Nonetheless, Harvey maintained a sober head when confronted with the suggestion that this financial development was but one aspect of a broader movement to a system of flexible accumulation in the 1980s. Considering the debate on this issue, he attempted to tread an even pathway between, on the one hand, those who argued that the introduction of new technologies in the 1970s and 1980s had allowed the 'reconstruction of labour relations of the production systems on an entirely different social, economic, and geographical basis' and, on the other, those who maintained that the ideology of flexible accumulation was not premissed on a deep economic transformation of the system, but did act to legitimise the idea that nothing could be done against the tide of neo-liberalism.[35] For his part, Harvey believed that while the ideology of flexible accumulation could best be understood as a capitalist strategy designed to increase profits by winning workers to the idea that, in Thatcher's famous phrase, 'there is no alternative', it could not be reduced to such a strategy: something had changed at the level of the labour process. Indeed, the important changes to the labour process had made it harder to sustain 'unionisation and traditional "left politics"'.[36]

Revisiting these arguments a decade later, Harvey made two points that are of relevance to this discussion. First, he suggests that the left's embrace, including his own, of the concept of globalisation in the 1980s and 1990s 'made us weak opponents of the politics of globalisation particularly as these became more and more central to everything that US foreign policy was trying to achieve'.[37] The implication of this suggestion was that even he, in his relatively sober analysis of the economic changes of the previous two decades, had been partially swept along with the globalisation rhetoric that originated with the neo-liberals. Nevertheless, this admission did not lead Harvey to reject his earlier, pessimistic, analysis of the political consequences of the economic changes that had occurred over the previous decades: 'The workforce is now far more geographically dispersed, culturally heterogeneous, ethnically and religiously diverse, racially stratified, and linguistically fragmented. The effect is to radically differentiate both the modes of resistance to capitalism and the definitions of alternatives.'[38] Moreover, deploying a revised version of Marx's model of class – where Marx had argued that opposing classes could best be understood as sharing contrasting relations to the means of production, Harvey defined class as 'situatedness or positionality in relation to processes of capital accumulation' – he argued that 'certain segments of the working class . . . [have] a great deal to lose besides its chains'.[39] Despite the pessimistic conclusions that could be drawn from these arguments, Harvey remains hopeful that 'alternative models of organising' could be constructed.[40] Indeed, he has recently suggested that it is the strength of the 'anti-globalisation movement' that it eschews 'traditional forms of labour organisation', and that the mass international anti-war movement realised in the demonstrations of 15 February 2003 'is a force to be contended with'.[41]

If Harvey therefore attempts to muster an 'optimism of the will' against the pessimistic conclusions implied by his intellectual analysis of the deep economic causes of the decline of the left, other Marxists have stressed the economic continuity between the modern and the post-modern conjunctures. For instance, Terry Eagleton locates the roots of post-modernism in the experience of defeat felt by the radicals of the 1968 generation: 'whatever else postmodernism may spring from . . . it is also, and centrally, the upshot of a political failure which it has either thrust into oblivion, or with which it has never ceased to shadow box'.[42] More specifically, Eagleton has argued that 'after the debacle of the late 1960s, the only feasible politics seemed to lie in piecemeal resistance to a system which was here to stay. The system could be disrupted but not dismantled.'[43] In contrast to the small thinking of post-modernity, Eagleton juxtaposed the emergence of the grand narrative of anti-capitalism in the wake of the Seattle demonstration of 1999.[44] However, despite the rhetorical appeal of this argument, Eagleton's analysis of the defeat out of which post-modernism emerged is, as Anderson argues, 'presented as a playful parable rather than actual reconstruction'.[45] Nonetheless, Anderson is quite wrong to suggest that Eagleton's analysis was the 'most sustained reading of postmodernism as the product of political defeat', for, as he himself points out, Callinicos 'advances a closer analysis of the political background to the postmodern'.[46] Unfortunately, Anderson does not engage with this reading of the defeat out of which the post-modern emerged, preferring to hack away at the straw man of Eagleton's parable.

Like Eagleton, Callinicos essentially explained the reception of post-modernist discourse in the 1980s as a consequence of the toll taken by the defeat of the radicalism of the late 1960s and early 1970s on a social layer who, in the 1980s, benefited from the rise of the 'new middle class' under Reagan and Thatcher. Following Mike Davis's analysis of the emergence of a 'overconsumptionist' regime of accumulation in America in the 1970s and 1980s, within which there occurred 'an increasingly political subsidisation of a sub-bourgeois, mass layer of managers, professionals, new entrepreneurs and rentiers',[47] Callinicos argued that the new middle class benefited from Reagan's and Thatcher's 'reorientation of fiscal policy' towards, in part, 'a redistribution from poor to rich'.[48] However, the emerging hegemony of post-modern discourse in the 1980s could not be reduced to this economic process. Rather, post-modernism grew out of a conjunction of two forces: 'the prosperity of the Western new middle class combined with the political disillusionment of many of its most articulate members'.[49] Following the analysis outlined in Chris Harman's *The Fire Last Time: 1968 and After*, Callinicos paid especial attention to the growing sense of defeat experienced by the generation of 1968,[50] arguing that the rise of post-modernism in the 1980s could best be 'understood largely as a response to the failure of the great upturn of 1968–76 to fulfil the revolutionary hopes it raised'. What is more, he explained the defeat of this period of struggle not as a direct consequence of a deep-seated economic transformation of capitalism but in primarily political and sociological terms:

> The failure of these struggles to make any long-term inroads into the power of capital was a contingent one, reflecting not the immanent logic of the system but the dominance of the Western working-class movements by organisations and ideologies which, whether stemming from social democratic or Stalinist traditions, were pledged to achieving partial reforms within a framework of class collaboration.[51]

Callinicos also argued that Anderson's pessimistic assessment of the collapse of Stalinism was predicated on the unwarranted presumption that the Soviet Union 'embodied a social system other than capitalism'.[52] By contrast, Callinicos followed Tony Cliff in characterising the post-1928 Soviet regime as a form of bureaucratic state capitalism.[53] Pointing to the predication by Lenin and Trotsky of the Bolshevik revolution on the gamble that October would foster similar revolutions across Europe, Callinicos commented that, while this wager 'was far from irrational . . . the fact remains that the Bolshevik regime . . . did not succeed in breaking out of its isolation'.[54] Moreover, while Callinicos explained the rise of Stalinism as a consequence of the isolation of the Soviet regime after the October revolution, he refused to accept that the defeat of the revolutionary wave beyond Russia in the post-war period occurred with fatal necessity. Rather, it was a consequence of the failure of the European left, generally, and the German left, more specifically, to realise the potential of the revolutionary opportunity offered it in the period 1918–23.[55]

So while Callinicos and Anderson agree that post-modernism, generally, and, more specifically, the appeal of Fukuyama's 'end of history' thesis are predicated on the defeats suffered by the left in the 1970s and 1980s, their contrasting interpretations of those defeats have led them to embrace very different strategic conclusions. Whereas Anderson insists that the left should accept, for the time being at least, that there is no systemic alternative to capitalism, Callinicos argues that Marx's vision of a revolutionary socialist alternative to capitalism retains its salience today.[56]

Statism and socialism

It is evident that the Marxist debate on post-modernity has been complicated by the inclusion of two ways of thinking about the defeat of the left: Callinicos concentrates on the bottom–up interpretation of the ebb and flow of the class struggle, while Anderson concentrates on the top–down story of the decline of social democracy and Stalinism. Anderson's political pessimism is therefore predicated on a reading of the collapse of the Soviet Union and the terminal decline of social democracy as evidence of the extinguishing of socialism as a viable systemic alternative to capitalism; while Callinicos's optimism is rooted in his argument that the defeats suffered by workers across the globe in the 1970s and 1980s did not mark a fundamental break in the history of capitalism.

In fact this debate draws our attention to the contested nature, even among Marxists, of the concept of *socialism* itself. One powerful way of highlighting the issue at stake in this debate is through Hal Draper's conceptualisations of 'socialism from above' and 'socialism from below'. According to Draper, those two models are in fact antonyms: Marx's democratic model of socialism from below is the opposite to the statist model of socialism from above associated with both Stalinists and social democrats.[57] By contrast, as I pointed out in chapter 5, Isaac Deutscher implied that the two models offer merely different roads to the same goal.[58] Moreover, Deutscher was aware that in classifying Stalin's conquest of Eastern Europe as some form of socialist transformation of those societies,[59] he was breaking with Marx's understanding of socialism as the self-emancipation of the working class: 'There is no room for classical Marxism in this cycle of revolution.'[60] On the basis of his interpretation of Stalinism, Deutscher came to the conclusion that the socialist project had no necessary anchorage in any particular form of agency. In 1965 he suggested that the locus of the struggle for socialism against capitalism had shifted from the point of production to the Berlin Wall: 'The class struggles of our time have degenerated into the unscrupulous contests of the ruling oligarchies.'[61]

The great strength of Deutscher's argument is that it highlights the theoretical innovation involved in classifying the Stalinist regimes as – even deformed – types of socialism: for this novel application of 'socialism' involves a clear break with Marx's vision of it as the self-emancipation of the working class. Of course, Marx may have been wrong to believe in the possibility of a non-statist alternative to capitalism, but at least this insight provides Marxists with a basis from which to reject Anderson's Deutscher-inspired pessimism.[62] This is not to suggest that Callinicos's optimistic alternative is necessarily more persuasive, for the divisions within the working class noted by Harvey and Anderson remain a serious question for Marxist theoreticians. Nonetheless, as the core of Marx's politics was aimed at overcoming divisions such as this, at least Marxists can begin to imagine a strategy for dealing with them.[63]

Conclusion

The statement made by Lukács in *History and Class Consciousness* with which this chapter opens suggests at least one sense in which there is a degree of continuity between the modern and post-modern worlds: intellectuals in both have tended to regard Marxism with ironic disdain. Nevertheless, the emergence of a global anti-capitalist and anti-war movement in the wake of the 1999 demonstration against the WTO in Seattle has once again created a space within which Marxist ideas can grow. For those ideas to move fully into the mainstream, however, requires the emergence of an international anti-capitalist workers' movement which might provide the existing movement with the social weight necessary to realise its aims: as Marx and Engels wrote in *The German Ideology*, 'the existence of revolutionary ideas in a particular period presupposes the existence of a revolutionary class'.[64] Nevertheless, such a movement will not grow as a mechanical response to economic developments, but will be built by ordinary activists. And while the main source of education for those activists will be their own experience of struggle, they will also benefit from the rich legacy of Marxist history, both as a supply of lessons from earlier struggles and as a fount of inspiration from which they might begin to imagine a better world.

Notes

1 The title of this chapter is borrowed from Paul Sweezy's collection of essays *The Present as History* (New York, 1953); Sweezy himself borrowed the title from a phrase in Lukács's *History and Class Consciousness*.
2 G. Lukács *History and Class Consciousness* (London, 1971 [1923]), p. 1.
3 P. Anderson *Considerations on Western Marxism* (London, 1976), p. 110.
4 F. Jameson *The Political Unconscious* (London, 1981), p. 9.
5 Rigby *Marxism and History*, p. 300.
6 R. Hilferding *Finance Capital* (London, 1981 [1909]), p. 23; cf. R. Hilferding (1941) 'The Materialist Conception of History' in T. Bottomore ed. *Modern Interpretations of Marx* (London, 1981), p. 127; see also L. Colletti *From Rousseau to Lenin* (New York, 1972), pp. 229–36; and Anderson *Arguments within English Marxism*, p. 6.
7 S. Perkins *Marxism and the Proletariat* (London, 1994), p. 11.
8 Fredric Jameson is distinguished professor of comparative literature at Duke University, NC.
9 F. Jameson *Postmodernism, Or, the Cultural Logic of Late Capitalism* (London, 1991), p. 1.
10 Ibid., pp. 35–6.
11 S. Homer *Fredric Jameson* (Cambridge, 1998), p. 108; E. Mandel *Late Capitalism* (London, 1975), pp. 118–21; M. Davis 'Urban Renaissance and the Spirit of Postmodernism' *New Left Review* no. 151, 1985, p. 107; A.Callinicos *Against Postmodernism* (Cambridge, 1989), p. 133.
12 F. Jameson *The Cultural Turn* (London, 1998), pp. 136ff.; P. Anderson *The Origins of Postmodernity* (London, 1998), p. 126. For the former's earlier attempt to provide his cultural theory with a material foundation borrowed from Baran and Sweezy, see F. Jameson *Marxism and Form* (Princeton, NJ, 1971), p. 36.
13 P. Blackledge *Perry Anderson, Marxism and the New Left* (London, 2004), pp. 150–5.
14 P. Anderson 'The Ends of History' in P. Anderson *A Zone of Engagement* (London, 1992), p. 343.
15 Anderson *The Origins of Postmodernity*, p. 73
16 Ibid., p. 84.
17 Ibid., p. 81.
18 Ibid., p. 92.
19 Ibid, pp. 89–92.
20 Ibid., pp. 93, 114.
21 Ibid., p. 104.
22 Ibid., p. 115.
23 Ibid., pp. 134–5.

24 P. Anderson 'A Sense of the Left' *New Left Review* no. 231, 1998, p. 81.
25 P. Anderson 'Renewals' *New Left Review* 2:1, 2000, p. 10.
26 Ibid., p. 7.
27 Ibid., pp. 11–12.
28 Ibid., p. 17.
29 Ibid., pp. 13–14.
30 Terry Eagleton was a professor of English at Oxford University, and has recently moved to take the chair in cultural theory at the University of Manchester; David Harvey is Distinguished Professor of anthropology at the Graduate Centre of the City University of New York; he was previously a professor at Oxford University.
31 Anderson *The Origins of Postmodernism*, pp. 78, 126.
32 D. Harvey *The Condition of Postmodernity* (Oxford, 1990), p. 121.
33 Ibid., p. 124.
34 Ibid., p. 194.
35 Ibid., pp. 189–90.
36 Ibid., pp. 191–2.
37 D. Harvey *Spaces of Hope* (Edinburgh, 2000), p. 13.
38 Ibid., p. 45.
39 D. Harvey *Justice, Nature and the Geography of Difference* (Oxford, 1996), p. 359; Harvey *Spaces*, p. 45.
40 Harvey *Spaces of Hope*, p. 50.
41 D. Harvey *The New Imperialism* (Oxford, 2003), pp. 189, 201.
42 T. Eagleton *The Illusions of Postmodernism* (Oxford, 1996), p. 21.
43 T. Eagleton *After Theory* (London, 2003), p. 51.
44 Ibid., p. 72.
45 Anderson *The Origins of Postmodernity*, p. 116.
46 Ibid., pp. 115, 78.
47 M. Davis *Prisoners of the American Dream* (London, 1986), p. 211, quoted in Callinicos *Against Postmodernism*, p. 163.
48 Callinicos *Against Postmodernism*, p. 164.
49 Ibid., p. 168.
50 C. Harman *The Fire Last Time* (London, 1988).
51 Callinicos *Against Postmodernism*, p. 168.
52 Callinicos *Theories and Narratives*, pp. 18–19.
53 A. Callinicos *The Revenge of History* (Cambridge, 1991), pp. 19, 29.
54 Ibid., pp. 26–7.
55 Callinicos *Against Postmodernism*, p. 60.
56 A. Callinicos *An Anti-Capitalist Manifesto* (Cambridge, 2003).
57 H. Draper 'The Two Souls of Socialism' in E. Haberkern ed. *Hal Draper: Socialism from Below* (London, 1992 [1966]). See more generally Draper's superb four volume study *Karl Marx's Theory of Revolution* (New York, 1977–90).
58 I. Deutscher, *Stalin* (London, 1966), p. 539.
59 In two essays first published in1966, he argued that the Stalinist states were, in fact, 'postcapitalist' states, 'halfway between capitalism and socialism': I. Deutscher *Marxism in Our Time* (London, 1971), pp. 239, 41.
60 I. Deutscher *Trotsky: The Prophet Outcast* (Oxford, 1987 [1963]), p. 519.
61 I. Deutscher *Marxism, Wars and Revolutions* (London, 1984), p. 87; I. Deutscher, *The Great Contest* (Oxford, 1960).

62 P. Blackledge *Perry Anderson, Marxism and the New Left*, pp. 98–9; 170–1; P. Blackledge 'Realism and Renewals' *Contemporary Politics* 7:4, 2001; see also P. Blackledge 'Marxist Interpretations of Thatcherism' in M. Cowling and J. Martin eds *The Eighteenth Brumaire: (Post)Modern Interpretations* (London, 2002).
63 P. Blackledge 'Marx and Intellectuals' in P. Reynolds and D. Bates eds *Marxism and Intellectuals* (London, 2006).
64 Marx *German Ideology*, p. 65.

Index